PREHISTORIC MONUMENTS OF THE
LAKE DISTRICT

PREHISTORIC MONUMENTS OF THE
LAKE DISTRICT

TOM CLARE

First published 2007 by Tempus Publishing Limited

Reprinted in 2015 by
The History Press
The Mill, Brimscombe Port,
Stroud, Gloucestershire, GL5 2QG
www.thehistorypress.co.uk

© Tom Clare, 2007, 2015

The right of Tom Clare to be identified as the Author
of this work has been asserted in accordance with the
Copyrights, Designs and Patents Act 1988.

All rights reserved. No part of this book may be reprinted
or reproduced or utilised in any form or by any electronic,
mechanical or other means, now known or hereafter invented,
including photocopying and recording, or in any information
storage or retrieval system, without the permission in writing
from the Publishers.

British Library Cataloguing in Publication Data.
A catalogue record for this book is available from the British Library.

ISBN 978 0 7524 4105 4

Typesetting and origination by Tempus Publishing Limited
Printed and bound by TJ International Ltd, Padstow, Cornwall

CONTENTS

	Acknowledgements	6
1	Introduction: Prehistoric monuments and the landscape of the twenty-first century	7
2	The principal types of evidence	10
3	North and West	24
4	The Long Meg area	44
5	The Penrith area	56
6	Moor Divock and Swarthbeck Gill	71
7	Shap and the eastern Lake District	80
8	The upper valleys of the Eden and Lune	97
9	Furness and South Lakeland	115
10	Thinking about the evidence	132
	Appendix	145
	Notes	146
	Bibliography	154
	Index	156

ACKNOWLEDGEMENTS

This book would not have been possible without the help of a large number of people. In particular I would like to thank the following for their help with the surveys: Geoff Thompson, Jack Otway, Martin Simpson, Keith Bracey, Charles Haddath, Graham Vincent, Phil Wheatman, Dave Wilkinson, Hannah O'Regan, David and Alyson. Nor would such work have been possible without the willing co-operation of landowners and farmers, including the National Trust, National Park and English Heritage.

Thanks are also due to Keith Barber for drawing attention to the site of Kitchenhill, to Vin Davis for his comments on the geology of Long Meg and Her Daughters and to the Chapter of Carlisle Cathedral for permission to reproduce drawings in the Machell manuscript. Thanks are also due to the Bodleian Library for permission to reproduce material there.

Again, thanks to Paul Kerigan, Sonia Lawson, Gwen Murfin, James and Sam Belbin, Phil Hull and Robert and John Heblethwaite who, along with many of the others, have tried to record the rising and setting of the solstice suns over the last three years. Therein lies a clue; this book has long been in the making so especial thanks to Aly and David for their work and patience over those years.

1

INTRODUCTION: PREHISTORIC MONUMENTS AND THE LANDSCAPE OF THE TWENTY-FIRST CENTURY

Stone circles, standing stones and burial mounds are part of our twenty-first century landscape. Some, such as the Goggleby Stone at Shap (*colour plate 1*), were amongst the first ancient monuments to be protected by parliamentary statute; although the Revd Lukis reported in 1884 that the farmer at Long Meg 'considered himself quite capable of looking after his own property'.[1] Today, that site is also protected and, as in Lukis' time, one of the best-known stone circles in Britain, after Stonehenge, as is Castlerigg. Perhaps not surprisingly, given its location within the Lake District and its mountainous background, Castlerigg receives thousands of visitors a year, and even as early as 1889, 'During the Lake season huge chars-a-bancs daily discharge large numbers of tourists and trippers at the circle'.[2] Now, too, hundreds of thousands pass Gunnerkeld (*1*) as they travel south along the M6, but how many people have actually noticed it, and how many have heard of or visited the standing stone not far from Mayburgh (*colour plate 2*)?

A primary purpose of this book is, therefore, to provide an introduction and guide to the monuments of the region – for both archaeologists and those simply interested in the landscape around them. For that reason, and in particular, to provide data for use by archaeologists, the book includes new, topographical surveys of many monuments, new sites and previously unpublished – or unrecognised – early records of some well-known monuments. A second purpose is, however, to *begin* to explore the relationship between the various sites and types of site. As such, it is hoped that the book will provide both an introduction and synthesis which can be used alongside those publications which have concentrated solely on 'stone circles'.

For convenience, the focus will be largely confined to the Neolithic and Bronze Age sites contemporary with the stone circles. Whilst these could, and almost certainly should, include settlement sites and burials in crevices, caves and unenclosed cremation cemeteries, space prohibits detailed description here. Consequently, although consideration of such sites will be returned to in discussion, the book concentrates on those sites which appear to have been intended to last, or be seen. Monumentality, therefore, is taken to relate to structure and visible form, and it follows that monumentality may have been an element in the banks, ditches and house forms of contemporary settlements; and again, such ideas will be returned to later.

It is, however, also the case that every stone circle, standing stone and burial mound which is part of our twenty-first century landscape was also part of the medieval landscape,

1 The Gunnerkeld circle adjacent to the M6

the Roman landscape and the later prehistoric one. Near Bewcastle, for example, an earthwork dyke appears to be aligned on and then bend around a large burial mound (*2*). Similarly, the circle of Long Meg is in uncertain relationship to a linear dyke,[3] whilst a parish boundary passes through the Studfoldgate circle.

As existing landscape features, therefore prehistoric megaliths and burial mounds could sometimes be used as boundary markers and/or have attracted speculation, legend and myth. Amongst these is the idea that some stones are petrified people, as at Long Meg and Her Daughters. Of course many 'early' legends may simply be pure invention, but the possibility of 'folk memory' cannot be ruled out entirely. This is particularly the case if we are to assume that the building of the monuments themselves may have been part of the mythologising of the landscape.

As existing landscape features, some sites, including caves, continued in use after the Bronze Age. This can cause problems of interpretation. Were some secondary burials, such as those on Sizergh Fell, simply the utilisation of a convenient landscape feature or structure, or was it intentional; a recognition of an old monument, perhaps even a continuation of earlier activity, albeit in different form? Again, was the Roman coin found in the centre of King Arthur's Round Table simply lost or a deliberate deposition?

Our ability to correctly interpret the archaeological record is, however, hampered by the fact that whilst some sites have survived into our twentieth-century landscape, others have been lost. Consequently, the record consists of two principal sources of evidence; those sites which have survived physically in our landscape, whether as standing stones or cropmarks, and those which have survived only in the notes and writings of earlier workers. And amongst the latter, we must include excavation accounts for the latter process is a destructive one; the excavator being the last person with access to the primary evidence.

2 A dyke on Bewcastle Fells is aligned on, but avoids the mound of Tower Brae (top)

There, and in other secondary evidence, we are of course dependent upon the writer or reporter for the details of the physical data surviving. However, it is necessary to note that the evidence observed and reported may not be all of that which had survived, or was available. For example, in the writing of this book, the author checked, again, early accounts of Shap Avenue which he had last used thirty years ago, only to find that he had previously missed a drawing of the site. Equally, in some accounts, more might have been reported than actually survived.

The point is that in an ideal world archaeological methodology is a two-stage process; the reporting of the evidence in as full and accurate and dispassionate way as possible, and then, and as a separate process, its interpretation. For example, the writer used to show evening classes a photo of a mound on the banks of Coniston Water (*colour plate 5*), asking them what they saw. Almost invariably, someone would suggest they saw a Bronze Age barrow, reasoning that it was a mound which looked round, and round mounds tend to be Bronze Age in date. Of course, it is not possible to know the plan shape from the photograph, so that even the first step in processing the information had been affected by their subconscious and interest in the prehistoric. In reality, the mound is a bloomery – an early slag heap, the remains of early iron smelting – something which would have been apparent had they been able to walk over the site on the ground.

It follows that our ability to interpret and understand data is enhanced by being able to see the evidence ourselves. Above all, this book is intended to facilitate that process, to contribute to a better understanding and enjoyment of the monuments.

2

THE PRINCIPAL TYPES OF EVIDENCE

EARTHWORKS AND STANDING STRUCTURES

As noted in the introduction, prehistoric monuments can still be seen in our own landscape. They are visible as bumps and hollows, or as stones standing upright or fallen – and here our interpretation or assumptions might begin to influence our reading of the evidence. It is, for example, almost impossible to know without excavation whether some of the 'boulders' forming monuments, such as the circle at Oddendale, are as they were originally positioned or whether they originally stood upright; a situation which has implication for how *we choose* to shade individual stones on plans. And how, without excavation, do we interpret a stone like that shown in *colour plate 6*? Is it prehistoric or a more recent 'cow scratcher'? Again, without excavation, we cannot always be sure that a 'site' is man-made or natural. Near to Urswick, in Furness, for example, there is an arrangement of limestone blocks (*colour plate 7*) which could be the remains of a megalithic tomb with astronomical alignment[1] or simply part of the adjacent limestone pavement. Again, the stone located at Annaside, south of Ravenglass, in 1923, and thought to be the remains of a circle reported in the eighteenth and nineteenth centuries, was considered by the Ordnance Survey to be a 'free standing erratic'.[2]

Whether that was the case or not, it is evident that prehistoric people appear to have treated some erratics as they would standing stones. At Broomrigg, south-east of Carlisle, for example, a beaker had been placed against one such boulder, and the recognition of other erratics as 'thunder stones' – most noticeably in the Shap area – reminds us of the kind of thought processes which might have been in the prehistoric mind.

Similarly, prehistoric peoples may have regarded some natural mounds in the same way as artificial tumuli. At How Hill, south-west of Carlisle, for example, urns were inserted into a large glacial mound, just as 'secondary burials' were made in some burial mounds; a situation which may explain why 15 per cent of all chance finds of burials/urns within the region have come from sand and gravel quarrying (TABLE 1).

Nevertheless, it is also the case that, without excavation, we cannot be certain whether a mound, such as that in *colour plate 8*, is natural or not. And, for the reasons given above, even when we are certain a mound is natural in origin, we cannot be certain it was not used or regarded by prehistoric peoples as artificial, or a monument in its own right.

TABLE 1

Number of chance finds excluding axes

	sand/gravel quarry	collecting/quarrying stones	railway	road repair and building	building	agriculture	other	as % of all chance finds
pre 1900	4	3	1	5	4	12	12	76
1900–1950	1					3	1	9
post 1950	3		1	1			3	15
total	8	3	2	6	4	15	16	
As % of all chance finds	15	5.5	3.5	11	7.5	28	29.5	100

On Sizergh Fell, for example, there is a large, perfectly round mound from which it is possible to watch the midsummer sun setting over the Langdale Pikes, near to the Neolithic 'axe factories'. However, whilst everyone agrees the mound appears to be solid limestone, it is also necessary to agree with the comments made in 1904 that 'it is not at all improbable that … traces of interments may yet be found in the crevices of the rock'.[3]

The same author also warned of more general problems of site recognition within the region. Amongst them is the problem of recognising whether a cairn or mound 'was thrown up 20 or 2,000 years ago'. Here, he may have had in his mind the case of the spectacular site of Old Parks, north of Long Meg, where a few years earlier a cairn, covering a line of carved stones, had been sold to the County Council for road metalling on the assumption that it was a 'clearance cairn'.

AIR PHOTOS

The same problems apply to the features recorded on aerial photographs. Without excavation, it is not always possible to be certain whether a feature is natural or built, nor what its age and purpose was. For example, amongst the various 'cropmarks' recorded in the vicinity of Long Meg in 1983, were two ditches which appeared to be parallel and with a central axis which would pass through the Long Meg monolith. At first sight, this seemed to be a cursus or avenue; a type of Neolithic monument hitherto absent from the region. However, the fact that one ditch was much straighter than the other, and on some of the photographs appeared to have others at an angle to it, suggested it was a drainage ditch, presumably of different date to the other linear feature.

3a and b Two cropmarks sites. *Above left:* (a) A possible ring ditch beneath a Roman fort turned out to be a Roman signal tower. *Above right:* (b) Ring ditches below the Roman civil settlement at Brougham

In this example, two aspects of aerial photography are apparent. Firstly, that not all features may be present on a single photograph; some may be visible (or disappear) when the site is photographed from a different angle. Secondly, without excavation, we make assumptions and presumptions about the type and date of features recorded.

One other example may serve to illustrate how we choose to interpret the data. Figure 3a shows a Roman fort, discovered to the south of Hadrian's Wall in 1976, and with a circular feature which could be reasonably interpreted as a ditch in one corner. This author concluded the latter feature was a possible prehistoric 'ring ditch', but a colleague who was interested in windmills thought it was the remains of just such a structure, whilst a Roman period specialist thought it the remains of a Roman signal tower. Subsequent excavation proved him correct, but there are two earthwork sites – Appleby golf course and Middleton Hall – which, although considered signal towers, are more likely to be prehistoric.

Figure 3a also illustrates the fact that cropmarks do not occur in root crops. Moreover, not all areas of cereal crops produce cropmarks. For that reason, and given the limited arable land within Cumbria, much of any buried prehistoric archaeology may not be available for identification by aerial photography. On the other hand, parch marks in grassland can sometimes reveal remarkable data, as at Long Meg in 1983 when this author, and others, recorded a ditched enclosure adjacent to the stone circle.[4] In some areas, aerial photography *has* therefore contributed significantly to our understanding of the prehistoric landscape. It has, for example, demonstrated the existence of new monument forms such as pit alignments, a possible cursus and 'short cursus'/mortuary enclosure[5] within the region, and that barrows with ditches were more common than previously thought.

At Brougham, ring ditches (3b) can be seen to be overlain by the lanes and field boundaries of the Roman *vicus* or civil settlement, demonstrating what has long been suspected; that the prehistoric landscape on the valley floors and lower ground within the region has been ploughed out or buried by later processes (some natural), unlike in some uplands.

However, it is also important to note that some earthworks have survived on valley floors whilst some sites have probably been lost from the high ground. Nevertheless, the ring ditches, recorded by aerial photographs at Brougham, provide a context for the Neolithic Peterborough pottery found during alterations to the A66 in 1966 and 1967.[6] Together, they demonstrate intense Late Neolithic and Bronze Age 'ritual' activity which was previously unsuspected. In how many other areas does such evidence and activity remain undetected?

CHANCE FINDS AND EVALUATION

Chance finds may be like the tips of icebergs; the visible part of a much larger body of information which we cannot see. Examples of this type of evidence are the urns from How Hill (above)[7] and the cist discovered at Shap Beck, in the building of the Lancaster–Carlisle railway.[8] Taken together, and with individual artefacts, such as, stone or bronze axes, such finds form a significant proportion of the database available for the Neolithic and Bronze Age within the region.

Many of the finds occurred during 'improvement' and in other agricultural and industrial activities of the eighteenth and nineteenth centuries (TABLE 1). However, chance finds still occur; sometimes, as in the past, as a result of development or land use, but also as a result of the use of metal detectors. However, whether the find was in the past or present, as an artefact or structure, the problem is the same – there was no systematic survey or record. We know what was found, and where, but little of its context.

More recently still, archaeological evaluation, in advance of the determination of planning applications, has provided further evidence of the iceberg of data hidden below the present landscape. It is perhaps not too much of an exaggeration to suggest that the information provided by evaluation, and what used to be called 'rescue archaeology', is transforming the data available and, consequently, our understanding of the Neolithic and Bronze Age within the region. Nevertheless, evaluation provides as many questions as answers. At Allithwaite, near Grange Over Sands, for example, evaluation allowed recovery of urned cremations[9] but did not allow investigation of whether they had been placed within a formally defined enclosure or simply placed at one point in the landscape; questions posed 100 years before by the chance finding of similar groups of urns at Garlands and Aglionby, near Carlisle. There is, therefore, a need for 'research agendas' to inform, if not continue, the work of evaluation.

LITERARY SOURCES AND EARLY ACCOUNTS

As at Garlands and Aglionby, much of the evidence relating to the Neolithic and Bronze Age consists of museum objects, early accounts and excavations. Indeed, these may be the only source of information. For example, the only evidence for a stone circle at Sandford, in the Eden valley, is the note and sketch of Thomas Machell, who wrote c.1690. Inevitably, questions about the accuracy of what was observed and reported must be asked and these must take account of the fact that one 'description' may not be based on new and personal observation, but simply on an already existing – and unacknowledged – source. Nicholson and Burn's account of the remains in Leven's Park, published in 1777, for example, is almost exactly that published by Edmund Gibson in 1695, whilst their account of Raisbeck was, in turn, 'lifted' by Whellan in 1847.

The problem of ascertaining what might have existed, and what early writers *chose* to record, is well illustrated by a comparison of the previously unpublished drawings of Mayburgh, by Machell and Stukeley (4) with that of Pennant (5a). Stukeley, for example, shows two stones in the entrance, one beyond the extant, 'central' standing stone and two others within the interior. The drawing was made in 1725 and can be compared with his written account published after his death in 1776, where it is stated that there had been an inner and outer circle, and 'one stone, at least, of the outer circle remains by the edge of the corn, and some lie at the entrance within, others without, and fragments all about'. However, both Dugdale and Machell's illustrations clearly show only two entrance stones (albeit, Dugdale has them on the outside whilst Machell has them on the inside) and four in the centre with none at 'the edge of the corn'. Is it possible that *both* Dugdale and Machell chose only to plan those which were upright, or was the outer fallen stone depicted by Stukeley and interpreted as the remains of a second circle, one of the four central ones simply displaced after being felled? This is a question now almost impossible to answer without excavation, but a closer inspection of Machell's sketch reveals what may be a prostrate stone outside the entrance and where Stukeley placed one of his.

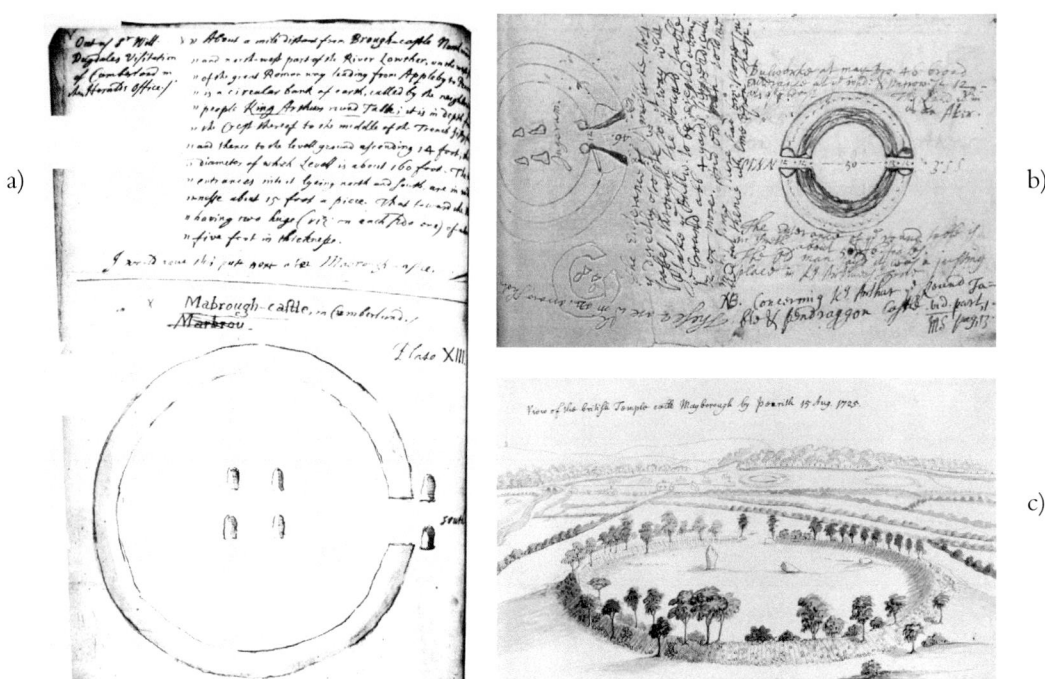

4a-c Early records of Mayburgh. (a) Dugdale (b) Machell (c) Stukeley. Dugdale and Stukeley are reproduced with permission of the Bodleian Library, University of Oxford. Stukeley's drawing is in Ms. Top. Gen.b.53. Fol.15v

The principal types of evidence

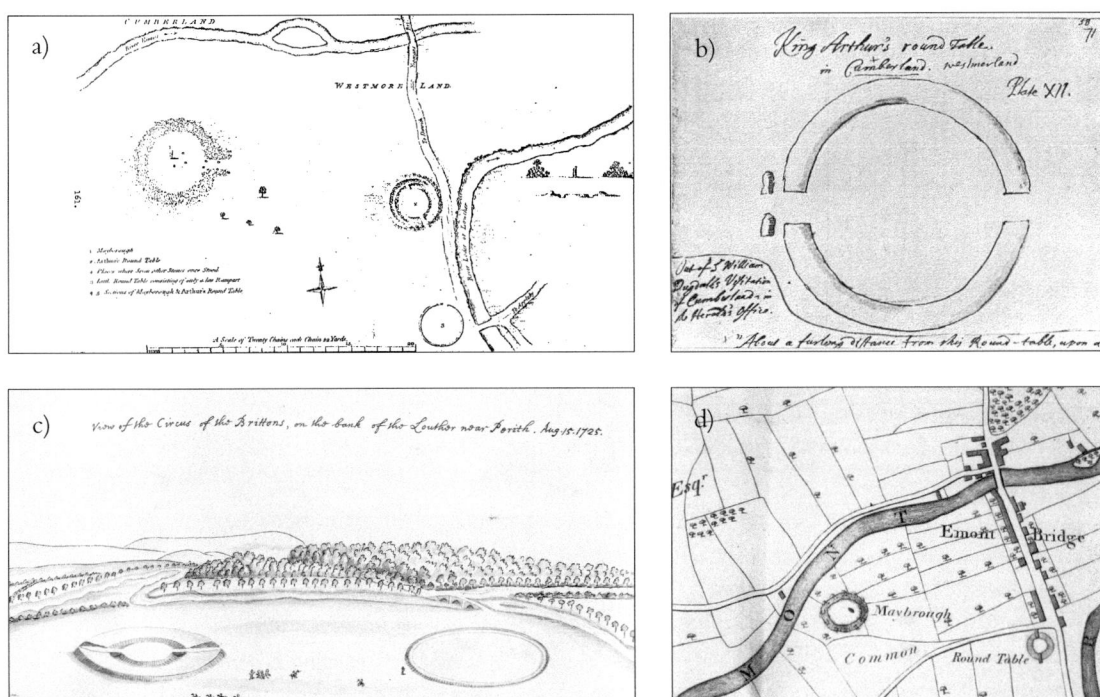

5a-d Early records of King Arthur's Round Table. (a) Pennant (b) Dugdale (c) Stukeley (d) Clarke. Dugdale and Stukeley are reproduced with permission of the Bodleian Library, University of Oxford. Stukeley's drawing is in Ms. Top. Gen. b53. Fol.13v

Did Pennant see four stones on his visit of 1769, or is his published plan an interpretation of the surviving evidence? In recording the position of four central stones, was he using Dugdale's plan, or was he simply making a guess at the position of the stones based on Stukeley's account? Certainly Clarke's map (5d) shows only one stone, but its accuracy is questionable, given that the bank has no entrance. However, if we allow that Pennant's plan may in part be a 'reconstruction', can we be certain that Dugdale or Machell actually saw four stones or were they too recording what was said to have existed? If the latter were the case, it might explain why one of them had two entrance stones on the outside and the other had them on the inside.

That Pennant had, however, undertaken some original fieldwork is suggested by the fact that he does not repeat Stukeley's assertion of a second circle, and his overall plan is more accurate than Stukeley's. In particular, he shows the bank having two projections at the entrance – a reasonable representation of the form of the earthwork surviving today – whilst Stukeley's bank (4c) is of the wrong proportions and does not show the bank increasing in height at the entrance. If, however, Pennant's depiction of the Mayburgh bank is more accurate than Stukeley's, should we also accept his depiction of the bank at King Arthur's Round Table continuing across the northern entrance, whilst Stukeley, Dugdale and Machell show a gap?

It will be evident one of the problems of early accounts is that it is not always possible to reconcile the details of one description with those of another. Nor can we always be certain that they were recording what they saw, not what they thought they saw. Taylor,[10] for example, reported an avenue and number of small circles on Moor Divock which no one else has been able to find, so that we are left wondering if they really did exist or whether he selectively recorded a few of the many stones which still project from the surface when the bracken is at its lowest. Similarly, we do not know whether, in reporting three concentric, buried circles at Yamonside,[11] he had probed the ground in a statistically valid sampling strategy or simply where he thought there should be stones.

A third problem, however, is the accuracy of the dimensions recorded. For example, Nicholson and Burn state that the Raisbeck tumulus, near Tebay, was 100 yards in diameter; an extraordinary, though not impossible size, so they may have meant, circumference. Again, we might suspect that in some cases the height stated is not a vertical one but one measured along the slope. At Mayburgh, for example, Dugdale states that 'from the crest to the skirt' the bank is 'about sixty foot and the perpendicular is about twelve foot ...'.[12]

A similar problem exists with compass bearings. When, for example, the report states a cist was 'east–west', do they mean exactly east–west or just approximately so; and if the latter, how big was the variation? It is also sometimes difficult to recognise what type of artefact is being depicted, or described.

At the same time, while eighteenth and nineteenth-century 'improvements' and development were leading to chance finds, a number of excavations were undertaken for 'scientific' purposes. In 1766, for example, the Society of Antiquaries was sent an account of the 'opening' of one of the barrows on Sandford Moor, in the Eden valley. The phrase 'opening', used in a number of similar accounts, suggests that the sites could be seen as boxes and excavation, the means of getting at the contents. Even a century later, the techniques of Canons Greenwell and Simpson, as evidenced on Moor Divock and at Mazonwath, seem to have involved 'driving' a trench towards the centre of the mound and 'exploring' the latter until the number of finds appeared to have been exhausted. However, nothing can match the excavation of a mound on Aughertree Fell (*colour plate 8*), near Caldbeck, where excavation (later than the time of Greenwell and Simpson) involved digging by lantern.

Whilst accepting that modern techniques and methods evolved from such beginnings, the fact is that much of the information relating to the burial mounds of the Lake District comes from the work of Canons Greenwell and Simpson in the Eden valley and of the Furness Field Club, as well as individuals motivated by those activities (TABLE 2). This means, that not only do we have little *clear* information about the structure of the monuments, but it is sometimes difficult to be certain what was encountered, at least for purposes of modern interpretation. The Furness Field Club, for example, excavated in the early part of the twentieth century, but with one exception, published neither sections nor plans; although, they did recognise the importance of the 'section' – on one occasion the 'plan of work' involved excavating spits 'to move the whole mass of the barrow about three feet down hill'.[13]

TABLE 2

Excavated sites excluding evaluation and cairnfields

	Sites partially dug for research	Sites wholly dug for research	sites partially dug for rescue	sites wholly dug for rescue	Total	%
pre 1900	46	5	2		53	61
1900-1935	4	8			12	14
1936-1970	12	3		1	16	18.5
1971-		1	1	4	6	7
Total	62	17	3	5	87	
%	71	19.5	3.5	5.5		

Sometimes, the problems of identifying, recording and interpreting structures, sequences and other evidence can be demonstrated to have been hindered by the size of the area excavated. Perhaps the best example of this is King Arthur's Round Table (KART) where the site was trenched by R.G. Collingwood in 1937. Working less than a decade after the discovery of Woodhenge, one of his aims was to discover whether a similar structure might have existed at KART. In that hypothesis he was not disappointed, as the Interim Report published in 1938 noted. However, re-excavation on a larger scale by Bersu, just before the outbreak of War,[14] showed that some of the postholes of 1937 were in fact animal burrows, some of which fortuitously occurred in straight lines. Here, surely, is a lesson for us all and a cautionary tale for evaluation and research strategies based on 'sampling'.

Finally, it is necessary to note the problems of interpreting the tantalising, but brief accounts of Canon Greenwell. In a number of mounds, he found scattered bones which he interpreted as being the result of earlier excavations. In some cases this explanation may be correct, but the modern excavations on Hardendale Nab,[15] near Crosby Ravensworth and at Borwick,[16] just to the south of Cumbria, demonstrated discrete areas of bone within the cairn structures, raising the possibility that similar deposits existed in Greenwell's sites and that such deposits represent a local tradition.

LOCAL TRADITION AND PLACE NAMES

Information about some sites comes from hearsay, and it is often not readily apparent what value we should attach to it. For example, when Gibson noted there were two 'heaps of stones' inside the circle at Long Meg, 'under which they say there are dead bodies bury'd',[17] should we conclude that excavation had taken place and burials found, or was he reporting an assumption and inference? Certainly we must hope that any buried there were dead.

How, too, do we interpret the legend of the Long Meg stones, namely that they were petrified people? Is it a distant folk memory and thus *evidence* of prehistoric activity, or simply a later explanation or inference? Camden, writing 400 years ago, certainly considered them to be explanations invented at a later time for, 'in the ages following … when they could not declare the trueth they laboured to bring foorth narratives, devised of purpose, with a certaine pleasant varietie to give contentment … '.[18] Such an explanation must surely apply to the site in Leven's Park, reported in a later edition of Camden and 'said to have been anciently a Temple dedicated to Diana',[19] for it is most unlikely that a single and specific Roman dedication would have survived 1,200 years.

That is, however, not to deny that some 'Celtic' customs and beliefs do appear to have survived that length of time. May Day and Halloween are the most obvious, but they are also days which had a wider European, and not just Celtic significance. Stories of malevolent little people or fairies may also be of later, pan-European origin, and their only relevance here is in their incorporation in place names leading us to identify possible sites; although Elf Howe appears to be a natural glacial mound, a reminder that most names are very probably no more than one of the 'narratives, devised of purpose', noted by Camden. Indeed, place name elements, such as 'how', or 'howe', and 'barrow' simply mean hill, whether artificial or natural, and sometimes, as in the case of Whit*barrow* Scar, they are substantial hills.

Similarly, it is unclear whether the word or phrase 'stone' in some place names refers to natural phenomenon or to the former existence of a monument. There is, for example, no evidence, other than the place name, for megaliths having existed at Ringlen or Ringingstone, near Egremont, and it is certainly impossible to know whether the stones – if they existed – formed a circle (as has been suggested) rather than another type of monument.

EVIDENCE FOR DATE

The introductory remarks to Camden's *Britannica*, published in 1610, recognises one of the fundamental problems posed by the remains which could, and can be dug up or observed in the landscape: 'who were the most ancient and very first inhabitants of this Isle … ?'[20]

Camden, and subsequent antiquarians and archaeologists, like Stukeley, worked within the framework offered by 'holy scripture', or the Bible. There, it was possible to total up the ages of the descendants of Adam and arrive at the date when God created the earth. It followed that everything recorded and uncovered by archaeology, and considered to be pre-Roman, fell within a 4,000-year period and had existed before or after the great deluge of Noah.

Use of the Bible and such models did not, however, resolve the fundamental problem of whether the stone circles and burial mounds were pre-Roman or post-Roman. Stukeley believed the sites were pre-Roman, and his drawings of Mayburgh and Long Meg dated to 1725 referred to those sites as 'British' and 'Celtic', respectively. Most other antiquarians agreed, but within the model provided by classical authors this allowed them to be associated with the druids. The mound at Hesket Newmarket, for example, was called Druid's Grove, whilst on Hodgson's map of 1828, the Standing Stones on Moor Divock was called Druid's Cross. Such ideas have not entirely disappeared, and visitors to Long Meg will find the County Highway's signpost pointing to 'The Druid's Circle', whilst that on Birkrigg Common appears in some archaeological literature, as 'Druid's Circle, Birkrigg'. Conveniently, there are enough stones at that site for the individual letters of the word 'Druid' to be sprayed on each separate stone.

An alternative view was that the sites were post-Roman and 'Danish'. For example, Pennant, who considered the Castlerigg circle to be 'druidical', argued that the stones at Shap were 'Danish'. 'That this monument was Danish may be inferred from the custom of the northern nation of arranging their recording stones in forms they seemed to determine should be expressive of certain events'.[21] Whilst the logic of this argument is not wholly clear, the principle of establishing the antiquity of a site *by analogy*, or *by association* with similar evidence of known date elsewhere, is one which is frequently used in archaeology, even today. However, when early accounts speak of 'Roman' objects being found in a site, we cannot always be certain that they did not simply mean 'old', or 'ancient'.

As well as dating by association and analogy, the observation of stratigraphy and, in particular, stratigraphic relationships, allowed early archaeologists to suggest that some forms of evidence were earlier, or later, than others. By the mid-nineteenth century, for example, it was generally accepted that 'long barrows' were earlier than round ones. Most importantly, stratigraphic observation provided the basis for dividing prehistory into 'three ages': Stone, Bronze and Iron. *Relative* to the others, the Iron Age could be demonstrated to be the latest. However, it was possible to find in some parts of the world cultures which were still 'in the stone age'. In practice, a *relative dating* system only works within a limited geographical area, and even then not always perfectly, especially when mixed with ideas of 'cultures'.

It also became apparent that some European groups using stone tools sometimes had access to copper or gold 'ornaments'. Consequently, new terms, such as chalcolithic (essentially 'copper age'), were adopted, whilst the stone age was subdivided first into an Old Stone Age (Palaeolithic) and New Stone Age (Neolithic), and then again into an Upper and Lower Palaeolithic with a Mesolithic between the Palaeolithic and Neolithic. However, what could not be determined was how long each of these periods had lasted. In the mid-nineteenth century some argued that the Neolithic had lasted just 500 years, others said that it had lasted 5,000 years.

It was not until after the Second World War that *absolute dating* techniques became available. Of these, the most commonly used is that of carbon 14, or radiocarbon dating. However, few radiocarbon dates were obtained for sites in the area during the 1950s and 1960s. In part, this may reflect the relatively high costs at that time, the relatively large quantities of organic material required and, last but not least, the relative paucity of sites being excavated. In contrast, the last decade or two have seen a number of more accurate, low-cost dates from much smaller quantities of material from the increasing number of sites excavated (see Appendix, p.145).

It is, however, important to recognise that, despite the development, refinement and increased application of such dating techniques, archaeologists still use the methods and phrases of the Three Age System whilst waiting for the absolute dates to come back from the lab, and as a convenient means of grouping data for discussion purposes. The danger is, however, that organising data and discussion within such convenient frameworks may obscure patterns and practices which reflect continuities within prehistoric society whilst requiring us to think of them as linked to technologies.

Nevertheless, there are problems associated with the radiocarbon dates available from the area. Perhaps the most important is the possibility that the material being dated is contaminated, or residual. At Hardendale Nab, for example, two very different radiocarbon dates allow that either the first phase mound was Neolithic in origin, and had then stood for 1,000 years before the next phase of activity, or that the bone in it had been scraped up from an older surface.[22] Similarly, a wide variation in dates from one cremation at Allithwaite has been explained by some of the charcoal being from the heartwood of the tree and thus much older than some other charcoal.[23]

More fundamental to understanding the monuments is, however, the small number of available radiocarbon dates. Consequently, we are still reliant on relative dating, such as association with a cultural object for many sites. Whilst these show that a number of burial mounds, such as Wiseber and Sandford, may have a post Roman phase and some cists may be Roman or later, the problem is establishing the actual age of the prehistoric artefacts. In that respect, the few radiocarbon dates available for collared urns and other artefacts within the region are extremely useful. Similarly, new radiocarbon dates require us to challenge assumptions developed in the nineteenth century. For example, the idea that a flexed skeleton found during evaluation work at Levens was typical of those normally associated with Bronze Age burial was proved wrong when the radiocarbon dates showed it to be 'late prehistoric'.

Nevertheless, the fact remains that there is neither cultural material nor radiocarbon dates available for the henges and large diameter circles within the area. The idea that they are amongst the earliest in the British Isles is, therefore, based on typological features, and that is a methodological approach not without its own problems.

ENVIRONMENTAL EVIDENCE

Whilst a consideration of environmental evidence may not relate to the actual *form* of the monument,[24] it is necessary if we are to understand the monuments fully. For example, any astronomical alignments would not have been possible if the sites were built deep in woodland. Interestingly, evidence that the prehistoric environment was very different from our own had been noted as early as the seventeenth century,[25] and Nicholson and Burn stated confidently that 'in the time of the druids' Shap had been 'shaded with wood, as this place of old time appears to have been, although there is now scarce a tree to be seen'.

Their evidence appears to have been fossil tree trunks 'commonly' found in the mosses and such remains, together with those of plants, seeds and charcoal, are referred to as 'macrofossils'. However, whilst such evidence has occasionally been sought and used, most systematic investigations of the palaeo-environment have been based on micro fossils and pollen, in particular.

Much of the early pollen work was concerned to demonstrate that the general vegetation sequences recorded elsewhere also occurred within Cumbria, and two consequences were that many sites examined were in, or adjacent to, the Lake District massif with the resulting records representing 'regional pollen rain' and vegetation rather than localised and site specific landscapes.

There were, of course, exceptions to this and some of the general investigations, such as the work of Pennington, at Barfield Tarn,[26] and of Oldfield and Stratton at Urswick Tarn,[27] also took place in the vicinity of known monuments. However, the suggestion of Pennington that the circles on Burnmoor were built within a forested landscape needs to be questioned, given that the sites are more than one mile and on the other side of a hilltop from the basin yielding the data. Equally, the recognition of clearings elsewhere does not necessarily mean that any monuments in that area were built within those clearings. There is therefore a need for future work to collect evidence from the immediate vicinity of the monuments. Equally, there is a need to recognise that the early Neolithic landscape was not one of unending homogeneous forest cover but a mosaic, and that increasingly throughout the period of the monuments discussed here the forest cover or wildwood[28] became even more fragmented.

The idea that the vegetation always had been 'fragmented', with a 'mosaic' of species and habitats, is not difficult to understand. Throughout Cumbria, interrelated factors, such as hydrology, slope angle, geology, soil, aspect and height above sea level, would have meant that the wetter parts of some valley floors and sides were characterised by carr woodland, whilst the adjacent dried slopes carried oak, ash and hazel with birch and, perhaps, pine on the higher slopes, and on the very highest parts little or no woodland. Indeed, it appears that some species presently found on the top of Helvellyn, and on other summits, must have survived, isolated in those refuges for more than 12,000 years.[29]

A similar interpretation can be applied to rare plants on the limestone escarpment which separate the upper Eden and Lune valleys.[30] There, however, anthropogenic activity may have played a part in the survival/distribution of certain species, for on Bank Moor the palaeo-environmental record suggests there has never been woodland cover because humans burnt the vegetation from time to time.[31]

However, as with many palynological studies, we are unable to say how extensive the open countryside of Bank Moor was. Certainly the evidence from Hardendale Nab and Oddendale demonstrates that by the middle Bronze Age the high limestone escarpment was open country. In contrast, at the beginning of the Neolithic, the lower ground in the vicinity of Sunbiggin Tarn carried heavier woodland; although, by the late-Neolithic, nearby Mazonwath, was 'open' countryside. Such forest reduction would have been aided by grazing farm animals, and today the unenclosed commons of the limestone escarpment between the Eden and Lune valleys are almost wholly devoid of trees.[32]

The present scant tree cover and large fields to the south and east of Long Meg suggest that area, too, may have been unenclosed common until a few hundred years ago.[33] Indeed, it is possible that the present distribution of monuments may reflect the former distribution of common land. For example, the ground around Castlerigg was only enclosed in the eighteenth century, and later still at Castlehowe and Harberwain Rigg. Again, the lost Sandford circle was on common land, as were King Arthur's Round Table and those at Broomrigg and Grey Yauds. Significantly, the disappearance of the latter coincided with 'improvement' of the former common, whilst Hodgson[34] thought the flora of Broomrigg related to improvement there.

But forest loss, coupled with climatic deterioration, had one other important implication for our understanding of the monuments and their distribution; it was accompanied by hydrological changes, soil degradation, erosion and deposition. As a result, the character/classification of the present soil may not have a direct bearing on the distribution of prehistoric monuments; although, a positive correlation may exist because later land use, related to later soil character, has skewed the preservation or identification of sites. It is also possible that the ground on hilltops and slopes is now lower than in prehistory, whilst Neolithic and Bronze Age valley floors may be buried. Excavations in advance of road works at High Crosby, for example, revealed a Bronze Age palisaded enclosure buried beneath valley silts, up to one metre deep.[35]

In some coastal valleys the buried land surface may be the result of sea level changes, and it should not be assumed that the present coast is that of the Neolithic and Bronze Age. At the beginning of the Neolithic, for example, sea levels may have been up to three meters below present. Equally, rising sea levels may have caused some low-lying coastal areas to flood so that the circle at Grey Croft may have overlooked an estuary or wetland rather than the present valley floor.

It is certainly necessary to recognise that the prehistoric landscape included more wetlands and tarns than at present. There was, for example, a tarn with open water to the south-east of the Castlerigg stone circle at the time of its building and use,[36] whilst there was still a tarn near Gutterby in the eighteenth century.

Such areas have a potential to provide evidence other than that relating to past vegetation. In the case of Sunbiggin Tarn, for example, 'two pairs of bull horns, jumped together in the position of fighting' were found *c.*1730[37] and, in the case of Ehenside near Sellafield, Neolithic pottery and timber objects, including a hafted stone axe, were recovered when a tarn was drained.[38] Taken together, such evidence demonstrates that wetland areas, whether open water or bog, were foci for beliefs and ritual practices alongside contemporary monuments, and it is, therefore, interesting to note there was a standing stone near Ehenside Tarn. However, it is also true that any reed beds around the tarns would probably have attracted ungulates and therefore hunting, land use and settlement strategies.

Some floodplains and valley floors may have been similar open areas within the wildwood mosaic and the deposits there, as in the case of other wetlands, may contain macro fossil remains such as seeds, as well as pollen and sediments.[39] Such data suggests that extensive, if localised, environmental change occurred about 3200 BC. In part, this may have resulted from an expansion of farming but it also occurred at a time of possible climatic deterioration, reminding us that it is often not easy to differentiate anthropogenic and environmental changes. More importantly, the environment of the monuments and the monument builders was not static, but dynamic, and it included (now) extinct animals, such as aurox, wolves and bears; a landscape of danger and uncertainty.

For all of these reasons, we need to envisage the monuments in a very different landscape to our own. Today it is difficult to imagine a landscape without much grass. Equally, a forested landscape would have been one in which visibility was reduced and views of a distant horizon may have been a rare experience. Consequently, those places where such views existed – mountain tops, and the edge of the sea, floodplains and tarns – must have been special places. Indeed, work north of the Solway[40] suggests that different monument types might have had different 'viewsheds'. Equally, movement through such landscapes would have been difficult, so that humans and animals may have used the same routes or followed streams and rivers, and tended to meet in those areas which were open or obvious points within the mosaic which was the wildwood. Within such an environment, the existence of particular places or locales where activity was concentrated rather than spread evenly across the landscape, might be expected; as indeed, might the 'persistence of place' from the Mesolithic into the Neolithic and beyond.

It follows that the monuments cannot be studied simply as constructions, rather, we must see them within their landscape – and in particular, their original landscape. But that raises the question of how prehistoric peoples saw their world and how, if at all, their monuments and practices related to such perceptions and interactions.

3

NORTH AND WEST

TOWER BRAE AND BEWCASTLE FELLS, NY 56857282

Tower Brae is probably the most accessible and one of the most impressive monuments in the Bewcastle Fells area. It is a much disturbed round mound, probably originally between 15m and 20m in diameter located in a prominent position just above a break of slope, and visible from both the lower ground and surrounding ridges.

From the site, the summit of Baron's Pike is visible to the north-east. The site there is a low bowl-shaped mound with a steep-sided ditch and causeway on the south-west. The character of the ditch raises questions about its antiquity, and the site is generally regarded as a Roman signal tower. However, it is possible that the midsummer sun would have risen over the site when seen from Tower Brae.

The forested area, north of Tower Brae, now obscures the sites of Lamb Crag and Shiel Knowe excavated in the 1930s. Of these, the site on the slopes of Lamb Crag was described in an unpublished note as 'Cairns, two long. One of these excavated. Cremation trench. Circular stone over whitish greasy material. Two fragments of burnt (?) bone. "Horse-shoe" circle of unknown date, cairn or circle? Fragment of cordoned beaker'.[1] By 1972, the site appeared to consist of one circular and one elongated heaps of stone. Amongst the stones forming the latter were two possible uprights which may have formed part of a long cist or been within the trench mentioned above.

The site at Shiel Knowe[2] was, in contrast, on the valley floor. It had been a mound built at the intersection of three natural ridges, but part of the artificial structure had already been destroyed prior to excavation. The latter revealed a roughly central cist containing two food vessels. The cist may have contained a cremation, and a hollow near a second (smaller) cist, also containing a food vessel, appeared to have been the site of a cremation pyre.

The second cist had been placed at the edge of the mound of sand which contained the 'central' one. Although this sand mound was considered natural, the published section records an old surface suggesting that the monument was of two periods, with the smaller cist placed at the edge of an existing, albeit natural, mound. If so, the gravel and stones sealing the central cist may have belonged to the second phase with the cover of the central cist originally being flush with the contemporary surface.

CARDURNOCK PIKE, NY55885200

This cairn, located just above the break of the slope, but not on the summit of the Pennine edge, is visible from a large lowland area; from the sites of the Grey Yauds and Broomrigg circles and from the ridge itself. A disturbance on the northern side is either a shepherd's shelter or rooms built by the miser who is said to have lived here. It is now impossible to be certain what the original profile was, but there appear to be carefully pitched stones within the body of the cairn and there is a possibility that the site contained a skeleton.

On the lower ground, and in the area from which the site is visible, there were a number of other sites, including those at Leafy Hill, near Castle Carrock, excavated by Greenwell.[3] The first was a beaker inhumation within a cist set into a natural mound. The second was a small diameter mound covering an oval pit with a cremation and flint knife.

SOLDEN HILL AND BROADFIELD, NY4144

Early antiquarians reported a number of sites in the area of what, in medieval times, had been Inglewood Forest. Of these, the most tantalizing were reported in the vicinity of Broadfield.[4] First was a large boulder, and although the published sketch suggests it an erratic, and there were other stones nearby – amongst which, it was suggested, it was possible to detect an avenue – such a stone is now unusual in that area. Second was a circular bank within which there appeared to have been a circle of 'erect stones'. The bank was some 20m in diameter, and the soil between the stones and centre of the site was less stoney than elsewhere and contained a 'large amount' of 'ashes'. Within this area were three cists. These details suggest that site may have been a ring cairn, although the published plan shows a penannular bank.

In their account of the area, Britton and Brayley[5] described a third site called Solden Hill. This had been a mound some 13m in diameter with a 'circle of granite stones on top'; an arrangement which might be compared with that of the Standing Stones on Moor Divock. When dug, several cists 'containing a great variety of human bones, skulls, jaws etc.', were found within the mound.

CARROCK FELL, NY343336

This mountain, located on the eastern edge of the Skiddaw-Caldbeck massif, is visible from Broadfield, many parts of the Eden valley (*colour plate 3*) and beyond the Solway. Its distinctive profile includes two small peaks, one of which is an artificial cairn. The whole of the summit is enclosed by a bank or wall which has numerous gaps. Collingwood[6] interpreted the site as a hillfort slighted by the Romans, but the possibility that it is a Neolithic 'causewayed enclosure' needs to be considered, especially as rock for stone axe production may have been acquired nearby.[7]

Whilst such a juxtaposition has been noted in some southern examples, the significance of this site – if it is a causewayed enclosure – is that the gaps are in the bank rather than

GREEN HOW, AUGHERTREE FELL, NY25803746

This indistinct hilltop enclosure has been described as a possible causewayed enclosure,[8] but possible gaps in the bank are difficult to identify on the ground. To the west, it is difficult to separate from a linear dyke, and the most obvious part of the earthwork is the southern sector where it is almost on top of the hill. In short, the earthwork circuit does not enclose the hilltop, rather it seems to include a small steep-sided ridge in its western half.

The linear dyke, referred to above, is part of a complex of similar earthworks on the unenclosed common, and some may be part of the landscape associated with three settlement sites, one of which has a distinct droveway. These lie on the northern facing slope, and the associated field system probably overlies the site of the burial mound excavated in the area by lanthern.[9] The urns were said to have been 'arranged in a circle'. It is unclear which site was excavated but there are at least five mounds on the northern slope, whilst that shown in (*colour plate 8*) lies to the south, apparently unexcavated.

CASTLERIGG, NY29132363

Although the location of this site makes it the best-known monument in Cumbria, it was sufficiently remote for Camden to omit it from his description of the county, and it was not until the eighteenth century that the first accounts appear. Of these, Pennant's picture (*6*) is perhaps the most illuminating, for it shows that some of the stones have been subsequently re-erected at some time. That same picture appears to show a fallen stone beyond the circle, to the south-east, but it is not shown on his stylised plan. Nor does that plan show an outlier to the west, where Hutchinson, writing twenty years later, says there was one 'three paces' beyond the circle and opposite to the rectangle.[10] Without excavation or geophysical survey, therefore, the original arrangement of stones must remain uncertain, as must the existence of a porch like entrance and another larger circle 'in the next pasture toward the town'.[11] It is, however, evident that the inner, rectangular arrangement of stones – the antiquity of which has sometimes been questioned – was in existence prior to 1725.

The rectangular area was trenched in 1882, and the limited report noted that natural was about 35cm below present ground surface, 'with the exception of a small portion at the west end where the black soil mixed with stones continued to a depth of three feet.'[12] Within this feature, which may have been a pit, there was some burned wood or charcoal and 'some dark unctuous sort of earth'. The depth of soil in the remaining area is perhaps somewhat surprising, and it may relate to the fact that the rectangle is located in a depression.

North and West

6 Pennant's picture of Castlerigg, showing that some stones have actually been re-erected.
Reproduced with permission of the Bodleian Library, University of Oxford from Gough's Scotland

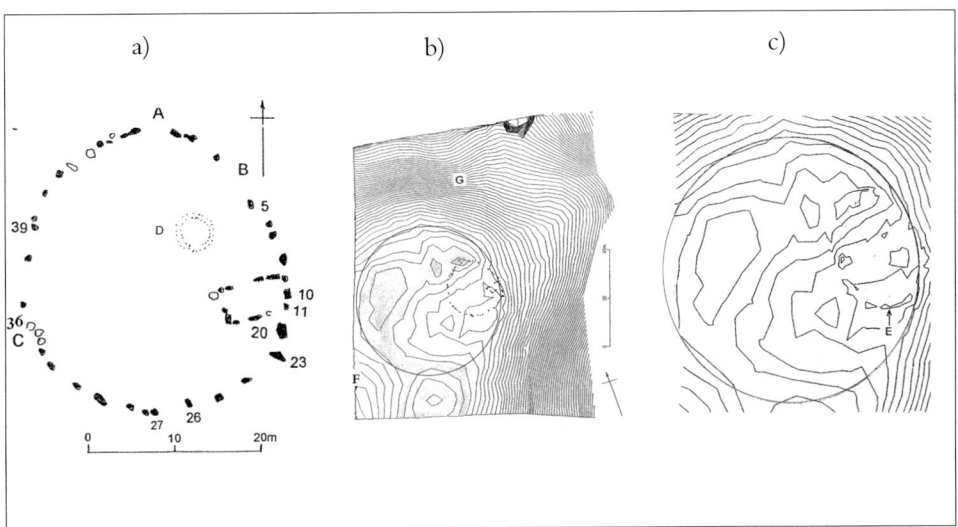

7a-c Castlerigg today. Given the ridge and furrow in the field, the survey points were taken half-way up a ridge to smooth out the effects of those earthworks

Apart from the rectangular area, there are a number of other features to note:
- The circle has a clearly denoted 'entrance' A (7a) flanked by taller stones with closely spaced ones beyond them,
- contrasting with large gaps such as that at B,[13]
    which in turn contrasts with closely spaced stones such as those at C.
- There is a symmetry of stone shapes and sizes either side of the entrance which is best appreciated from the interior of the circle.
- Two stones (23 and 26) are arranged 'radially'.
- Within the circle there is at least one small mound with surrounding ditch D.
- The circle is not located in the centre of but to the side of the hilltop (7b). As such, it is both at the edge of a steep slope and in a hollow but with its entrance on one of the highest parts of the hilltop;
    as a result, when seen from the north, only a few of the stones are visible; with those in the eastern half being more visible than those in the western half.
- The long axis of the rectangle of stones is that of the hollow in which the circle is located.
- The almost flat hilltop is almost circular in plan (7c). Although this must be natural, the fact that its diameter is about three times that of the stone circle allows us to speculate whether there was another monument, such as a circular palisade.
- As Burl noted, there is a bank at E (7c) beyond the stones, but this feature is most evident across and beyond the entrance where it appears to relate to agricultural activity.
- That activity is visible as ridge and furrow, and was probably responsible for the discovery of the stone axe now in Keswick Museum, and said to have been found 'in the vicinity of the monument'. Note that it may not have been found within the circle as sometimes stated.
- There is now an outlier to the south-west F in (7b). This was 're-erected' in 1915, before which it was difficult to find and 'completely covered in grass'. The latter is consistent with the plough marks on the stone, and its antiquity must be questioned.
- The northern approach corresponds to a subtle hollow G in (7b) which may be the result of erosion by feet, raising the possibility that it relates to focussed prehistoric movement of the kind which saw the building of a road and ceremonial approach at Durrington Walls.

Today, once the hill has been ascended, it is not merely the circle which becomes visible but the panorama of mountains and valleys. The possibility that stone circles replicate or reflect the horizon has been discussed by some authors, but there appears to be no close correspondence here between the height or shapes of stones and the distant summits. Skiddaw, for example, does not appear to be marked. In contrast, Anderson argued that sunrise on 1 May was over the very distant Fiend's Fell with such an alignment passing, remarkably, through Long Meg and Her Daughters.[14] Other orientations which might relate to something like the (later) Celtic calendar have also been proposed with midsummer sunrise/midwinter sunset being through stones 5 and 22,[15] but the medial line of the rectangle has no known astronomical orientation, although it does point to Great Mell Fell.

In 1995, a spiral 'carving' was recorded on stone 11 which occurs to one side of that medial line. However, recent analysis suggests that the spiral, which was never seen after the initial records, was modern and transient; perhaps painted in yoghurt by someone unaware of the problems it would cause.[16] Equally, some, or all of the putative carvings, subsequently identified on stones 10, 23, 27 and 36 may be natural in origin, whilst the date of the diamond on stone 36 is uncertain. However, a number of stones have natural banding, with that of stone 20, including white quartz, and stone 39, a vulva shaped inclusion, so that the natural patterning, texture or colour of a stone may have been a factor in its selection and placement within the monument (*colour plate 4*).

GREAT MELL FELL, NY39682537

A low, flat-topped mound is located to one side of the summit of this isolated hill which is a prominent landscape feature visible from the Castlerigg stone circle. Indeed, the rectangle within that monument is not aligned radially but points towards this summit.

The mound, some 80cm high and 8.5m in diameter, is within, but not quite central to, a circular enclosure formed by a low bank with inner and possibly outer ditch.

LITTLE MELL FELL, NY42322401

Although not marked on OS maps, a low, flat-topped mound is located on the summit of this hill. It is, however, unclear whether the profile is original or due to the moving of the OS trig point in 1952, when a collared urn was found.[17]

ELVA PLAIN, NY17693172

The remains of this circle are located at the western end of the steep-sided ridge, south of the river Derwent and north of a flat valley floor, which, in the Neolithic, was probably open water. It is, therefore, somewhat surprising that the site is not itself prominently located and, unlike the circle at Castlerigg, is built on a slope (*8*). Despite that slope, the stones — assuming they are in or near their original positions — form an almost perfect circle, but there is now no evidence for an outlier to the south-west.[18]

The stones lie adjacent to a footpath and are best appreciated by approaching from the west. There, at the end of the track from the farm, it can be seen that the ground to the west slopes down; that the monument is almost on a localised watershed above the head of a small steep valley which falls to the east.

Given the existence of the latter, it is somewhat surprising to find that Bassenthwaite Lake is not visible, although it can be seen from a few metres to the east of the circle. Was there some other factor influencing the position of the site? The most obvious one is afforded by the prominent crag on the skyline to the north-west where the midsummer sun might have set. There is a small stone directly east of the circle, (*8A*), but this does not appear to be visible from the circle whilst that at *8*B appears to have no astronomical significance. However, a line from the assumed centre of the circle through B would pass across the eastern end of Wythop Woods through Castlerigg to the summit of Great Dod beyond.

Around a number of the stones in the circle are others, apparently the product of ploughing, and there is a slight lynchet (*8*C) immediately beyond the lower stones which may have resulted from such activity or be the remains of a bank-like feature of the kind visible at Long Meg and Castlerigg.

EWANRIGG AND MARYPORT, NY035353 AND NY047377

A number of monuments existed on the ridge of high ground visible from and to the east of the A596, south of Ewanrigg, part of Maryport. These included a settlement with drove road, a cross ridge dyke,[19] a ring ditch (all discovered by aerial photography) and a group of at least 28 burials (two inhumations and 26 cremations).[20] The latter were grouped in a roughly circular pattern around a high point on the ridge where there were the remains of a cist and cairn associated with food vessel pottery. Of the other burials, one was associated with beaker pottery, others with collared urns and others with no pottery.

Earlier evidence for prehistoric activity in the area was the nineteenth-century discovery of two cup and ring marked stones in a field north of the Roman *vicus*, which probably came from another mound or cairn. In addition, the Senhouse collection of *local* antiquities included several collared urns, the provenance of which is unknown.[21]

Both the cup and ring site, and Ewanrigg, appear to have been located near wetlands which developed when sea levels and the configuration of the coast changed.

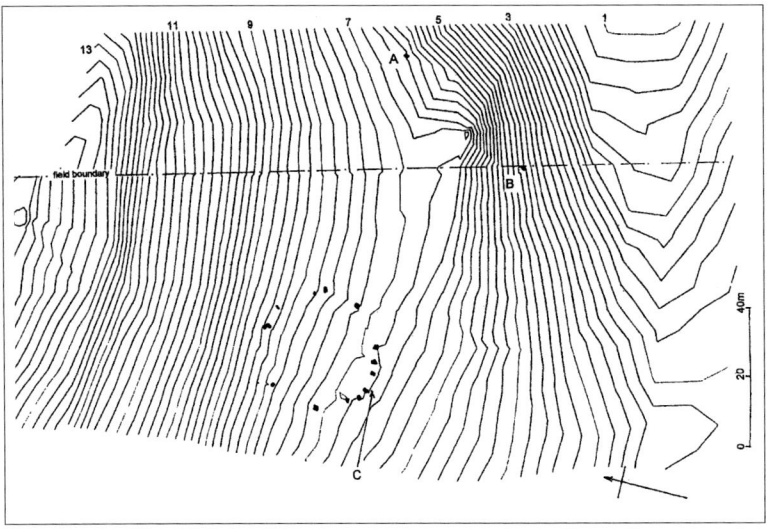

8 Elva Plain

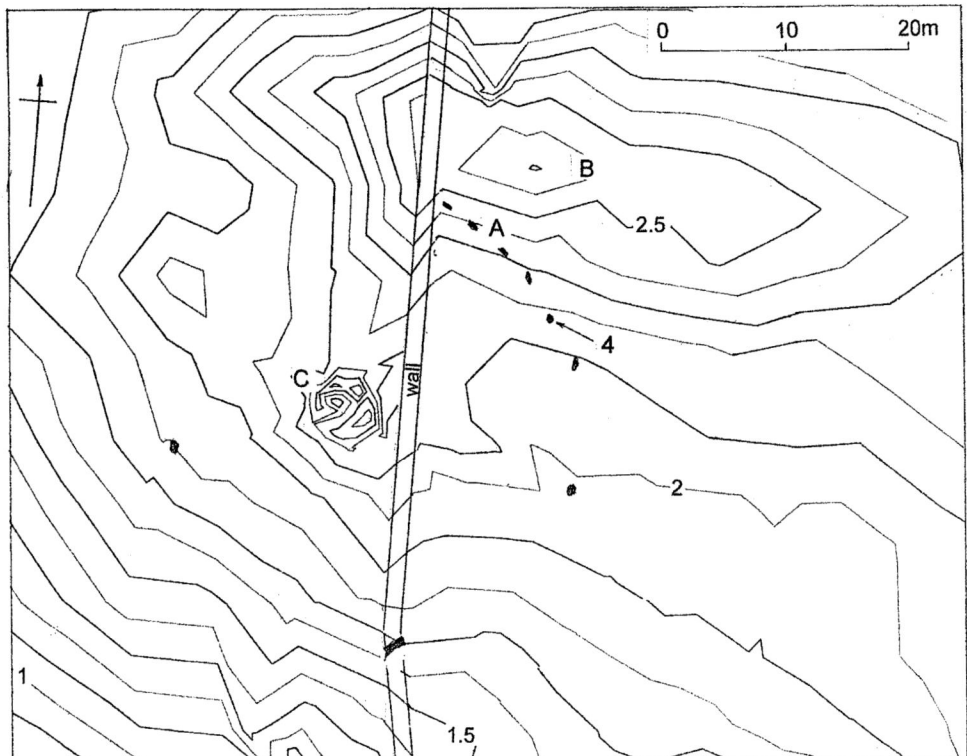

9 Studfoldgate

STUDFOLDGATE, NY04022235

The standing stones (9), which are on private land, appear to form an ellipse, but some of the stones at A do not appear ancient, so the monument may have been laid out as a perfect circle, 33m in diameter. Certainly, it is necessary to question the relationship of the stones to the low, but prominent ridge B and why the monument was not located on the flatter ground immediately to the south-east.

Within 'the circle' is a mound C, which was partly excavated and the remains of a possible kerb or cist uncovered. In addition, recent fieldwork has identified carvings (chevrons) on stone 4 and, nearby, possible burial mounds and a stone which may have been used for finishing stone axes.

The mounds, like the circle, are located on a ridge with spectacular views across the lowland to the north where there is considerable evidence of prehistoric activity. For example, a stone circle was reported at Lamplugh, whilst at Dean there is a possible standing stone, a cup and ring marked boulder, and possibly the remains of another circle.[22] An encrusted urn was found at Branthwaite, and further urns were found in cutting the railway at Ullock where, within 'bowshot', there was reputed to have been a circle of large boulders. By 1876, however, the latter had been either removed or buried, although two large slabs in the field boundary may be related.

BLAKELEY RAISE AND THREE OR FOUR LOST CIRCLES

The Blakeley Raise stone circle, with its central mound at NY06011403 was surveyed by Thom[23] and found to be typical of many others; the measurements corresponding to multiples of his megalithic yard and there being a stellar orientation which seems to have been singled out in other monuments. It is, therefore, somewhat surprising to note the contents of a letter written to the Ordnance survey in 1967. 'Originally it stood in the "infield" of "Standing Stones Farm" but in the eighteenth century was removed by the farmer, who used the stones for gateposts etc.. Whether all the re-erected stones came from the circle is not certain but … it is quite doubtful'.[24] Standing Stones Farm is to the south-west and, if any circle there was close to the buildings, it would have been within a valley rather than on a hillside like the present structure.

There was another (?) farm called Standing Stones, near Whitehaven, at NX989180, where, it is said, there was another circle 'anciently known as Le Whales'.[25] South of St Bees, at Ringing Stone, there is said to have been yet another circle, and there are certainly two large stones in the field bank.

Between there and Blakeley Raise is the town of Egremont, and on the common Hutchinson noted 'we observed several tumuli, particularly one of loose stones, 40 paces in circumference. Not far from it is a circle of large stones, 10 in number, forming an area 50 paces in circumference without any elevation of ground'. The common cannot now be identified with certainty. Did it include the Blakeley Raise area?

STOCKDALE MOOR AND SAMSON'S BRATFULL, NY099082

Amongst the mounds of the cairnfield are a number which appear to be well constructed. These might, therefore, be funerary rather than 'field clearance'. Samson's Bratfull – or *apronfull* – seems, however, an appropriate name for the large cairn at the head of a tiny valley and stream. It is some 25m long, 13.5m wide and 1.7m high and, although damaged by digging, there are no records of anything being found.

BURNMOOR, CENTRED NY173027

There are five stone circles above Eskdale (*10*); a pair on Low Longrigg at NY17250279, another pair above White Moss NY173241 and a larger circle referred to as Brats Hill NY17360234. A feature of them all is, however, the existence of one or more mounds in the centre of the circle. Those of the largest circle have been dug, two by a Mr Wright. These were found to cover a 'rude dome … of five large stones under which were burnt human bones' and 'fragments of the horns of the stag and other animal remains'. These remains suggest that the cairns are burial mounds and not part of the nearby cairnfields,[26] an interpretation supported by them possessing kerbs.

Williams, who reported the work of Mr Wright, thought there had been an outer circle and that tipped stone A (*10c*) had formed part of an internal rectangle very similar to that at Castlerigg. This interpretation was dismissed by Dymond[27] who pointed out that there were a number of stones scattered across the moor, and that probing had found no stones where the rectangle was supposed to be. Of the stones still visible near the circle, and shown in (*10c*), one, to the north-west, can be interpreted as providing an alignment on the midsummer setting sun, but it is no more than 0.3m high. A more obvious outlier is stone B (*10c*), but that has no obvious astronomical alignment; although, it is due north of the eastern cairn which is, itself, east of the centre of the circle. Nevertheless, stone B raises the possibility that some 'outliers' were in fact separate monuments.

Other stellar alignments have been suggested, but here attention is drawn to the fact that the two circles on Low Longrigg appear aligned on the top of nearby Boat How, whilst the midsummer sun would rise to the side of that hilltop and Sca Fell beyond.

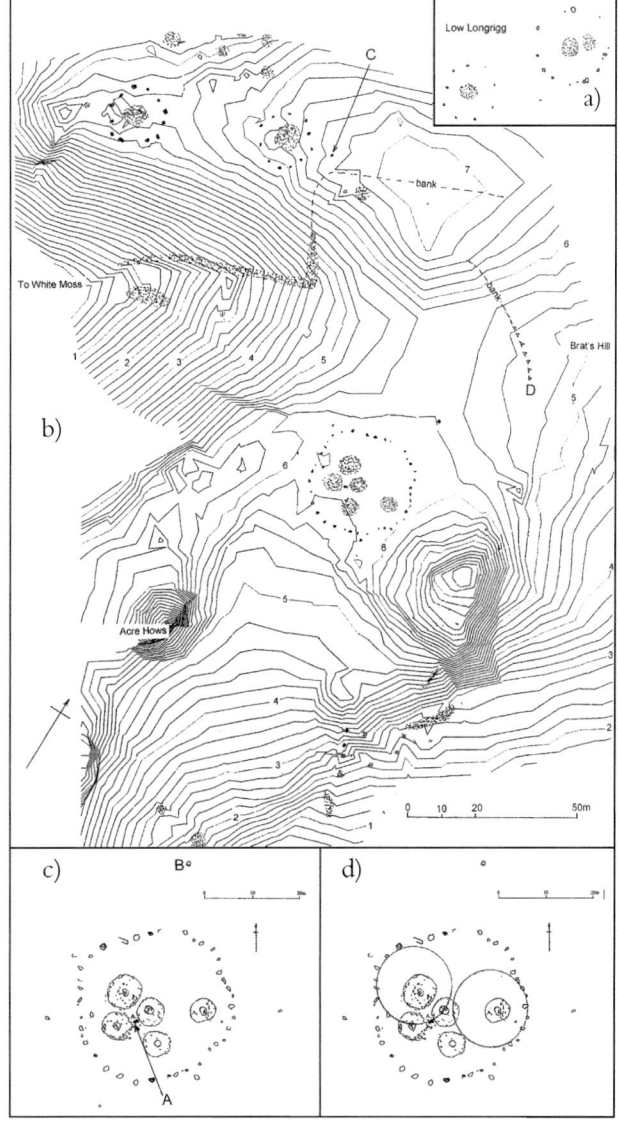

10a-d Burnmoor

It has also been claimed that the Brats Hill circle has a 'flattened' perimeter, again like Castlerigg and, as there, a response to the ground falling away from the monument. However, the ground does not fall away here (*10*b), and the 'flattening' is not obvious in the published plans, rather the perimeter consists of four arcs and stone A would lie on the perimeter of a circle drawn through one. This suggests that the monument may have been remodelled and may itself have originally been two separate circles (*10*d). Certainly stone A needs explanation.

Despite the curious arcs, it is also the case that the whole monument is roughly circular and the centre of the eastern circle on White Moss is 45 degrees from the centre of that circle. Equally, stone (C in *10*b) may mark the major standstill of the moon when seen from the same centre. However, the high ridge to the north would mean that midsummer sun would not have set along the 45 degree line, so that if it was real, the White Moss monument was erected at the point where midwinter sunrise occurred behind the centre of the Brats Moss circle, implying the latter is the earlier.

The stones of the eastern circle on White Moss are said to have been re-erected, and the ground within the northern half certainly appears to have been excavated. Somewhat in contrast, the northern half of the western circle appears to be higher than the ground outside, raising the possibility that the stones projected from a low platform.

A further feature of the circles is their different topographical positions. Whilst the pairs are on ridges, the larger circle is in a col between high points. One reason for the latter might be that the knoll, Acre Hows, allowed the site to be located from afar, especially for anyone coming along the path from Burnmoor Tarn. Another possibility is that the circle was avoiding what is now boggy ground to the north and south, but whether such wetland developed after the building of the monuments is unclear. In part, however, the wetland appears to have accumulated behind the lynchet – part of the cairnfield – at D in *10*b. As such, it is a reminder of the deterioration in soils which appears to have begun at the time of, or just before the start of the Neolithic.

What then was the vegetation at the time of the building of the monuments? Pennington[28] argued that they had been built in a forested environment on the basis of the palynological evidence from Burnmoor Tarn, but the pollen diagram may not be representative of the landscape immediately around the monuments. Moreover, if Acre Hows did serve as a marker, then it would be because the landscape was more open than previously assumed. Of course it is possible that the larger circle was located in forest and near to the knoll at the top of the valley leading to Mitredale and the coast. In short, the moor may have been accessed from Mitredale rather than Eskdale, as at present.

GREY CROFT, NY03330240

Although all but one of the stones of this circle 1 (*11*a) was 're-erected' in 1949,[29] the site is worth visiting. It can be reached by footpath from the road north of Seascale, and from there the stones can be seen silhouetted against the sea.

The work of 1949 included excavation of the central area and two peripheral trenches, and led to the discovery of an oval, central cairn with larger boulders around the edge.

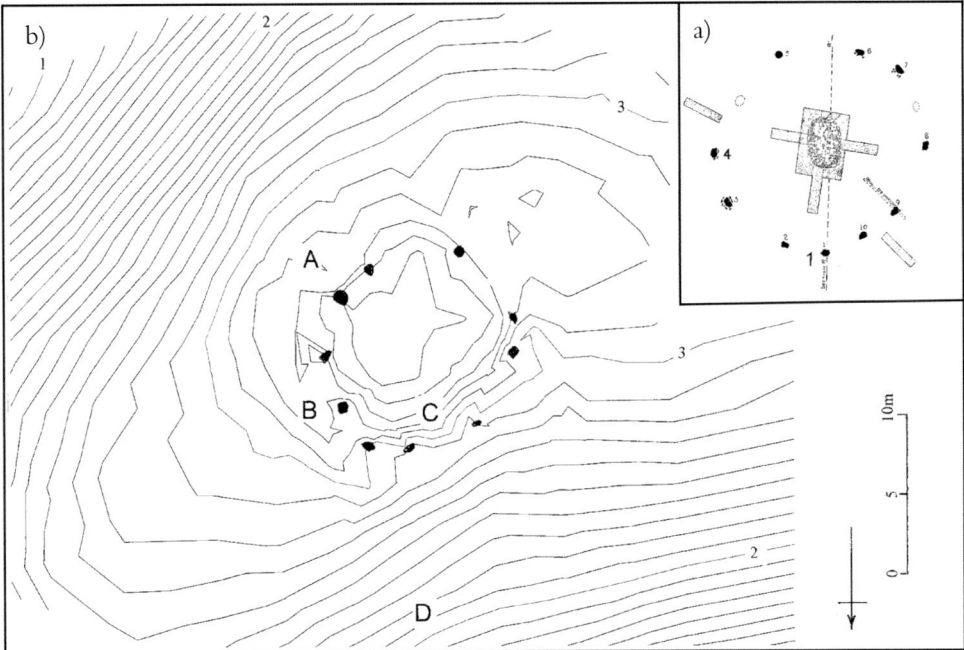

11 Grey Croft today. Inserted is the published plan of the areas excavated

Sand below the cairn contained calcined bone fragments and some macrofossil plant remains, including 'six hawthorn berries'.

The central cairn is reminiscent of the monuments on Burnmoor but is not visible in the present monument. Rather, the whole of the interior appears to be a low, if hummocky, mound which has been exaggerated at point A (*11b*) by modern agriculture, whilst at B it appears to have originally extended beyond the circle. Moreover, the form lines at C show that the mound is higher on that side by virtue of the circle not being in the centre of the low ridge on which it is located.

The present appearance of the site is not inconsistent with the sections of 1949 where the central cairn is shown below the surface of a gently sloping ridge. However, given the existence of that ridge, it is not clear how material would have accumulated around the cairn, unless deliberately placed there. The significance of the latter is twofold. Firstly, the monument may be of two periods, with the form of the second monument somewhat different to the first. Secondly, the broken lignite ring, picked up in one of the peripheral trenches, is likely to have come from that secondary mound, whilst the broken stone axe, found near stone 4, may also have come from that structure or a wholly different context. Equally, if the mound at B indicates the original extent of the mound, then the pits into which the stones had been felled must have been dug through it.

It will be evident from (*11a*) that there appears to have been no excavation around the stones, rather they were found by probing the ground and, where packing stones did not exist below the stones to guide re-erection, weathering was taken into account on the assumption that the prevailing wind direction has not changed in 5000 years. Consequently, the form and present appearance of the circle should be viewed with some caution.

The probing also located an 'outlier' – stone 11 – '70ft to the north' of stone 1. Omitted from the published plan, it must have been in the vicinity of D and appears to have been visible in the 1960's when Thom claimed it was aligned on the star Deneb.[30]

In the vicinity of point D, the stone would have stood above the steep slope of the small valley which lies to the north. The latter, and its stream, are worth close inspection, for at the seaward end the northern side curves round into what appears to be an old coastal cliff. Whilst the southern side is obscured by the golf course and possible former sand dunes, the topography suggest that the monument was erected on a low ridge, a short distance inland from the point at which a small valley and stream debouched onto the beach; a natural focal point in the landscape.

GRETIGATE, NY058037

The footpath between Seascale Hall and Gosforth passes the end of a shallow valley between glacial hills where three possible stone circles were described for the first time in 1961.[31] One of the circles, the largest (31m in diameter), was represented simply by a curved field boundary, but the others consisted of partly buried stones.

Amongst these stones, two circles, one with a diameter of 20-23m and one of c7.3m, were traced and excavated. Inside the larger was an area of cobbles, three areas of burnt earth, two holes containing carbonised wood and a 'worn down tooth'. A cobbled area within the smaller site yielded two small flint flakes, small carbon deposits and an egg-shaped granite ball.

The stones of the larger circle were still visible in 1972 when it was apparent that they could be interpreted as forming a circle of different configuration, but today none are visible in the dense undergrowth.

KIRKSANTON AND A BURIED LANDSCAPE, CENTRED SD1283

The standing stones at Kirksanton (*colour plate 9*) are on private land but adjacent to a public footpath, at SD13608110. The site was first described by Hutchinson as 'a small tumulus on the summit of which are two huge stones pitched endwise … about 15ft asunder. Near adjoining to this monument, several other stones stood lately placed in a rude manner'.[32] In 1874, a cup mark was discovered on the inner face of the eastern upright.

Today, there is only a slight rise between the stones so that the dimensions of Hutchinson's mound remain unknown. However, on an aerial photo (*12a*) there appears to be a ring of pits around the stones (arrowed). The cropmark enclosure A is one of several in the area, but other cropmarks include 'timber henges' or roughly circular palisaded enclosures with internal and concentric pits. One of these is adjacent to an area which produced sedimentary and macro-fossil evidence for an intensification of late Neolithic agricultural activity.[33]

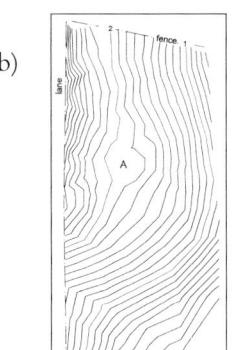
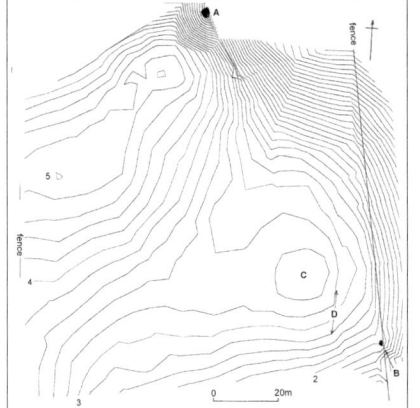

12a-c A buried landscape. (a) Cropmarks at Kirksanton. (b) The site of the Gutterby circle. (c) The site of the Annaside circle. A is the erratic previously considered to be part of the circle

In addition, there were three stone circles in the area: at Annaside SD09888528, Hall Foss SD112871[34] and Gutterby SD10608488. At the latter – also known as Kirkstones – thirty stones[35] formed part of two concentric circles with the inner one having 'two sides, very entire … opposite each other',[36] an arrangement echoed in the timber structures. Two hundred yards south of Gutterby, there was also a large cairn, some 13.5m in diameter 'surrounded with large stones at the base'.

Neither the cairn, nor the circle has survived, but the topography, where the circle is said to have stood, A (in *12*b) suggests the outer circle could have been 20m–28m, and the inner one 14m. These dimensions are similar to Oddendale and, as there, we might suspect the stones were not very large, for none are conspicuous anywhere in the vicinity. Likewise, at Annaside, the one possible stone which may have come from the monument B[37] (in *12*c) is not large. There, however, the circle may have had a central mound C, but the latter appears truncated by ploughing along line D.

Together with a ring ditch and collared urn, these monuments are evidence of intense prehistoric use of this narrow lowland strip; an intensity of land use confirmed by the palaeo-environmental evidence noted above. In that context, attention is drawn to the proximity of the above sites to an extensive wetland area extending north from Kirksanton, part of which, at Gutterby, was a tarn producing 'large quantities of leeches'.[38]

LACRA, CENTRED SD149812

The four megalithic monuments here are located on terraces amongst the rocky knolls of the ridge end, high above Kirksanton. They are on private farmland, but two of the sites – 'A' and 'D', to use the nomenclature of 1947[39] – are visible from the public footpath. From there, too, it is possible to see the earthwork remains of two settlements; that of Kirkstead marked on the OS map and that at SD148811.

'Circle A' is nearest the present farm buildings and what must originally have been a spring. Although apparently incomplete, all but one of the stones lies close to the perimeter of a circle, 17.5m across. A feature of the site, commented upon in the nineteenth century, is the clustering of stones A, exactly east of the centre (in 13a). In addition, there is an apparent outlier B, but there are other stones on the ground nearby e.g., at C. The marshy ground to the south separates this site from 'circle D'.

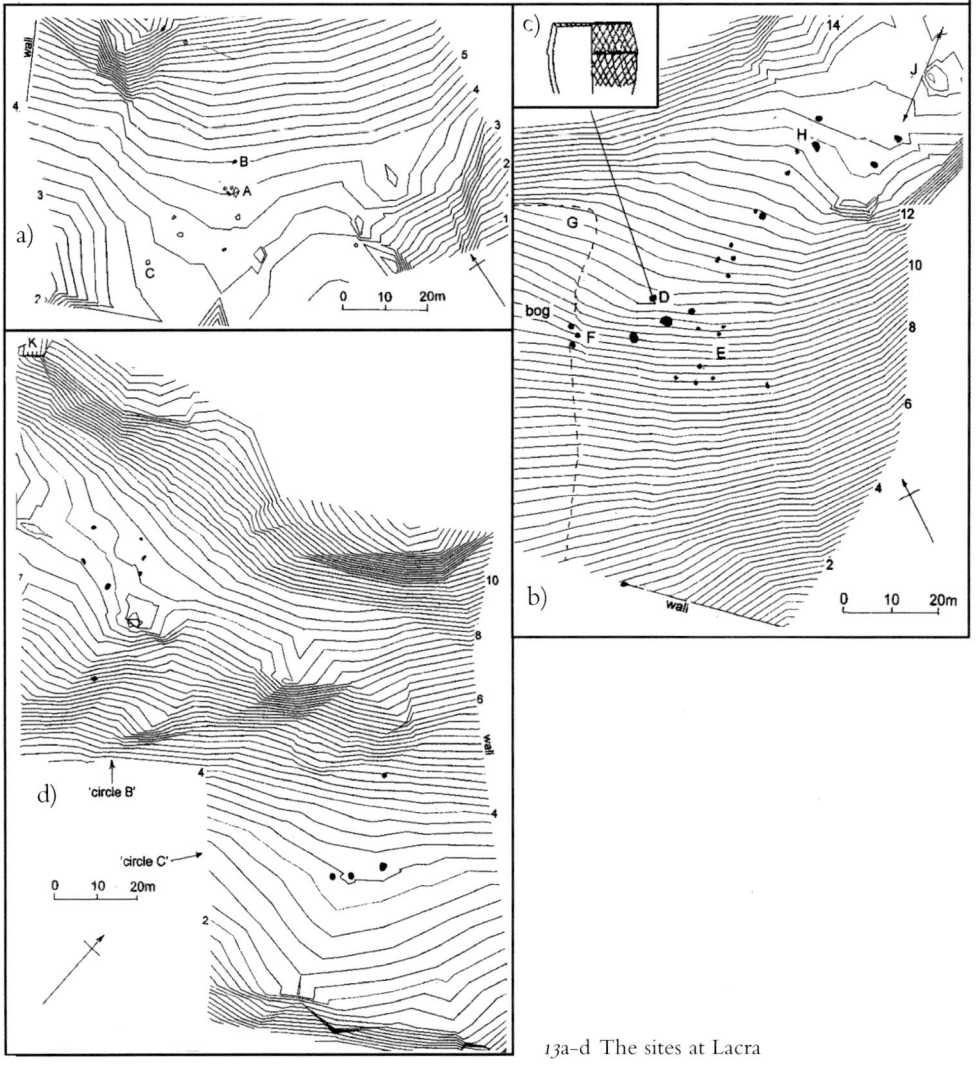

13a-d The sites at Lacra

Although described as a 'circle', there is no clear pattern amongst the boulders of site 'D', and it is perhaps unfortunate that the excavations of 1947 did not look for stone sockets. However, the trench adjacent to stone D in (*13b*) showed that boulder had not been placed in a socket, although an inverted urn had been placed against it (*13c*). Consequently, the stones were considered the remains of a circle about 15m across, and with a possible concentric circle E, whilst the stones at F were interpreted as the possible remains of another smaller circle, but they are adjacent to the boggy area and this seems unlikely, even allowing for changed soils and hydrology. It will also be apparent that the main group of stones are not located in the centre of the terrace but to one side, a situation which may be explained by the proximity of a putative spring G.

The second principal feature of site 'D' is the line of stones stretching north-eastwards. It was interpreted as the remains of an avenue in 1947, albeit with some caution. In fact, it is possible to suggest the stones form two separate alignments ending in the two prominent stones at H. However, there are two more horizontal stones beyond them and a few more on the same alignment as the break of slope at J, as if one row continues much further north-eastwards. It will also be evident that stones H are at the edge of a large area of relatively flat land and that they, together with the horizontal stones, may have formed another circle 17m across.

'Circle B' (*13d*) is also not located on the largest area of available flat land; land from which the Kirksanton stones are visible. The site is, therefore, not the most obvious location to build in, especially as 'circle C' is not intervisible. It is, however, possible that the midsummer sun sets over a grouping of natural rocks/outcrops at K.

Whatever the explanation, the site is the most complete of the circles, and the excavations of 1947 revealed that there had originally been 11 evenly spaced uprights, a central cairn with sort of kerb and, possibly, groupings of stones at the cardinal points. In contrast, 'circle C' consists of three stones with a possible fourth, and if they did originally form a circle then there must have been a large number closely spaced.

SWINSIDE, SD17168818

One of the first accounts of this site describes it as 'a small but beautiful druidical monument ... circular about twenty yards in diameter' with stones from 'six to eight feet high, all standing and complete'.[40] Today, some of the stones are horizontal but the adjective 'beautiful' is still applied by many who toil up the track to visit the site and enjoy both the site and views.

Topographically and, particularly when seen from the east and at a distance, the site can be described as being within, or at the edge of a semicircular embayment in the side of Black Combe. The latter, some 600m high, forms the south-western 'corner' of the Lake District massif and is a prominent mountain visible from high ground in the vicinity of Wigan and Chorley, more than 70kms away. Closer to, however, the Swinside circle can be seen to occupy flat ground within a valley. From here, the valley opens to the south-east but the ground to the west of the circle rises another 160m to the summit of Raven Crag, whilst the view to the south is blocked by the slopes of Knott Hill.

As noted above, not all the stones are now standing; a situation which raises the question of whether some have been deliberately felled since Hutchinson's time or whether they have fallen as a result of chance or agricultural operations. Chance seems, however, unlikely, as some appear to be half buried and, indeed, were it not for Hutchinson's account one might have assumed from their character that they had fallen centuries ago. Dymond[41] thought they had collapsed as a result of 'the usual cause – the sheltering of sheep under the lee of the larger stones', and reported that one leaning member had been protected by a bank of cobbles in the late nineteenth century.

In addition to the fallen stones, there is a large gap on the eastern side A (14a) and the (relatively) widely spaced stones along this eastern arc are echoed by the arrangement of stones diametrically opposite at B. Dymond trenched gap A but could find no evidence for stones having stood there. However, a principal characteristic of the remainder of the perimeter is the fact that many of the stones are contiguous, forming a solid perimeter not seen in other circles in the region. Dymond described this arrangement as a peristalith and stone 'fence', and the effect would have been more impressive had other stones stood in the hollows recorded in 1900. Significantly, no hollows were noted in arcs A and B, so that they can be seen as dividing the perimeter into two, almost equal halves.

The stone 'fence' is perhaps best appreciated when looking northwards from point C where the stones are also reminiscent of the uprights of a palisade. A similar impression is provided by the arrangement of stones around the porch-like entrance and anyone looking into the circle from there has the impression of looking along a passage into an enclosed space; a view reminiscent of that obtained at the Clava cairns, in north-east Scotland.

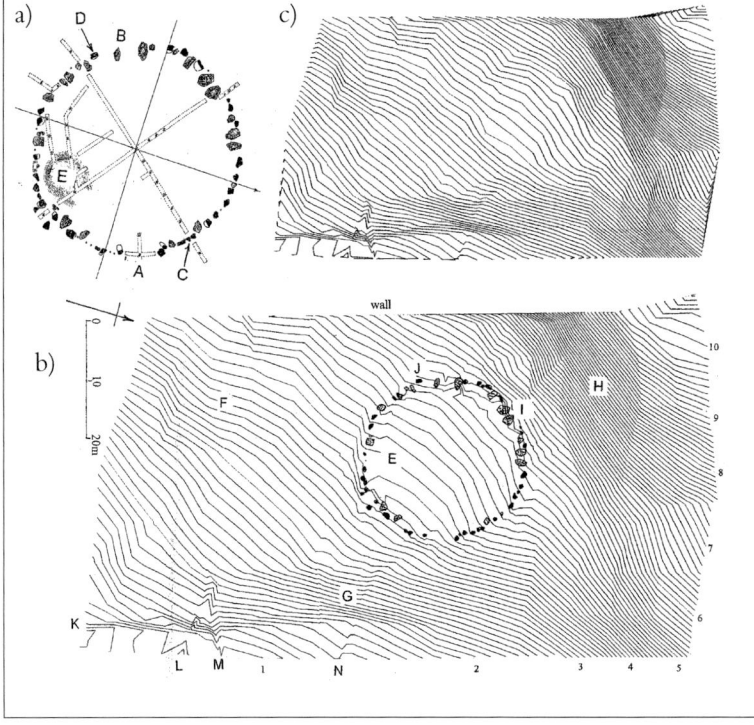

14a-c Swinside. a) is based on Dymond's plan and shows his excavations, in b). K–N are linear features resulting from agricultural activity

The porch-like entrance of the circle is, however, paralleled by that at Long Meg and faces south-east, providing thereby a general alignment on the midwinter rising sun.[42] If that was intentional, then anyone standing in the centre of the circle would, on a clear day, have seen it rise over an unnamed hilltop on the far side of the Duddon estuary, behind 'The Kirk' on Kirkby Moor; although, that monument does not appear to be located precisely on such an alignment. Equally, anyone standing at the centre of the circle would, if vegetation and weather conditions permitted, see the midsummer sun rise over the distant, pointed summit of The Caw, and this alignment may be reflected in the arrangement of stones at C.

Two other features of the stones must be noted. Firstly, that although 'a thorough and repeated scrutiny' by Dymond 'failed to detect any archaic marks upon the stones', the carving of an *Ankh*, the Ancient Egyptian symbol of Life, was found on one stone in 1952.[43] Secondly, it is important to note the colour, patterning and texture of the stones. This is most evident in the case of upright D *(colour plate 10)*. Weathering, and the rubbing of animals have, however, almost certainly changed the original colour of the stones, but even so, Dymond noted that they were still 'variously tinted'. That some may, originally, have been light blue is suggested by a newly moved stone on the approach track *(colour plate 4b)*.

It has already been noted that Dymond trenched the site with little result. He also investigated the small mound at E, but again the results were inconclusive. Nevertheless, the feature, which has otherwise not attracted attention or comment, might be compared with the 'ring ditch' in a similar position at Castlerigg. In addition, there is another previously unrecorded mound outside the circle at F *(14b)*, and it certainly should be considered a possible 'burial' mound; although, without excavation, an alternative explanation might be that it is material cleared from the nearby stream.

This stream is one of several local topographical features that require recognition. In particular, attention is drawn to the fact that, as *(14b)* demonstrates, the circle is actually located on a gently sloping shelf above a short steep slope G and, most significantly, built up against an even steeper slope H. What is, however, not clear is whether the northern edge of the circle is actually cut into the bottom of the slope with the interior of the circle effectively terraced into the hillside. At I, for example, there is a faint hollow which continues at J and could be explained by soil accumulation against the circle after it was built just beyond the steep slope. However, the situation is complicated by the apparent bank around the base of the stones.

Dymond does not refer to any bank, but it cannot be an extension of the small bank which he reported had been built because the hollows he recorded are within it. Moreover, it seems to have been in existence by 1821, for Housman[44] noted that 'the larger stones are 50 in number, with an infinite number of smaller ones scattered about their bases'.

Perhaps, significantly, the bank appears to be absent along the eastern arc of the circle in the vicinity of gap A and there the perimeter appears to be a terrace. Indeed, when viewed from C, and elsewhere, the impression is of a terraced interior. However, one of the objectives of Dymond's excavations was to investigate whether the surface of the circle had been levelled, and he could find no evidence for that; a conclusion consistent with the evidence presented in *(10c)*. Nevertheless, the form lines recorded there do suggest that the interior may have been scraped level; an explanation not incompatible with the evidence found in the excavations. It is, therefore, most unfortunate that the more detailed records implied in Dymond's numbers on his plan have not apparently survived.

As noted above, the stones viewed from C appear to form a wall and this might reflect the wish of the builders to exclude those outside. However, if that were the case, it is odd that there should be the gaps at A and B. Moreover, anyone standing on the high ground above H can see the whole circle, its interior and the principal viewshed down the valley.

This raises the question of why the circle was built so close to a steep slope, especially as there was 'flat land' available around F. Possible reasons would appear to be that:

a) The builders wanted to incorporate/build up against the higher ground of H.
b) The builders wished to accommodate some other, now invisible/unrecognisable landscape feature.
c) The builders needed to be in this position to get an astronomical alignment.
d) There was some other structure already in position; perhaps the other, larger, but less intact circle to the 'south' which Hutchinson thought he saw.

Unfortunately, apart from that one reference, the latter site is otherwise unknown (but see Ash House, below). There is no obvious platform like that at Swinside, to the immediate south, although there are a number of other stones, all apparently natural/erratics, on the surrounding slopes.

These stones, and the large boulders in the base of the wall adjacent to the extant circle which appear to be 'clearance' of similar boulders, provide further context in which to view the extant circle. They require us to ask how prehistoric people themselves regarded the stones scattered across the hillside and, in particular, how their own selection, transport and erection of some was regarded or justified. Were the stones themselves important and regarded as having special properties?

ASH HOUSE, SD193873

Two boulders stand on a hillside between rocky outcrops from which it is possible to obtain views of the Duddon Estuary. The 'southern' stone has grooves which appear to be artificial and to have resulted from rubbing/abrasion. The 'northern' is juxtaposed with an old field boundary A (15a).

When the site was first described by Marjorie Cross and W.G. Collingwood,[45] it was considered to be the remains of the second circle alluded to by Hutchinson in his account of Swinside and described by Housman; 'Not far from (Swinside) we see a second circle of stones, situated on rising ground, which is dry, and seems to have been levelled for the purpose. An opening towards the south-west affords views of Duddon Sands. This, though on a more pleasing situation, appears to have had less attention paid to it; the stones are small and few in number, only 22 appearing above the surface'.[46] However, no other records of this site exist, and Dymond, who surveyed and excavated Swinside, had concluded that 'there seems to be no reason for believing that either of these topographers had themselves seen the *locus in quo*', and that local tradition referred to the non-megalithic remains at a place called Gornal Ground, south of Broadgate, and the lane north to Swinside.[47]

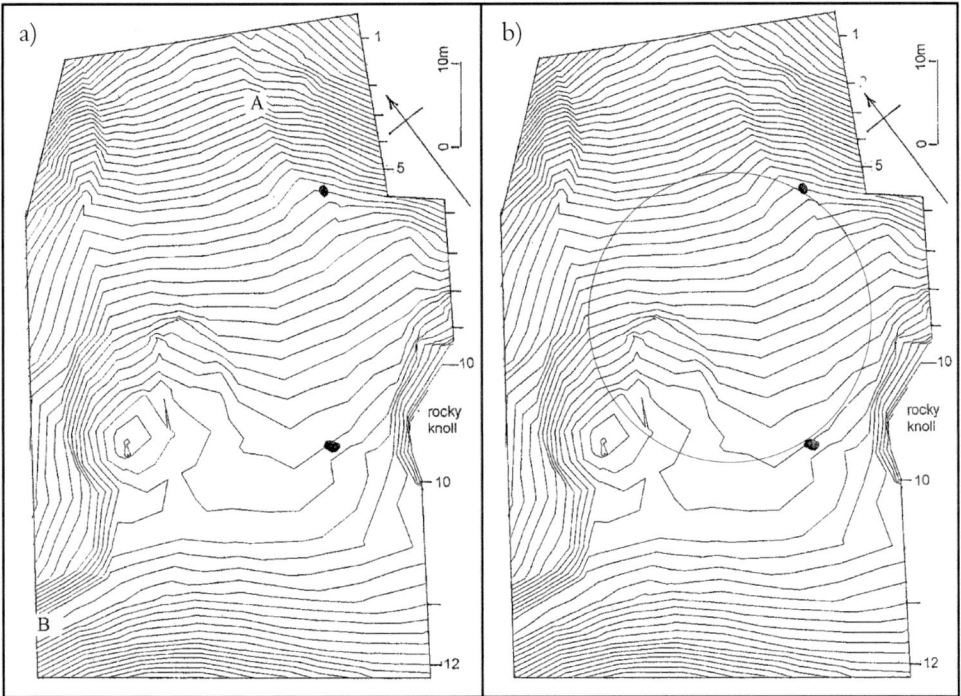

15a and b Ash House. B is an old trackway

Significantly, W.G. Collingwood had excavated a (bloomery) mound at Gornal Ground for Dymond and been party to collecting local hearsay on the matter of lost remains, so it was probably then that his attention had been drawn to the site at Ash House.

Cross and Collingwood stated that 'a level platform still holds two of the stones' but, as (15) shows, the ground is far from level; indeed there is no level ground, nor is there a view of the sands, unless one stands on top of, or beyond the principal rocky outcrop. However, Elva Plain is on a hillside, and it would have been possible to fit a circle with a diameter of 100ft between the rocky outcrops (15b). In addition, a line between the stones runs north-east to south-west, i.e. the stones appear to be aligned on the rising of the midsummer sun and on the setting of the midwinter one. It is also of interest to note that there is a small wetland area (former tarn?) at the base of the steep slope to the north, and that the stones are near the remains of a magnificent summer house. Could the stones have been erected at the same time as that structure?

There would appear to be no reason for that, except for the explanation of the *Ankh* carving on Swinside put forward by Plint, in 1972.[48] He thought the carving was influenced by the introduction to H. Rider Haggard's, *Ayesha*, where reference is made to a house on the Cumberland coast behind that which was a hill with a stone circle on the crest, because he had ascertained (significantly from Marjorie Cross) that H. Rider Haggard's brother (and possibly the author himself) used to stay in nearby Broughton, in Furness. Should the stones at Ash House – on a slope with views to Broughton, in Furness – be seen in a literary context?

4

THE LONG MEG AREA

LONG MEG AND HER DAUGHTERS, NY 571372

Here, the phrase, Long Meg, simply refers to the monolith, for it is now known that there are a number of other sites within the vicinity,[1] and it is possible that the monolith was originally erected at a different time, or conceived as a separate monument to the stone circle.

The earliest description of the megaliths known as Long Meg and Her Daughters is that provided by Camden who noted that there were two 'heaps of stones' considered to contain burials within the stone circle. These were described by John Aubrey as being of 'cobble stones, nine to ten foot high' and his sketch[2] shows two small pimples within a ring of stones. These had, however, been removed by the time of Stukeley's visit; although he noted that there were 'two roundish plot … more stoney and barren' than the rest of the area, as if 'places of burning the sacrifices, or the like'.[3]

In one of two sketches made by Stukeley (*16a*), there appears to be a wall, A, west of the Long Meg monolith, a hedge dividing the stone circle and a road outside the circle, to the east. Today, the prominent earthwork approximately parallel to the present road and its associated trees must be the remains of the hedge, whilst the footpath to and from Glassonby is all that remains of the road. However, the present road was in existence by the time of the first Ordnance Survey, and Lukis noted that when it was built 'two of the stones of the ring were displaced'.[4]

Two other features of Stukeley's drawings require comment here. Firstly, he shows another circle, B, to the south-west. The precise position of this has been lost but he described it as a 'circle of lesser stones, in number twenty; … fifty five feet in diameter; and at some distance above it … another stone placed, regarding it as Meg does the larger circle'.[5] Secondly, the same drawing also shows a curious mound, C, to the north-west of Long Meg and apparently obscuring the wall in an area of rough ground which once carried trees.

Later, antiquarians added little to the observations of Camden, Aubrey and Stukeley until the discovery of carvings on the face of Long Meg. These have been subject to more recent, detailed scrutiny[6] and decoration found on a number of other stones[7] (*16b*). In addition, it is now recognised that there is a bank around some of the stones of the circle,[8] and that there was a ditched enclosure contiguous to the stone circle[9] (*17*).

The Long Meg area 45

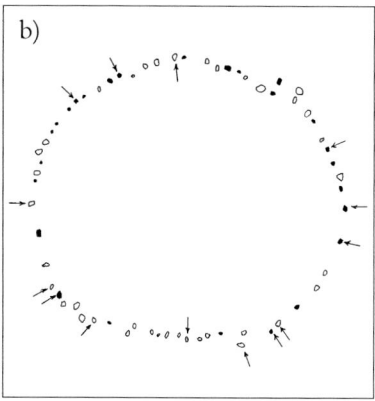

16a and b The character of Long Meg. (a) One of Stukeley's sketches of Long Meg made in 1725. Reproduced with the permission of the Bodleian Library, University of Oxford, from Ms. Top. Gen. b53. Fol.13v. (b) The character of the extant stones, showing which ones appear decorated or have specific textures; based on Beckensall 2002 and TCWAAS3, IV, 1-26

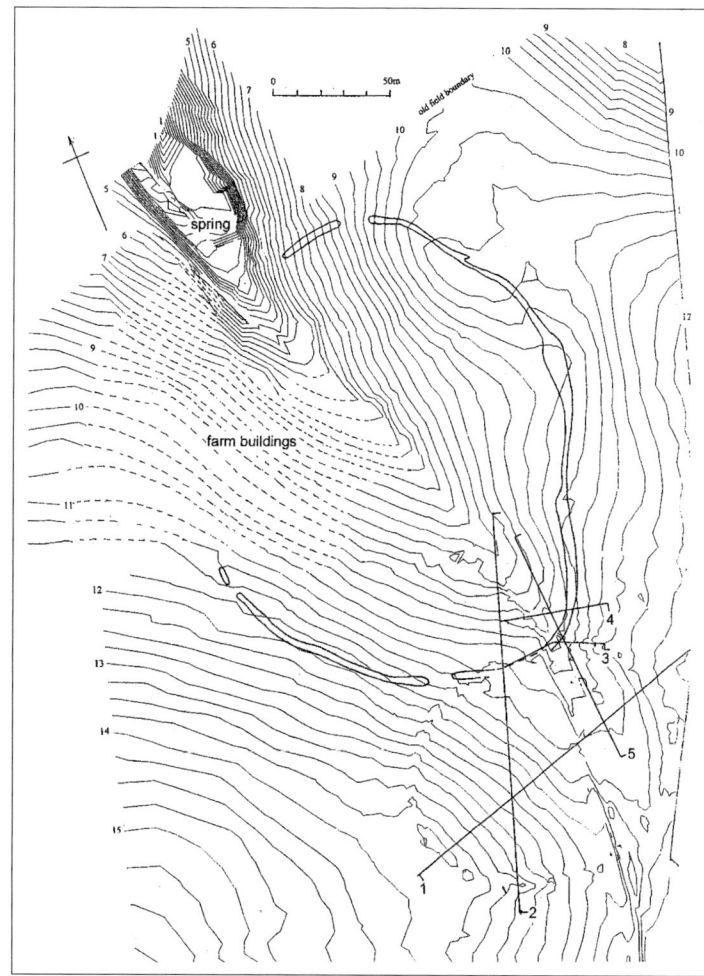

17 The topography of the ditched enclosure and megalithic sites at Long Meg showing the position of the sections (*18c*)

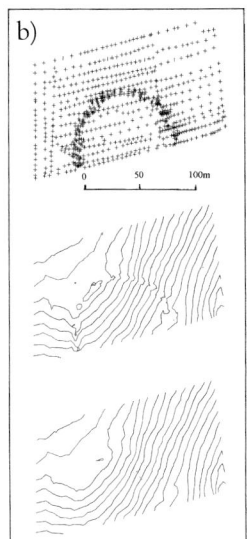
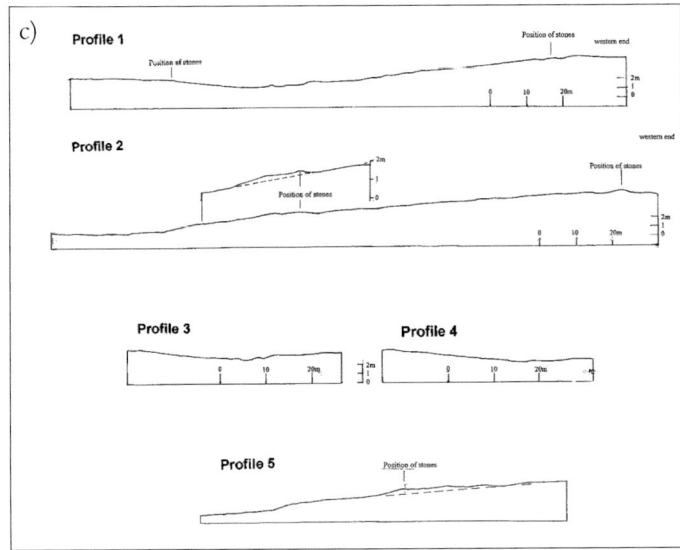

*18*a, b and c The Long Meg bank. (a) Low level sun light shows narrow ridge and furrow, but no bank. (b) points at which height readings were taken, the topography including readings on the bank, the topography without readings on the bank. (c) Profiles across the circle

The antiquity of the bank is unknown, but it is more extensive than previously thought and appears to include the area of the four portal stones. This suggests that it may be the result of ploughing, but it is significant that the feature does not show on air photograph *18*a. If ploughing was the cause of the feature, then it belongs to a period earlier than the narrow ridge and furrow recorded there.

Both contouring and profiles across the site (*18*) demonstrate that the south-western, north-eastern and eastern arcs of the circle also correspond to breaks of slope and the 'contour' lines change direction within the circle. It follows that the ground surface within the circle had been altered prior to the narrow ridge and furrow, but whether the process was one of ploughing, prehistoric activity, or both, is impossible to determine without excavation.

Deliberate scraping or hollowing of the stone circle's interior would have emphasized the perimeter of the monument and the surveyed profiles e.g., profile 1 in *18c*, show there are hollows inside and outside some lengths of the bank, suggesting that it too may have been created by scraping up material. However, profile 2 in *18c* shows the 'bank' has the same profile in that part of the circle contiguous with the ditched enclosure, suggesting that the two features cannot be contemporary. In short, if *all* the stones of the circle were erected in a bank, then those in the northern sector cannot have stood on the lip of an *open* ditch or have fallen as a result of subsidence of ditch fill. This suggests that if the bank is prehistoric, it was added later when the ditch was no longer open, or that the latter feature was deliberately infilled.

One further observation about the bank needs to be made. Where the stone circle crosses the lowest ground, the perimeter (and thus the putative bank) is a terrace (profile 5 in *18c*). Whilst this may be the result of accumulation from ploughing, it is also possible that the putative 'scraping' of the interior included an attempt to level up the enclosed space.

Whatever the explanation, the stone circle was not built on level ground, such as that to the west of the monolith, nor was it built on the hilltop occupied by the small, lost circle of Stukeley. Rather, its topographical position appears to be dictated by the proximity of the ditched enclosure, implying that the latter was indeed earlier.

The ditched enclosure encompassed a valley (*17*) which, at its northern end, was up to 5m deep. In addition, it appears to have been sited in relation to springs, there being one in the narrow, steep-sided valley to the immediate north and, possibly, another within the enclosure itself. Interestingly, the stone circle was laid out across part of, and included the head of the same, shallow valley as the ditched enclosure. This is best seen in profile 1 (*18c*), and it provides a further context, if not explanation, for the perimeter of that monument coinciding with a break of slope. Certainly, it is no longer possible to describe the stone circle as being built on a slope.

In this context, attention is drawn to the fact that east of the present farm the position of the ditched perimeter, like the stone circle, coincides with a slight change in the angle of slope. It is also the case that the ditch may be discerned faintly against the stone circle when viewed from the south-east corner of the farm wall. The significance of this, and the possible existence of a former spring within the enclosure, is a statement by Stukeley. According to him, there was 'not far hence towards Glassonby' the 'very fine spring … and higher up the field is a large spring, intrenched about with a vallum and foss of a pretty great circumference, but no great depth'.[10] In short, the ditched enclosure may have still been an earthwork in 1725.

Whether that were the case, or not, it appears that one of the principal factors in the location of the monuments was the valley and the presence of springs within it. However, it is also significant that, northwards, the valley leads steeply to the river Eden, and a confluence which is not an ordinary one. The valleys meet between sandstone cliffs just below the only natural waterfall in the middle course of the Eden, where the floodplain of the latter is dramatically narrowed by those cliffs and where there may originally have been outcrops of gypsum. Gypsum, which is still mined in the Eden valley, was used to whiten the banks of the Thornborough henges in the vale of York, and the use of white materials such as quartz has been noted elsewhere.[11] Consequently, it is necessary to consider the possibility that the putative banks of the ditched enclosure and stone circle may have been white.

Whilst the possibility that the colour and texture of stones was a factor in the selection and arrangement of stones will be returned to again, it is necessary to note here that the Long Meg monolith differs from all the other stones in being *red* sandstone. As such, it again links the monument to the river Eden, the nearest outcrop of red sandstone. However, without petrological analysis, it is not possible to match the monolith to any known rock outcrop or source.

Such an analysis must surely be part of future research, but it seems fitting to conclude consideration of the Long Meg megaliths by noting that the owner in the late nineteenth century had 'a special aversion ... to geologists, many of whom, without leave, chip fragments from the stones'.[12]

MAUGHANBY OR LITTLE MEG, NY 57693749

This small stone circle or oval (*19*) is located some 650m north-east of the Long Meg stone circle. Although it is on private ground, the stones are visible from the nearby road and from there, too, the topographical position of the site is best appreciated. It stands on a very slight ridge amongst gently undulating glacial deposits and, were it not for the plantation, Long Meg would be visible on a distant slope (*colour plate 11*).

The circle was discovered in the middle of the nineteenth century when a mound, said to be *c*1.3m high, was removed. According to the workmen, burnt bones and charcoal were found in the mound. 'Burnt bones', together with a 'coarse pot', were also found in an oval cist set into the old ground surface at the centre of the site.

The pot has not survived and indeed only fragments were given to Canon Simpson for him to display to the Society of Antiquaries when he first described the site.[13] There he stated that the pot had stood at the east end of the cist and the report says it was unornamented (*19*b). Simpson also exhibited a rubbing of the co-joining spiral and concentric circles found carved on one boulder (*19*d) but he also mentioned that 'on another stone that has stood on the west side of the circle there is an incised circle eight inches in diameter with some indistinct marks in the middle'. This carving, illustrated by Sir James Simpson in 1867, is no longer evidence, but in 1902 a cup and ring marked stone in Penrith Museum (*19*c) was also stated to have come from the cist.[14] However, as Simpson did not mention the latter its provenance must be questioned.

Unfortunately, the problems of interpreting this site are not confined to the type of urn or to the number of decorated stones. There is a problem with the actual number of stones forming the monument. Simpson reported that eight stones had been found, but a plan by Dymond, exhibited by Lukis in 1884, showed eleven stones. Today, the monument appears to be much as Dymond recorded it. So, how do we reconcile the evidence? The easiest solution is to suggest that Canon Simpson missed three smaller stones: 1, 5 and 6 of Dymond's plan; especially as they are upright, and Simpson seems to state that only one stone was erect – almost certainly stone 11.

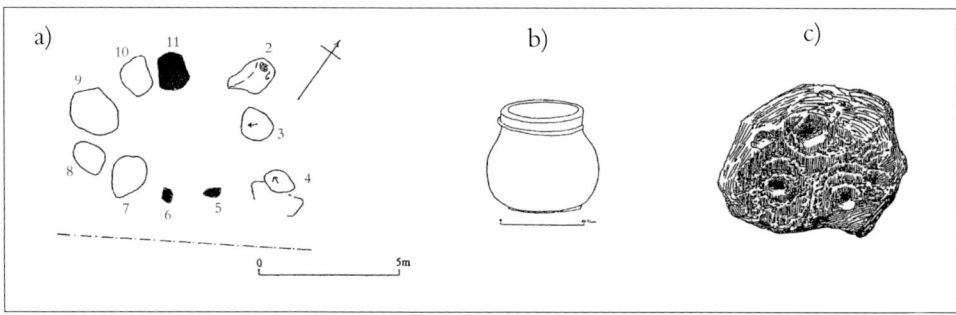

19a-d Little Meg. (a) The site today using the stone numbers of Dymond. (b) The drawing of the urn, said to come from the Thompson manuscript

It may be that Simpson saw the site before the mound had been wholly removed and the smaller uprights exposed but, whatever the explanation, the curious fact is that the mound only 'partially covered' the larger stones and only one, possibly two, of them were 'still standing … the others had either entirely or partially fallen'.

Amongst the latter, Simpson was probably thinking of stone 7 which, like Lukis, we might describe as an upright, or consider tipped or a boulder in its original position. But what does 'partially covered' mean? Did only a few stones, 11 and possibly 7, or most stones protrude from the mound like those of 'The Standing Stones' on Moor Divock? Against the latter interpretation is the reported height of the mound, for unless the latter was very steep sided, it is unlikely that the stones could have projected from a mound 1.3m high. However, if they were within the mound, or even partly projecting from it, there is the question of how some were found 'entirely or partially fallen'.

Dymond's plan implies that stone 2, that with the decoration, was one of those judged to have wholly fallen. Its shape, however, allows us to suggest that if it stood upright it would have been with the narrow end embedded in the ground and the carvings looking inward, and to (perhaps significantly) the south-west, to Long Meg. So, when and how did stone 2 fall? Were some of the stones deliberately felled prior to construction of the mound? Alternatively, are we right to assume that here, and elsewhere, all stones stood upright; that the preference was to have uprights rather than 'boulders'?

Clearly, small-scale excavation would allow this question to be tested, but what such work would not tell us is whether the carvings were already on the stone when it was brought to the site.[15] However, it is worth noting that the carvings on stone 2 are remarkably sharp, suggesting they had been protected by the mound almost immediately after carving.

One further observation can be made about the site. It was noted above that it stands on a low ridge and that Long Meg might have been visible, but both attributes probably existed elsewhere in the immediate vicinity. So, why build here? Whilst chance is one possibility, another is that the site was specifically located in relation to Long Meg especially since, as already noted, carved stone 2 may have faced in that direction. If it was intended to see, and be seen, from Long Meg, then the landscape between the sites must have been open country.

But *if* Little Meg was deliberately located in relation to Long Meg, why was it not built along the midwinter/midsummer alignment of that monument? Three suggestions can be made. Firstly, the midwinter/midsummer line was considered too 'sacred' to be used. Secondly, that such a line was not visible in the contemporary land use/vegetation. Thirdly, that there was another, existing monument on that line and the centre of a crop mark (SMR 968) may be it. Certainly, it is necessary to recognise that 'in former times there were two smaller *stone-encircled* cairns in the locality' of Long Meg; 'one has disappeared, the other is near a fence'[16] (this site; my italics).

It is apparent, therefore, that Long Meg needs to be considered in a wider landscape context than previously adopted. Indeed, Simpson reported the existence of another cairn about 'one hundred yards' east of Little Meg. But which, if any, is that mentioned by John Aubrey in his description of the Long Meg stone circle; 'In ... a barrow not far hence, was found (not long since) an urne under square stones'?[17]

GRAYSON LANDS, GLASSONBY, NY 57293934

This site, which is on private land but visible from the road, overlooks a small valley, the northern side of which is Old Parks. Seen from the road, it is a low, flat-topped mound. It probably possessed a similar form prior to excavation in 1900 when Ferguson noted that 'one can trace a stone circle or fence within its circumference'. Certainly W.G. Collingwood, who published an account of the excavation, reported that 'the surface of the tumulus was fairly level and defined by a layer of stones which seemed to have been broken intentionally, as if the whole had been gone over with a hammer'.[18] Given this character, and allowing for the depths of the old ground surface recorded by Collingwood, the site can be described as a platform at the end of a low spur (*20a*).

Collingwood reported that the uprights – the geology of which he tried to identify – had been 'set on edge on the natural ground ... Not sunk in the soil but propped with the small cobbles which form the tumulus'. Consequently, there were no sockets to indicate whether other stones had stood in the gaps of his 'continuous fence' (*20b*), but he believed there had been some removal of stones. In particular, he was told of one which had been 'over three feet long, about six inches thick, and two feet high, of red sandstone with a spiral or concentric circles'.

Within the 'circle' was an area of charcoal and a glass bead (*20c*) 'near the original surface', and set into the latter was a cist which 'had been opened and rifled long before'. Outside the central area two cremations were found; one placed in a hole in the old ground surface and the other in an inverted urn (*20d*). Anatomical examination of the cremated bones suggested that those associated with the urn had belonged to an adult and the other cremation that of a younger person or woman.

What is not clear from Collingwood's report is whether the urn was in a pit, or not. If not, then either it must have been contemporary with the building of the cairn or inserted at a later time, as might the other cremation. Collingwood was, however, not the excavator, and a year later Canon Thornley – under whose 'care' the work had been done – published a short paper on ring-marked stones, including one in position at this site (stone 28, *20*b).

The fact that the urn and known carving occurred in the same – and south-east – quadrant may be significant in suggesting continuity between the building of the monument and the assumed insertion of the secondary burial. Equally, the fact that the upright stones were not in sockets, but supported by the cairn material, raises questions about the constructional sequence. As (*20*b) implies, the stones could have stood upright against a bank of cairn material allowing the central area to be open for some time, or the uprights could have been the kerb of a cairn around which was added later material, perhaps at the time of the two cremations. In the latter case, the decoration would have been hidden in a manner echoing arrangements in some megalithic tombs; a comparison which raises the question of whether the decorated stone was reused from somewhere else.

In that context, it is interesting to note that the present field is also reported to contain a ring ditch, said to be the terminal of a cursus.[19]

OLD PARKS, NY567399

(a) NY56993987
The Ordnance Survey record this as the position of the large cairn destroyed in the nineteenth century and note the presence of a ditch visible on an aerial photograph.

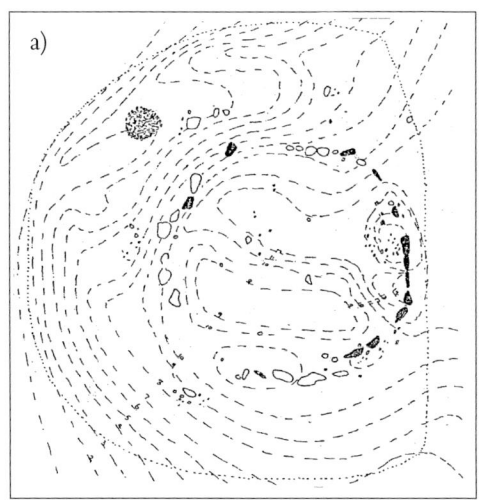
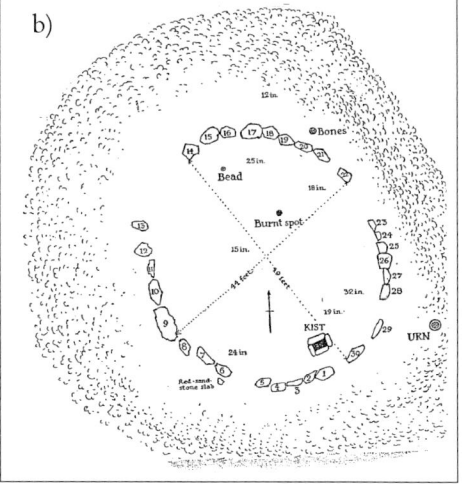

20 Grayson Lands. (a) form line survey from Clare, 1973. (b) after Collingwood

No ditch is mentioned in the early accounts,[20] but then they were simply reports of a site which had been destroyed for road metal.

The cairn, which had been thought to be recent field clearance, was recorded as being 1.2m high and oval in plan (some 26m x 20m), with the longer axis east–west. Below the cairn was a line of five decorated stones orientated north–south (*21a*). To the west of the standing stones were 32 deposits of burnt bones in 'holes scooped in the ground and in some cases accompanied by fragments of urns,' including some of a 'thinner paste, being probably of the class known as drinking cups', presumably beaker ware. A complete but broken urn was also found and, in separate places two 'pygmy' cups, one containing twelve 'shale' beads. Near to this cup was a deposit of burnt bones covered by a slab; the only deposit apparently so treated. The small vessels and beads are shown in (*21b*) together with what might be the urn. Two more 'shale' beads and 'a hard pebbly stone, roughly cylindrical and a little more than a half inch each way drilled trough with a large hole' were found between 1902 and 1904.[21]

To the east of the standing stones there were two pits, both orientated east–west. The larger was approximately 2.5m x 1.45m, and 1.3m deep, whilst the other is said to have had 'the dimensions of a modern grave'. This feature was apparently not investigated by Ferguson, but in one corner of the larger, 'under a flagstone were some burnt bones and ashes'. The implication of Ferguson's account is that the pits were found filled with material similar to the rest of the cairn.

He also thought that the pits had originally contained inhumations, and that the deposits of burnt bone in the western half of the cairn were secondary burials. Given that he noted many had been found near to the periphery, this seems a reasonable interpretation, but the overall distribution of them implies knowledge of the structure beneath the cairn. That is also suggested by his reporting that the small vessels were approximately 'north' of the line of standing stones.

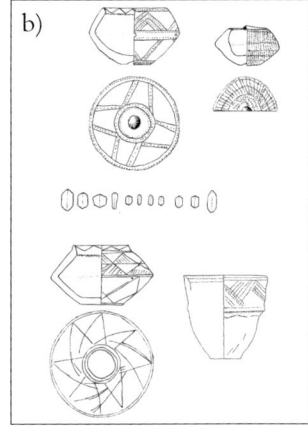

21 Old Parks. (a) One of two photographs of the wall published by Ferguson. (b) the finds in Carlisle Museum

(b) NY56883988

Ferguson also noted 'a granite monolith in the next field 106 yards due west' of the cairn. No longer visible, it was said to be some 1.4m high.

BROOMRIGG, NY548467

During the 1930s, 40s and early 50s, a local archaeologist, Kate Hodgson, described and excavated a number of sites on a shoulder of high ground between the river Eden and steep side of the Pennines. Today, the area is forested, and the descriptions and illustrations here are derived from her work.[22]

Site A was an arc of stones which may have formed a circle some 58m across. The uprights appeared to have been 'hammer dressed' and 'provision may have been made to place an urn against the outer side of one stone'. Beyond the arc were five other uprights, and whilst Hodgson thought three of them formed an alignment, it is possible the other two also did.

Site B (22a) was a circle of seven stones less than 3.5m in diameter. Between the stones was a slight mound formed by a scatter of stones. In the centre was a conical pit which was 'lined with stones carefully fitted together' but thought to have been 'opened and robbed'. If this were the case, it is surprising that the early excavation cleared out the pit so precisely as to leave the lining intact. Similarly, the idea that a roughly 'carved' stone found 'near' the pit had been placed on top of the urn, *assumed* to have been originally in the pit, must be questioned. A pit outside one stone socket did, however, contain 'a small amount of charcoal'.

'About 25ft from circle B there was a tiny circle, B2, of small stones, four to five feet in diameter and surrounding a conical pit 1ft 10in. across, a miniature of that in circle B; the pit was partly cobble-lined, packed with and filled with the same black washed soil.'

Site C was, as (22b) shows, a sub-circular area of 14 stones inside which was a slight mound, like that of site B. In the south-west quadrant was a pit containing an empty cist and nearby the crushed bones of a 'foundation sacrifice'. In the south-east quadrant there were several cremations. One of these was in an urn with an accessory vessel 'very near … amongst further deposit of bones'. All the other cremations had been placed in pits, possibly in 'bags'. Thirteen jet beads and a V-bored button were also found.

Several aspects of this site are worth noting. Firstly, the section shows the 'mound', or pavement of stones continuing across the top of the pit so that the latter appears to have been undisturbed. Consequently, the cist either never contained a body or the acidic soil had removed all traces; an explanation which provides a context for interpretation of the other sites. Secondly, the published section also shows that whilst the cist was in a pit cut into the 'brash', the latter filled a hollow within the bedrock. Thirdly, and as Hodgson pointed out, the arc of stones adjacent to the cist were placed contiguously and may have belonged to a separate earlier monument. However, it is not clear whether the stone holes for such a monument were looked for. Fourthly, as the urn was not in a pit, it must have been protected by the layers which sealed the cist, suggesting it belonged to a later phase. Fifthly, and as Hodgson noted, the white sandy layer needs to be considered in the context

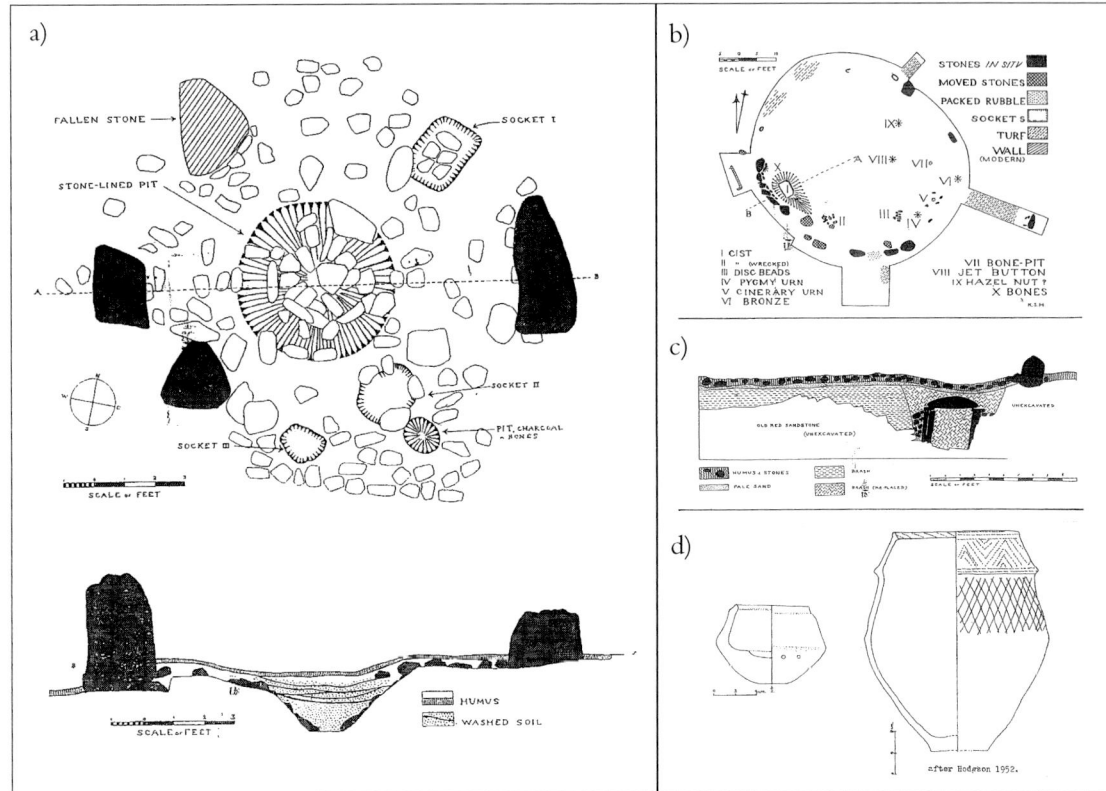

22a-d Broomrigg after Hodgson

of white materials elsewhere. However, here a caveat needs to be added, namely that it is possible the layer and its distinctive colour was simply the result of leaching.[2] Site E, a penannular bank and ditch some 50m in diameter, was not excavated.

Hodgson also recorded the existence of another small circle about five meters in diameter (site D) and, later, the finding of a beaker placed in a small pit against a 'glacial erratic in situ'. What is, however, not clear is whether this erratic was the standing stone (site J) or whether the latter was another site.

GREY YAUDS, NY545487

A circle of 88 stones, none more than 1.2m high, is reported to have existed on a shoulder of the ridge on which the Broomrigg sites are located. The diameter of the circle was said to be 52yds (49m) with a single stone about 1.5m high, 4.5m to the north-west.[24]

The area was also known as King Harry's Common, and in the eighteenth century Hutchinson noted, 'We scarce know a more desolate spot'.[25] As a result of enclosing and improving the common, this monument had largely disappeared by 1816. That process is evidenced by the large stones – presumably those of the circle - in the base of wall A (*23* and *colour plate 12*).

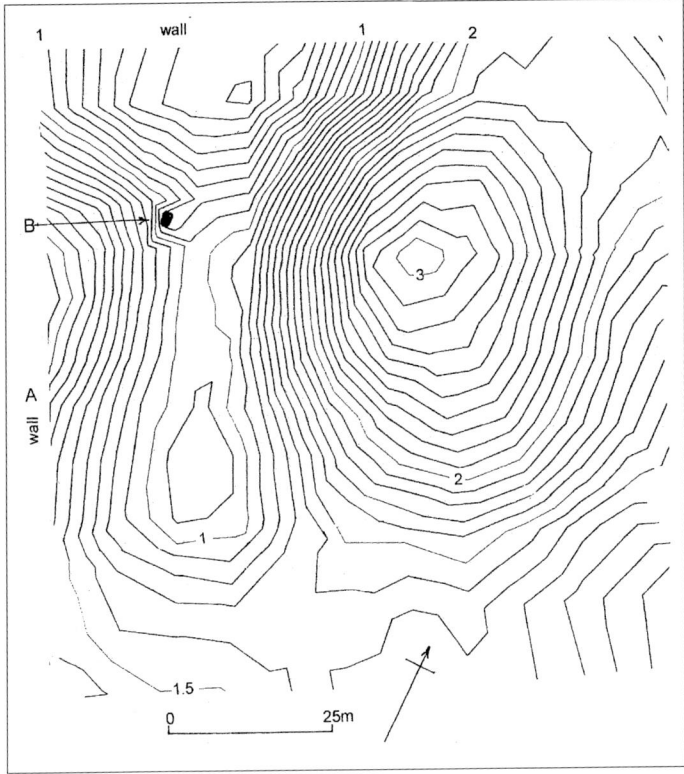

23 Grey Yauds

The single standing stone B has been assumed to be the outlier reported in the eighteenth century, but it is difficult to envisage a circle 49m in diameter to the south-east. If it did exist, and surround the hilltop there, then it would be more than 5m from the present monolith. It may, therefore, be significant that Hodgson[26] also reported the existence a 'more distant' outlier and two mounds, about '2,000ft to the south-east'. One other possible clue to the location of the circle may be provided by the fact that all the stones assumed to be from the circle are in the western wall A. Did the circle lie beyond there? If so, it would still have been on uneven ground.

Wherever the circle was located, it is possible that there was some intervisibility with the monuments at Broomrigg, for today the tree tops there are visible above the field walls. Whether this situation also existed with regard to Stone B is less clear and a notable feature is its location in a small valley. Consequently, where ever the circle was, no rising or setting astronomical body would have appeared to touch its top. This suggests the need to recognise that not all outliers had astronomical significance and may, indeed, have been regarded as separate monuments.

5

THE PENRITH AREA

It is tempting to say that Maybugh and King Arthur's Round Table (KART) are two of the best-known prehistoric sites in the north-west but that is perhaps an overstatement, as many people hurtling down the M6 are probably unaware of their proximity to the vast bank of Mayburgh. Nevertheless, that site, KART and the, certainly less well-known, Little Round Table (LRT), form a group which has been referred to as 'the Penrith henges'.[1] However, to see the three sites simply as a single group of one type of monument may be a mistake and rather than see them in isolation, it is possible – and almost certainly necessary - to see them in the broader context of a wider landscape of monuments.

MAYBURGH, NY51922845

The unique (?) feature of this site is the composition of the enormous bank, and some years ago a local quarry manager, letting his mind wander whilst I lectured the rest of his group, estimated that it contains some 20,000 tons of stone. Pennant[2] called it 'stupendous', but its pitted surface is the result of various depredations, some of which had occurred more than 200 years ago.[3] One original feature which appears to have survived such attacks is the increased height of the bank at the entrance; a feature found elsewhere, including KART. This is most obvious on the southern side, but also occurs to the north (24).

Where the stones were gathered from is uncertain. Many have suggested that the stones were collected from the river, but an alternative is that the bank was formed by excavation and re-arrangement of a glacial mound;[4] a construction technique similar to that of Irish sites of a similar appearance where the ground inside the enclosure was scraped up to form the bank.[5] Significantly, the local till does contain numerous 'cobble' stones of the kind forming the bank, but it is also true that it is precisely such material that would have been in the river bed 5,000 years ago.

The present stoney bed of the river can be seen in good sunlight from Eamont Bridge, itself, but the practicalities of extracting such material would obviously be a problem and two observations follow. Firstly, that if the material had been obtained from the river bed, then building the bank might have been thought of as bringing the river/water onto the land and a kind of inversion of the natural order. Secondly, comparison with existing areas of braided and abandoned channels would suggest that cobbles may have been lying on dry ground, such as Westmorland Holme east of the village.[6]

Following the early antiquarian records, the monument is generally considered to have consisted of the bank, four stones 'flanking' the single entrance, four central stones and an 'outer' circle. However, it will be evident from the earlier discussion that the only evidence for the latter is Stukeley, and his drawing allows for an alternative interpretation. On the other hand, the former existence of a circle of stones would explain why the ploughing of the interior – reported by Stukeley and visible as ridge and furrow – stopped several metres from the base of the bank creating a low terrace A (25). This ploughing also produced a bronze axe and probably explains the linear arrangement of the geophysical anomalies recorded by Topping.[7]

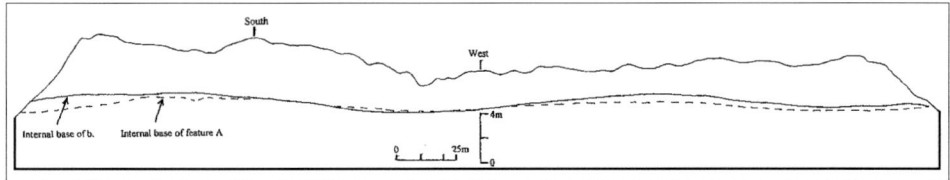

Above: 24 Mayburgh – the profile of the top and bottom of the bank – on the inside

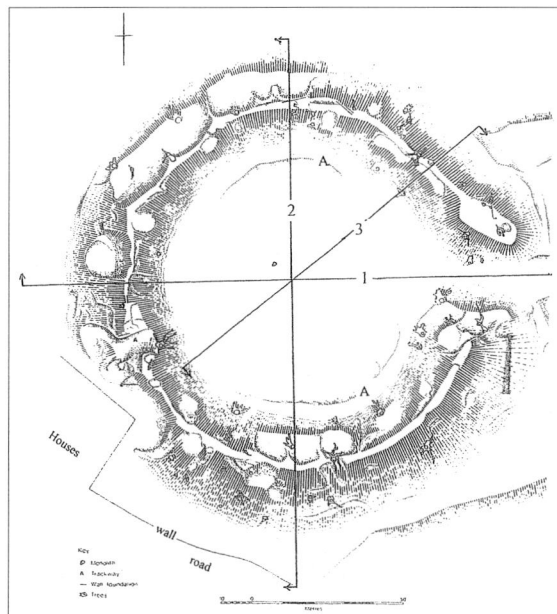

25a and b The internal topography of Mayburgh. (a) the inner 'terrace' A and the position of the profiles based on Topping 1992. (b) the dotted line is that of profile 3, showing how close it is to the other two and, therefore, how symmetrical the central area is

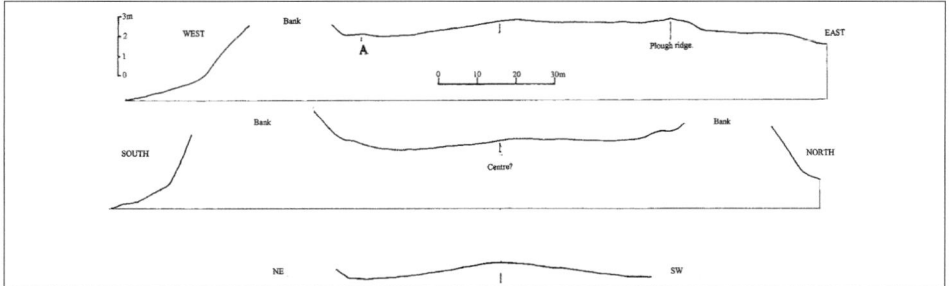

Here attention is drawn to the fact, noted by both Stukeley and Pennant, that the monument is located on a natural rise and that several features appear to result from this. Firstly, there are two low areas within the interior so that the central area is slightly domed. Secondly, the bank appears to be higher when viewed from the outside than on the inside and, thirdly, the top of the bank when seen from the footpath to the north appears to be horizontal, unlike the rise and fall of the ground surface.

The surveyed profiles confirm the above observations, and in particular the domed interior. However, the ground east of the centre, towards the entrance, is much flatter, and whilst this may be the result of ploughing and/or the continuation of the low terrace A, it may also be original. Equally, the original profile of the ground within the entrance appears to have been damaged or lowered in the relatively recent past, and it may be that it was such activity which led to the discovery of a fragment of a stone axe.

In addition, the profiles demonstrate that in a number of places feature A is in fact a low bank, not a terrace. This raises the intriguing possibility that if this were a bank and the location of a destroyed 'outer' stone circle, and there were four portal stones, Mayburgh may originally have been a stone circle very similar to that at Long Meg, with the great bank being added later.

The possible topography of the site, excluding the main bank, is shown in (26) and, although survey and interpolation of the results is complicated by the existence of the nearby houses and adjacent quarrying of the bank, it appears that the monument may have been built on a low ridge rather than hillock. It is also evident that the two high points in feature A occur on the axis of that ridge allowing, again, for the idea that part of the original ground may have been scraped up/dug away, as in some Irish sites. However, it seems unlikely such a process would have produced enough material to construct the main bank, rather it may have been used to 'level up' the indentations within the ridge.

Whether that is the case, or not, a dominant feature of the monument is the almost perfect circular perimeter of the main bank; a circularity which exists regardless of the rise and fall of the adjacent and underlying ground surface. Achieving this would not of course have been impossible if the stone were being tipped from above and, not withstanding the observation that the top the bank in the western and northern quadrants appears from a distance to be level, it does appear to consist of numerous, separate dumps. Some of these are evident in (24), but it is also apparent the highest point is not the bank immediately south of the entrance, rather there is a second point almost as equally high and almost directly south of the centre. This, together with the fact that the entrance is due east of that centre, thereby framing the rising of the equinoctial sun,[8] suggests that the monument may reflect the cardinal points, as do the Long Meg and Castlerigg stone circles.

Finally it should be noted that:
- The eastern 'sight line' would have passed immediately to the north of KART.
- One of the few external landscape features visible from the interior of the monument is the ridge top of Blencathra where the equinoctial sun may have been seen to set.
- Stukeley noted that there was a spring between this site and KART.

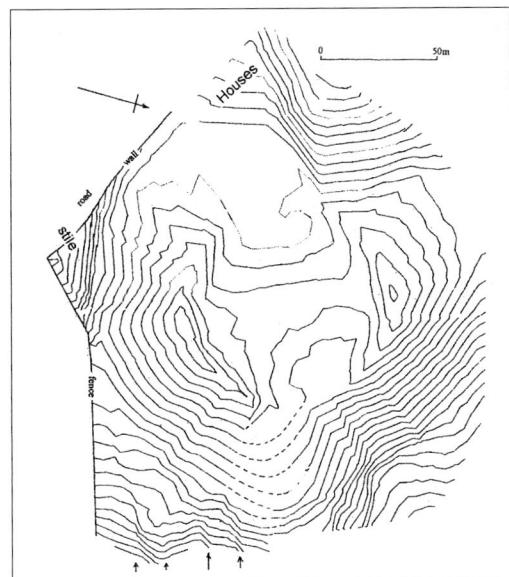

26 The possible original ground surface of Mayburgh, form lines at 25cm intervals

KING ARTHUR'S ROUND TABLE, NY 52322840

Whilst the spring, mentioned by Stukeley (above), is no longer in evidence, and much of the original terrain is obscured by buildings and roads, it is still possible to see that the location of KART is very different to that of Mayburgh. Whilst the latter was built on, or around, a high point in the undulating glacial terrain, KART was on a fluvio/glacial terrace below a prominent 'river cliff'. On this terrace, according to Stukeley, the marks of the tents of King Charles' Scottish army could still be seen in 1725.

Given the topographical differences noted above, it may be significant that the monuments themselves are different. Mayburgh is visibly constructed from stones and has no ditch, whilst KART was built from gravels and has a ditch. Whilst it is accepted that the newly built KART would not have had a grassy bank, the character of the latter would still have been visibly different from that of Mayburgh, and there are other features which suggest such differences were deliberate. Mayburgh, for example, has one entrance, KART has two. Mayburgh is an almost perfect circle while KART is not. The bank of Mayburgh prevents anyone seeing the interior, unless through the entrance or standing on the bank, whilst the interior of KART is overlooked by the high 'river cliff'.

This latter point is worth emphasising, for it provides a very different context for those discussions which have emphasised how henge banks appear to 'exclude'.[9] True, the bank at KART does create a perimeter beyond which some people may not have been able to enter, but it would not have prevented them from *seeing* what was happening in the interior. This point was in fact made by Stukeley, for his sketch (5c) shows people sitting on the 'cliff' top looking down on the various activities below. Indeed, it may have been this aspect of the topography which led him to interpret KART and the Little Round Table as being part of a 'circus', a single visible area for movement, and it certainly explains why he estimated 'the bank' (presumably the river cliff) could have carried 10,000 spectators.[10]

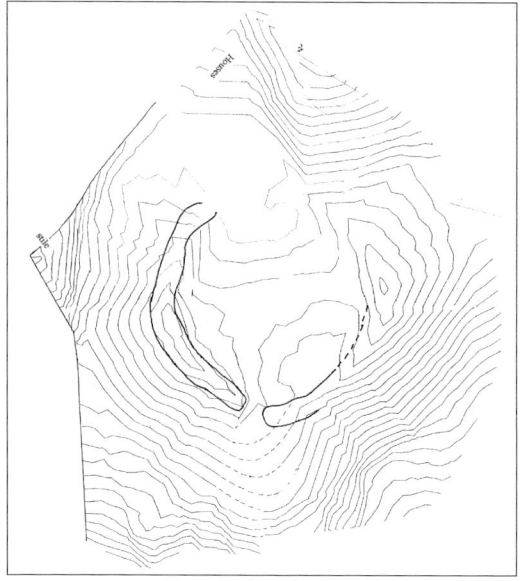 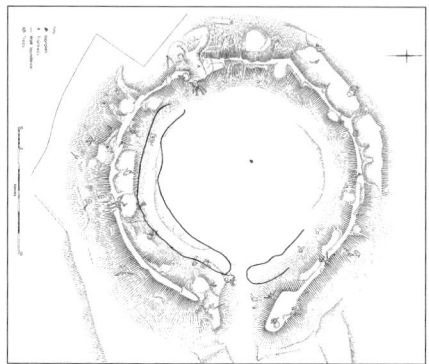

27 The external bank of KART compared with Mayburgh

Despite the differences between KART and Mayburgh noted above, there are similarities. In both, the banks appear to have increased in height, either side of the entrance, and KART also had portal stones, at least in its northern entrance (5b). In addition, excavation failed to find any evidence that the sides of the bank in the southern entrance had been revetted,[11] so that the form of the entrance was, albeit on a smaller scale, that of Mayburgh. These suggest, despite the contrasts noted above, the existence of local preferences or traditions and, therefore, underlying linkages.

Is it therefore coincidence that the *external* diameter of KART is almost exactly that of the *interior* of Mayburgh? This is demonstrated in (27), but the possibility that Mayburgh had a first phase consisting of a monument almost identical to KART is not supported by geophysical survey, which recorded no internal ditch.

The principal visible features of KART are the sub circular bank, the internal ditch and, in the central area, a low, circular platform or 'disc'.[12] At the present time there is one entrance, but originally there were two; the northern one being almost wholly lost to the road, with the only visible field evidence for its former existence being the early records.

Excavations demonstrated that the ditch had been cleared out, and its sides, but not apparently its bottom, recut c1800, so that the original dimensions of the ditch appear to have been similar to the present ones. Given that the bank was constructed of gravels piled around turves, and that it probably had a flat top,[13] just as the ditch had a flat bottom, the bank was in effect an inversion of the ditch.

Stukeley's drawing and account suggest that the bank had already acquired something of its present appearance by 1725, and it has been suggested that the irregular inner face of the bank is the result of the removal of standing stones, sometime prior to the record of Dugdale. Whilst this is possible, it may be significant that, as Topping's plan[14] shows, it is not merely the inner face of the bank which is irregular. Could the irregularities be, like those of Mayburgh, the result of former tree cover?

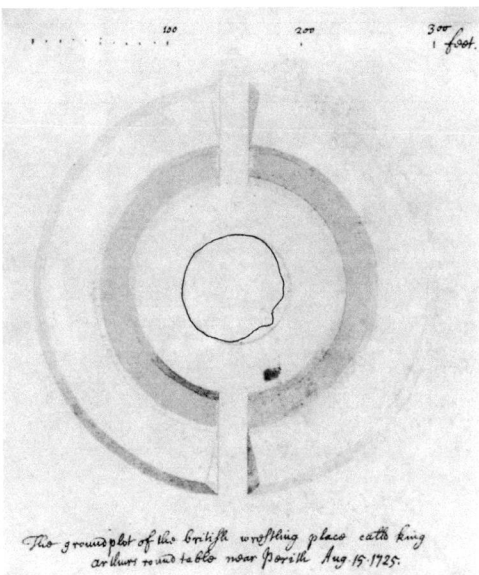

28 Stukeley's plan of KART overlain by Topping's plan of the central disc at the same scale

Stukeley's account refers to the existence within the central area of 'a circle … somewhat higher in elevation than the other',[15] and his plan of it looks remarkably like the disc visible at the present time (*28*). However, excavation demonstrated that the latter was, like the recutting of the ditch and the rest of the central area, the product of the creation of a 'tea garden'. Although memory and tradition suggested the garden was created *c*.1800, it may be necessary, in the light of (*28*), to revise interpretations. However, there does appear to have been a prehistoric, central mound covering a shallow depression. This may have been a grave but it was found to contain only hazel charcoal and a few bones of indeterminate character.

Amongst the material tipped to form the present disc were substantial splinters of a large stone of 'Borrowdale igneous rock'. One of these splinters is recorded as being 0.6m long, so that the original stone must have been large. Whilst this may have been part of a cist or covering for the central burial, the geology would suggest the stone was an erratic and therefore likely to be a boulder rather than a slab. Consequently, it is tempting to see some of the splinters as the remains of a portal stone.

THE LITTLE ROUND TABLE, NY 502278

This earthwork appears to have been less substantial than KART, and Clarke's map of 1789 (see 5d) does not show it. It is only thanks to Stukeley and Pennant that we know of its existence. According to them, it appears to have been a bank and ditch with single entrance, and excavation in the estimated location of the site[16] did find a prehistoric ditch. This probably had a bank on the outside and was thought to have a diameter of 48m. However, geophysical survey has suggested it was almost exactly twice that size, 92m.[17] As such, it was about the same size as the external diameter of KART, as Stukeley (5c) shows, but appears to have differed from that site in its possession of a single entrance and in having a V-shaped ditch.

EAMONT BRIDGE, ORMSTEAD HILL AND SKIRSGILL, NY 515290

Stukeley reported a cairn on the other side of the river from the above sites which 'in all probability was the funeral monument of the king that founded the temple and circus. Somebody has lately been digging away part of the barrow'.[18] Pennant also noted the site stating that 'Almost opposite Mayborough on the Cumberland side of the Eimot is a vast cairn or tumulus, composed of round stones, and surrounded with large grit stones of different sizes, some a yard square, which all together form a circle sixty feet in diameter'. Hutchinson repeats Pennant's account but says that the site was known as Ormstead Hill, and that the stones of the body of the cairn were visible 'where the turf is broken'.[19]

This is a site which has never been located, but on Stukeley's sketch of Mayburgh – and previously unnoticed – is just such a mound as he and Pennant describe (*29*). The sketch places it towards Eamont Bridge and above a cliff north of the river,[20] but what is not clear is whether that is the river*bank* or the earlier river*cliff* lying to the north, which is not otherwise shown. Nevertheless, in that position the site appears to have been a separate monument from the extant standing stone at Skirsgill (*colour plate 2*), just west of the M6/A66 junction, which must now be seen to have attracted no comment in the early literature. On the other hand, the area now truncated by the A66, and immediately east of its junction with the M6, appears to have been known as Orm*sett* Hill (my italics), and there was a tradition that there formerly existed a circle of stones 'at the north-west end' of the dry valley.[21]

29 Stukeley's Ormstead Hill. Reproduced with permission of the Bodleian Library, University of Oxford. Stukeley's drawing is in Ms. Top. Gen.b.53. Fol.15v

Clearly, it is difficult to reconcile the available evidence. It seems unlikely that Stukeley would have 'relocated' the site so that it could be included in a sketch showing the 'environs' of Mayburgh. The simplest conclusion is that there were at least two megalithic monuments north of the river and that Hutchinson's Ormstead Hill was not Sukeley's site. Whatever the explanation, no sites are shown on Clarke's map of 1789.

NEWTON REIGNY, MOSSTHORN AND SEWBORRENS, NY485302

The Ordnance survey records the site of a 'cairn' at NY48513047 and, nearby, two 'long cairns'. The latter, visible from the B5288, are two high and irregular oval mounds on a ridge within an undulating landscape of glacial deposition. Whether they, too, are natural is uncertain but they appear to have been dug at some point in the past. What, if anything, was found is unrecorded, but Whellan mentions the existence of several barrows - one of which contained 'urns' - at Newton Reigny, and it is possible the latter was one of the three sites mentioned above.

The beaker in Carlisle Museum (30a), said to have come from Newton Reigny, maybe one of the urns referred to by Whelan, but our understanding is complicated further by the Thompson manuscript. There, reference is made to the 'remnants of a stone sepulchral ring at Sewborrens', the farm to the south-east of the sites mentioned above, and to a buried 'stone circle' at 'the Riggs'.[22] Elsewhere in his manuscript, he describes 'a field or two south' of the long cairns, 'a standing stone eight feet high ... in the fence close to is another apparently about the same size cut in two ... in land adjoining are evidences that there had been more of similar size'. This would appear to be the monolith and boundary stone at NY48483012, but what is uncertain is whether this site is the same as his Sewborrens site, and whether the latter was the Ordnance Survey's destroyed cairn or a wholly different one.

The stone is located on a mound, but the latter does not continue beyond the hedge; rather, the latter is a lynchet at the base of which are a number of other large stones (just as Thompson described). Was this a megalithic monument, or could the 'fallen' stones be glacial erratics ploughed up and rolled to the side of the field? Against the idea of the standing stone being prehistoric is the fact that it stands almost at the centre of the mound and not at its base. But it remains to be explained why the boundary turns at the stone, at the centre of the mound. If the stone is not ancient, could it be that the boundary recognised the importance of the hillock, considering it a burial mound?

KITCHENIIILL, NY496346

This standing stone, one of the largest if not the largest in Cumbria, is best viewed from the adjacent road where it appears to stand at the side of a mound (*colour plate 13*). The latter is, however, a ridge which has been cut by the London–Carlisle railway line. Whether anything was found during the excavation of the latter is not, however, known.

Amazingly, the site was first reported during the writing of this book. Why it has previously escaped recognition is unclear. It certainly looks ancient. Perhaps we should

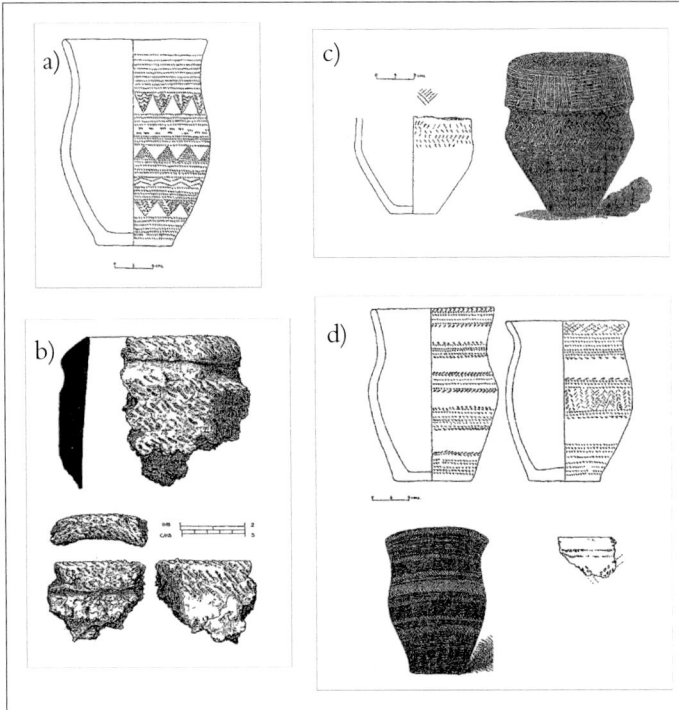

30a-d Pottery from the environs of Penrith. (a) Beaker from Newton Reigny. (b) Peterborough ware from Brougham, from TCWAAS2 LXXII. (c) The urn from the Brougham cist. (d) The two extant beakers from Clifton Cross, and the third as originally published

regard it as a monument to non-systematic field survey, just as Nicholson and Burn failed to record the existence of the Gamelands circle, even though one of them lived nearby. Whatever the reason for such omissions, it is a reminder that our distribution maps are partial and may bear little resemblance to original patterns.

BROUGHAM, NY535293

Four sites, or groups of sites, might be recognised here:

1. Aerial photographs (3b) record ring ditches in at least two locations adjacent to the A66 and in the vicinity of the Roman *vicus*. One group in particular is close to where some sherds of Peterborough Ware (30b) were found during road works.[23]

2. Further east and beyond the Countess Pillar, a cist was discovered in quarrying for sand in the nineteenth century. Inside was a contracted skeleton, beaker and 'food vessel', but the latter, never illustrated, are lost. On the floor of the cist were ashes, 'such as would result from the burning of dried grass in considerable quantities'.[24] The Ordnance Survey recorded the location as NY548267; a location visible from the busy and very dangerous A66 as a shallow valley in undulating glacial topography.

3. In 1889 at NY547280, in a field adjoining the previous site, a stone was ploughed up. 'In lifting the stone it was seen that it rested on the tops of three large cobble stones, which enclosed a space 2.5ft (75cm) in diameter'. Within the cist was an upright urn (30c) which contained a cremation.[25]

4. Taken together, these sites are evidence of relatively concentrated prehistoric activity in the area not far to the east of the 'Penrith henges'. In that context, it is interesting to note that Stukeley described sites in this area and his description is quoted in full here because the passage has previously gone unrecognised, perhaps because it appears unintelligible. Having described Mayburgh and KART, he states,[26] 'There is another Celtic monument in the fields beyond the Lowther and SE of the Countess Pillar … upon a fine dry spot of ground near the moors, marked out with stones set at equal distances. One points eastward … being above 100ft long, not a raised tumulus, but a pyramidal form designedly two sides of stones like an avenue. A little way above the head of this is another largish burial, and on a sort of barrow; it points differently from the former. Further on is an arc of a circle, consisting of four large stones equidistant, opening south[27] … . Further on is one side of a long burial like the first. There are many more such like hereabouts but ruinous … In the pasture on the eastern bank of the Lowther, in the way to Clifton, are several cairns … also many other monuments of stones, 3, 4, 5 set upright together'.

CLIFTON STANDING STONES, NY53132593

These (*colour plate 14*) must be one of the megaliths referred to by Stukeley, and in the nineteenth century they were variously referred to as Crummack Stone and Cromlech Stone; the latter suggesting that they were considered to be the remains of a tomb. Part of the site was, however, excavated in 1977[28] when the southern stone was re-erected. This work revealed a third stone which was thought to have been buried here after discovery during hedge removal, sometime between 1965 and 1969. Had the stone originally been a separate monument, one of the others alluded to by Stukeley?

The pit in which the third stone was buried had been cut into a small cairn which lay to the east of the paired stones. Although the upper part of this cairn had not survived, it was found to have been constructed of small stones 'laid in circles around a central area of larger stones, and surrounded by a kerb of small, unshaped boulders'. In the central area, and amongst these stones, was a large amount of burnt bone; apparently the remains of several individuals, 'though positive evidence of more than one body was absent'. Although the bone was lightly burnt, the small amount of associated charcoal had been subject to a high temperature leading to the conclusion that the material may already have been charcoal when used in the 'cremation'.

The stones were located on flat ground below a small ridge and not in the centre of the latter. Whilst it might be because the cairn already existed, the latter was, itself, built on the side of the ridge and not on the flatter ground available to the west. This suggests that the cardinal points may have been a factor in the layout of the features, and the stones do in fact have a north–south axis.

CLIFTON CROSS, NY52912756

This former mound was largely removed for agricultural improvement in 1880,[29] and today, the only evidence is a slight rise in the field boundary visible from the A6. This shows, however, that it was located on a gentle break of slope above the floor of the valley.

Underneath the mound were two cists partly sunk into the ground. One contained a contracted skeleton resting on 'fine black mould and sand', a beaker and a bone pin *c.*6.5cm long and slightly curved. The second cist contained two beakers, but a skeleton which had largely decayed. The beakers are shown in (*30c*), but the published account does not make it clear which came from which cist.

TRAINFORD BROW, LOWTHER, NY53692431

It is said that the surveyors of the Royal Commission disagreed about the origins of this tree clad mound, which had not been previously reported, and the subsequent description reads like a compromise. 'The wayfarer approaching the cross-roads nearly a mile ENE of Lowther Castle might eye suspiciously a long mound within the NW angle of the crossing but would probably conclude that it is nothing more than an old spoil-dump from the neighbouring road-cutting'.[30] Even today, and after the planting of the trees, it is easy to see why the possibility of a spoil dump was entertained. It is remarkably angular and has a similar length to the adjacent road cutting. However, the character of the mound prior to tree planting (*colour plate 15*) is that of the archetypal long barrow. One hundred and four meters long, it is orientated east–west, with the eastern end higher and wider than the western one, and with a transverse dip in the middle – a feature which compares with that at Rayseat Pike. And, is it just coincidence that the site stands within a limited viewshed from the Penrith henges?

The present Ordnance Survey maps mark the site as a 'long cairn' and that is surely the correct description, for a cairn is, after all, only a pile of stones.

HACKTHORPE, NY54802315

This burial mound was removed in the nineteenth century but its structures (*31*) were sufficiently important to be restated here. The mound was composed of soil, amongst which were bone and charcoal. The soil covered a stone circle with a diameter of 20m and almost eight meters from the centre was an inverted urn. Eight other cremations were found in a similar position and a further four near the centre. Each of these un-urned cremations had been placed in a pit covered with a dome of cobble stones packed with small flakes of similar material and with 'a covering of fine black mould'; an arrangement which suggests that they had been placed within an open circle sometime prior to the construction of the mound. At the centre was a two-tier cist. The upper one was empty but the lower one contained 'a large quantity of human bones broken into fragments'.

The Penrith area

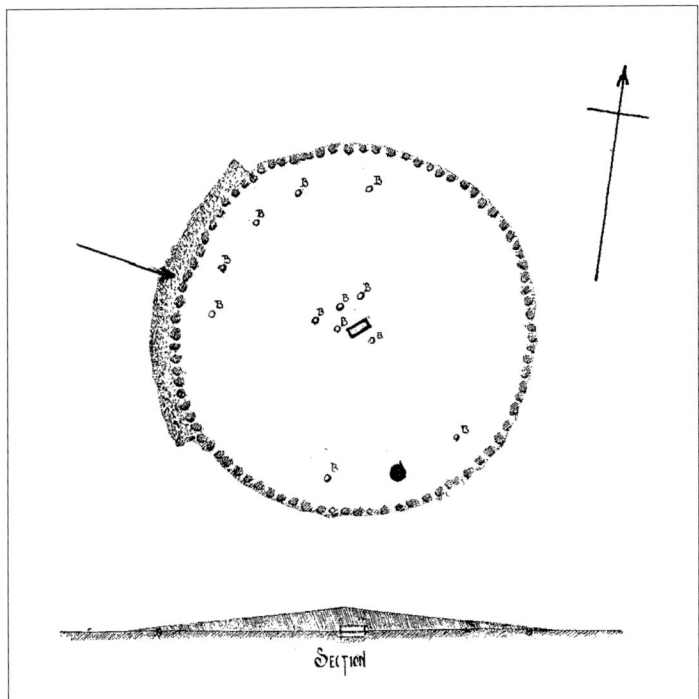

31 The published plan and section of Hackthorpe with the external platform arrowed

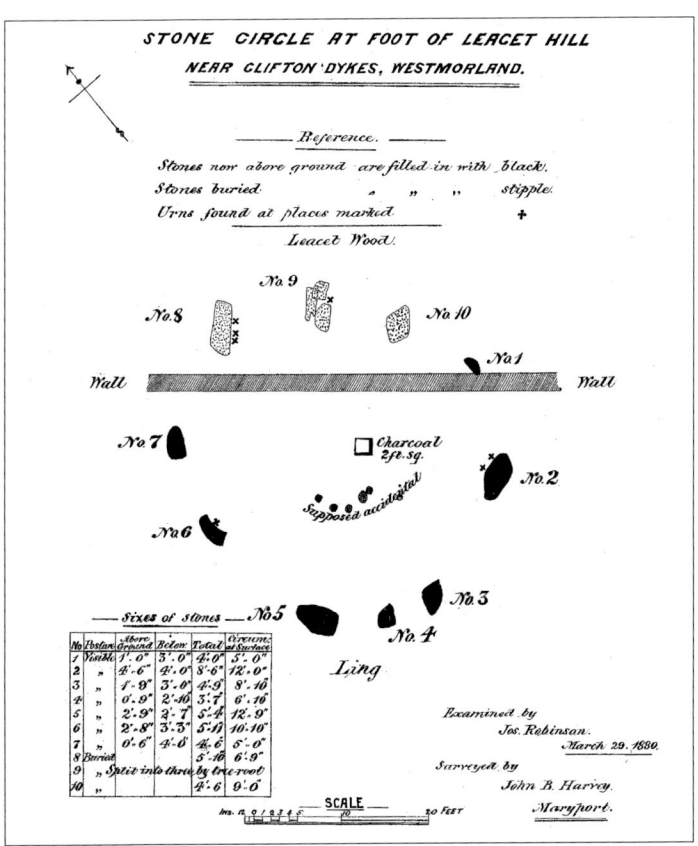

32 Leacet Hill as originally published

Three features suggest that the site was laid out with respect to the 'compass'. Firstly the burials only occurred in the NW and SE quadrants, with the urn exactly half way between two other cremations. Secondly, the ground in the NW quadrant appeared to have been baked hard. Thirdly, that there was a platform outside the western arc of the stone circle.

LEACET HILL, NY56292629

This site lies on private land and cannot be visited, although some of the stones are visible from Wetheriggs Pottery (*colour plate 16*). The existence of the latter is because of nearby clay and that, in turn, suggests the prehistoric site may have been near a former tarn. Equally, a field adjacent to the northern end of the pottery contains erratics of the type that would have been available both for use in this site, and others.

The original character of the site (*32*) is not wholly clear. The circle of stones encompasses the width of a narrow ridge at the bottom of the hillside. There is nothing to suggest that the interior of the circle was higher than this natural ridge, which runs NW–SE, but the south-western arc of stones – those still extant, (stones 2-5) – appear to surround a slight bulge or platform in the ridge.[31]

The excavators[32] reported finding three pots alongside stone 8 and another two by stone 2. The pots, which have since disappeared, were said to have consisted of five 'cinerary urns', one 'food vessel' and one 'incense cup'. There was also an area of 'calcined and broken bones', 0.9m x 0.3m, at the foot of another stone, and near the centre, 'about three feet from the present surface ... a layer of charcoal about a foot thick, interspersed with minute fragments of calcined bones'.

Given the present form of the monument, the central deposits must have been in a pit and, given the present topography of the site, it is reasonable to infer that the urn, said to have been 'about a foot below the surface', was also in a pit. However, other details of the account would be consistent with the latter, being placed on the old ground surface with a mound – the platform – built above.

In addition to this site, the excavators 'dug into a place on top of Leacet Hill, a saucer like place, with ditch around, like the so called "pond barrows" but found nothing other than bedrock, a little charcoal and a buckle from a lady's shoe'. This site cannot now be identified, but aerial photographs recording cropmarks in the vicinity led to an evaluation in advance of development. The results were the identification of a Bronze Age farmstead, a small cremation cemetery which was of similar age but not associated with pottery, and a pit alignment or grubbed out hedge.[33] For the dates see Appendix (p.145).

STONE CARR, MOTHERBY, NY41862810

Clarke[34] mentions that several 'urns, stone coffins and bones' had been found near the side of the road at Stone Carr, a place used 'time out of mind' for races and other sports, and, on the following page, describes what he thought to be a 'Druidical Temple'.

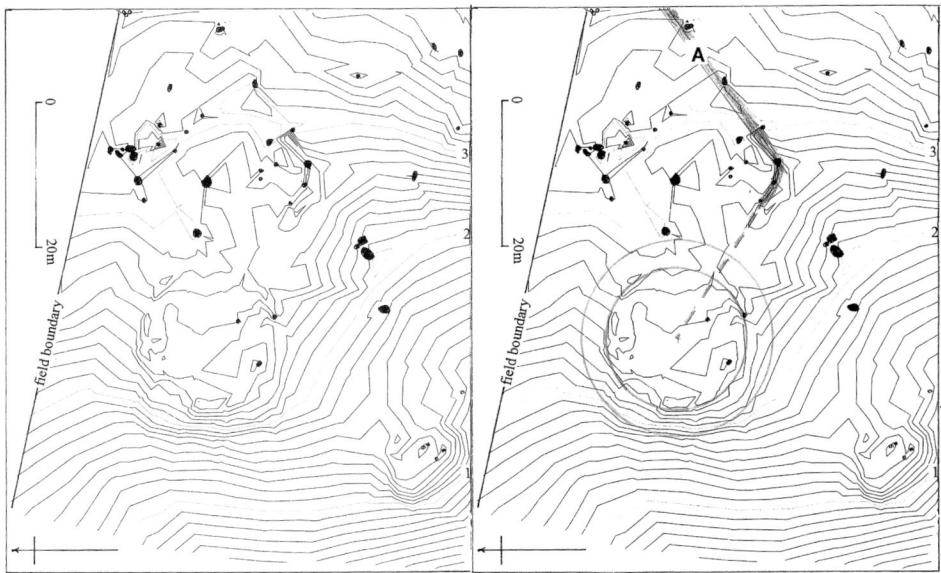

33 The probable site of the Motherby circle. The black stones are erratics

This included 'two large stones which form the entrance … and at the southern most point of the camp is a circle of large stones seventeen yards in diameter. This circle has been lately dug for treasure, but none was found, nor indeed anything but a vast number of bones'.

The precise location of these two sites has always been uncertain. Williams[35] reported that the circle had been destroyed by 1856, but that it had been an 'excellent peristaleth'. Whilst there are reasons to question his accuracy, with regard to other sites, it does appear that by 1876 little of the site remained.[36]

What is probably the site referred to by Clarke lies on private land but is just visible from the old A66 (*colour plate 17*). It appears to consist of a circular bank projecting, platform-like, from the hillside (*33*). The crest of the bank is about 17m in diameter, and a nearby linear dyke A is aligned on its centre. A noteable feature of the site, visible from the old A66 is that it is adjacent to an extensive area of glacial erratics. This poses the question of how prehistoric people regarded the latter and selected particular stones for use.

Equally puzzling is why the stones of the circle were destroyed/removed when those nearby were not – although some of the latter exhibit evidence of drilling. The conclusion has to be that the stones were deliberately targeted and this, in turn, raises questions about their visibility, and therefore size. Unfortunately, Clarke does not give their dimensions, but the present form of the monument is suggestive of a ring cairn, so that the stones were probably not standing as tall monoliths.

CISTS AND CUP-MARKED STONES

In addition to the two cists at Brougham, a number of other cists, or slabs, thought to belong to cists were discovered in the vicinity of Penrith during the nineteenth and early twentieth centuries. A significant number of these were decorated with 'cup marks', and it may well be that undecorated slabs, which had been parts of other cists, went unreported. In addition, however, to these finds several more stones with cup marks have been found within and near Penrith, and to these can be added what appears to be another cup mark on one, the western cross of the Giant's Grave, in Penrith churchyard.[37]

REDHILLS, NY50182777

One of the largest decorated slabs was that found at Redhills in 1881,[38] which appears to have covered a grave cut into the solid limestone. This pit had been 'partially lined' with 'cobble stones' and was filled with loose soil, some burnt 'wood' and a 'quantity of calcined bone'.

There was no evidence for a cairn or covering mound, but in his account, Taylor mentions several other possible sites which are otherwise unknown, unrecognised and unrecorded; 'a round cairn ... on the slope of the hill, three hundred yards to the south ... also near the top of the hill, not very far distant, what might be the remains of a small sepulchral circle, with some of the stones partially buried'.

In addition to these sites, an eighteenth-century account[39] refers to 'an ancient cairn' somewhere in the vicinity of Skirsgill, or Redhills. This site had been dug and was considered to be that of a Roman General because 'bones, urns and broken weapons were found'. Clearly the decorated slab was not Roman, but could the fill of the cist, described by Taylor, be that of a previously riffled monument?

6

MOOR DIVOCK AND SWARTHBECK GILL

Moor Divock is a saddle in the ridge forming the northern end of High Street and the eastern side of Ullswater; a position best appreciated from either the vicinity of the western banks of Ullswater or the A6 south of the Shap Avenue. However, the monuments themselves are probably best understood if approached from the unenclosed road above Helton village.

From Shap, Helton can be reached either through Lowther, with its putative long cairn, or via the hamlet of Bampton. There, worthy of note is the great width of the floodplain which must have been a significant feature in prehistoric times. Certainly, it is possible to imagine it being a relatively open area in the early Neolithic forest cover; an area carrying reeds and grasses favourable to browsing.

From Helton, the Moor is accessed by a steep road which leads onto the unenclosed common, and the principal sites lie along the bridleway to Pooley Bridge. This bridleway, which crosses the ridge, would appear to have its origins in a routeway as old as the monuments, for they are strung out along it. However, both were probably also influenced by the former existence of a tarn,[1] and it may be this, providing again a grazing resource, which influenced the location of the monuments.

THE COPSTONE, NY49602160

This is a somewhat enigmatic site in that it sometimes appears that the prominent monolith is set on the edge of an earthen circle and associated with other, much lower stones. That is how Greenwell described it, adding that it is 'about 68ft in diameter, the space within which is roughly paved with cobble stones'.[2] It is, however, unclear whether he actually excavated the site. Moreover, the site name implies a single monolith.[3] On the other hand, one problem of interpretation of the sites on the Moor, as a whole, is that the names are first recorded, no more than a couple of centuries ago. They may not be useful indicators of the original appearance of the sites.

Whatever the original form of the monument, the Copstone, itself, is visible on the middle distance horizon from many parts of the Moor and appears to mark the south-eastern boundary of the area of prehistoric 'ritual' sites. From the Copstone itself, however, it is possible to see the sites known as The Standing Stones and White Raise, and Taylor[4] thought they had been connected by an avenue of stones 0.3m–0.6m high, spaced at intervals of 2m–8m and 5m–8m wide.

FROM THE COPSTONE TO THE STANDING STONES

Although subsequent work has failed to prove the existence of this avenue, a walk towards The Standing Stones, especially when there is no bracken and the grass is shortest, does allow a number of small stones to be seen, and it is not difficult to imagine that *some* might have formed an avenue. Nevertheless, there is insufficient evidence 'to have any conjecture as to their having formed part of an artificial avenue'.[5] On the other hand, the walk from the Copstone towards the Standing Stones reveals two large stones (*34a*). These appear to be natural, but one has the impression that they are aligned with the other sites and that they are meant to be walked between. In short, whether the stones are natural or there was a formal avenue or not, they invite *procession*.

Taylor described the two stones as forming a 'circle' and 'cromlech' composed of one large boulder, 1.2m high and 4.5m in circumference, with two other stones about 1.2m to either side, forming a triangle which may have supported a capstone. Today, this arrangement is difficult to substantiate, but two further features of the site are worth noting. Firstly, they are due south of the mound on the hillside of Riddingley Top. Secondly, it can be argued that the northern faces of the stones are aligned on midwinter sunrise/midsummer sunset, with the latter occurring over the distinctive summit of Blencathra, or Saddleback.

THE STANDING STONES OR DRUID'S CROSS, NY49402196

This small stone circle, where the uprights appear to be erected on a small mound, is generally referred to as The Standing Stones, but on Hodgson's map of 1828 it is called 'Druid's Cross'. Although badly damaged by excavation, the mound appears to have originally had a level surface, and it will also be evident that because the monument is located on the end of a discrete spur (*34b*), the site appears as a platform from which the stones rise. However, because the monument was not built on the end or back of the nearby higher mound – presumably a deliberate choice – the area visible from the monument is limited.

One of the stones, A, carries a faint cup and ring carving,[6] and the site was excavated in the nineteenth century by Greenwell and Simpson. Apart from the obvious hole in the centre of the monument, their work appears to have included a trench and associated spoil heap B and C. They reported finding a central hollow 0.6m 'below the surface ... in the ground' in which there was a 'burnt body' and sherds of a vessel broken before deposition, and apparently brought from elsewhere. Above 'the burnt bones was a deposit of sand about three inches (7.5cms) thick, upon which was laid, on its side, and with the mouth to the west'[7] a food vessel (*34c*).

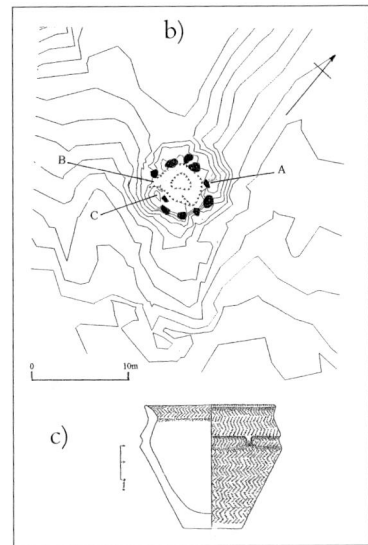

34a-c A line in the landscape. (a) The two boulders between The Copstone and The Standing Stones. (b) The Standing stones and (c) Food vessel

The sherds went to the British Museum, but this author has been unable to locate them. Nevertheless, they appear to have been an example of a practice noted elsewhere; the deliberate deposition of broken pottery. However, what is unusual is the fact that although food vessels were normally associated with inhumation burials, no such remains were encountered here. The simplest explanation would be to assume that the bones were lost to an acid soil but that process did not occur at White Raise. Could it be, therefore, that the intact vessel was deliberately buried by itself as an act similar to that which saw the deposition of the sherds? And in the absence of a detailed stratigraphy, might it be possible that there were two phases of burial/deposition and that this is not a single phase site?

SITE V, NY49312219

This group of standing stones visible from the last site has no name, despite being of considerable importance. Taylor, the first person to describe in detail the sites on the Moor, numbered it Site 5 and that is the nomenclature adopted here, but with Roman numeral to avoid confusion. Waterhouse follows the RCHM and Taylor's account[8] in describing this site as a stone circle; a somewhat surprising description given that the most visible part is *a line* of upright stones.

Detailed survey (35) and the first descriptions agree that the site consisted of a low mound 14m or 17m in diameter, possibly with a kerb of spaced boulders. Taylor thought there had been three low projections making the site a 'star shaped cairn', like White Raise, but the survey could not find these. There are apparent projections, such as A (35c), but they appear to have resulted from disturbance of the 'mound'.

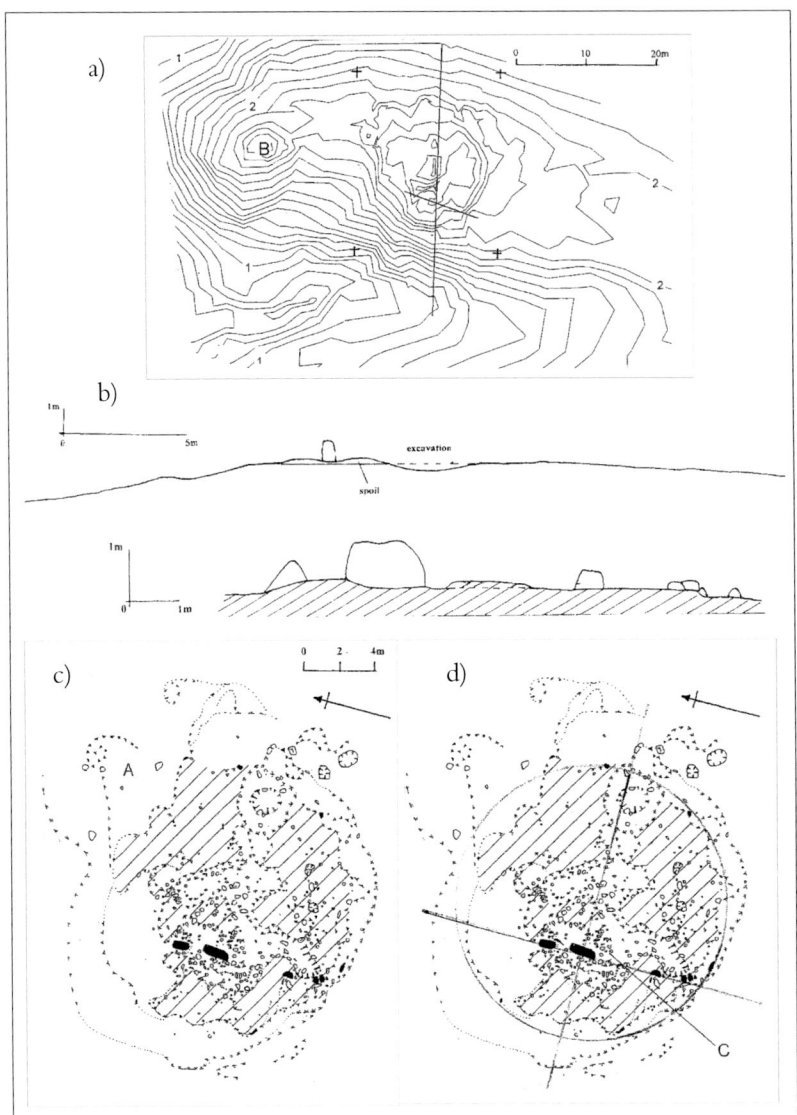

35a-c Site V, Moor Divock

The site appears to be deliberately located on a break of slope to enhance the platform-like appearance of the monument, and there is a small mound – probably a tumulus – to the north, B (35a). As figure 35d shows, the line of standing stones is orientated north–south and the largest of the uprights is on the east–west axis. Consequently, it is reasonable to suspect, as Simpson did, that there were once more uprights.

Simpson excavated the site[9] but someone had already disturbed it. The extent of their excavations can still be seen, and some of the material was piled on top of the platform (35b). It is also evident that some of the digging extended to the stones C (35d). Unfortunately, Simpson does not comment on the structure he found, but he did find an inurned cremation at the centre. The urn had been inverted but only the rim (which cannot now be located) survived.

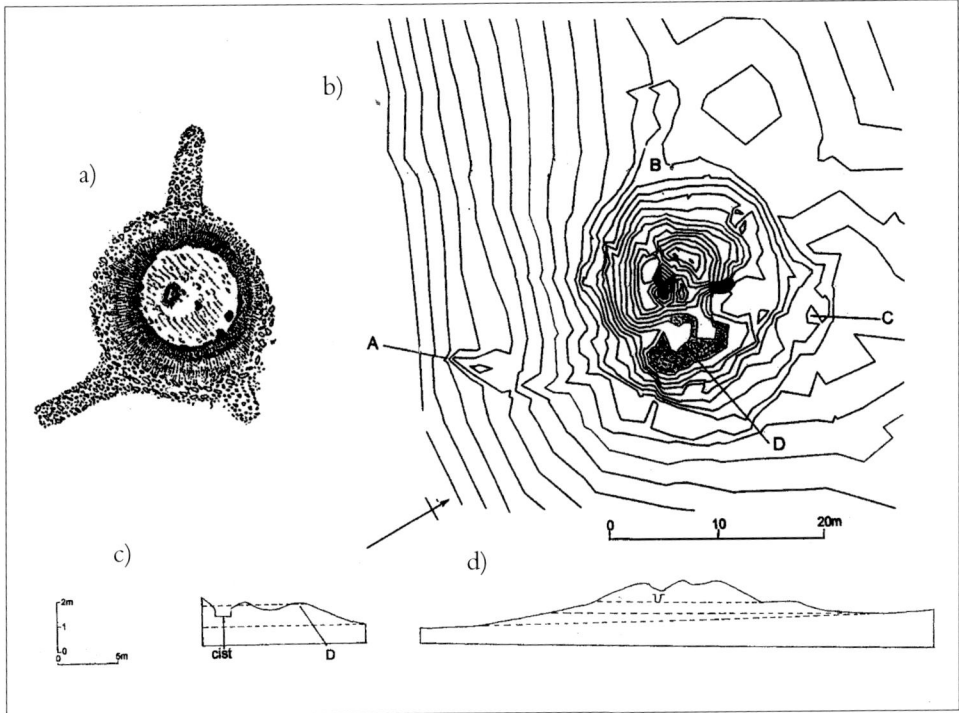

36 White Raise. (a) Taylor's plan. (b) The site today to the same scale; the probable, original flat top is shaded. (c and d) Profiles across the site suggesting that the cist was above original ground level and just below a flat top

FROM SITE V TO WHITE RAISE

The large mound of White Raise is clearly visible from Site V, and Taylor identified a number of small circles in the area in between. As with the avenue, which he thought led to them, it has been impossible to verify his findings. However, there is a small, previously unidentified cairn, probably representing 'field' clearance, and some alignments of stones can be suggested.

WHITE RAISE, NY48882245

The ruins of this large cairn bear witness to the techniques of early archaeologists, but they also allow us to see the cist in which Simpson found the bones of an adult. In addition to the cist, there is a large stone, one of several recorded by Taylor, as having existed below the cairn and apparently forming a line (*36a*).[10] However, the accuracy of his record must be questioned, as the three external projections which allowed him to refer to the site as a 'star cairn' are not quite where he sketched them.

Of these projections, one A (*36b*) appears to be the remains of a wall tangential to the cairn, and it is possible it, and projection B, were constructed for the protection of sheep, like the nearby bield. In that context, attention is drawn to the roughly rectangular area C, which may be a small pen or part of the original monument.

Whatever the age and purpose of these features, the main cairn appears to have been some 20m in diameter, but there is no clear evidence for the 'larger stones which may have bounded the base' noted by Taylor, nor for his inner ring. Taylor's plan does in fact show neither of these two features but gives the impression that much of the ground surface within the cairn had been excavated, leaving the rim untouched. In that context, it is interesting to note that when one stands to the north of the cist, the southern part of the cairn D appears to be relatively flat and reminiscent of the (suggested) original surface of Site V. The impression of a mutilated domed cairn may simply be the result of the piles of spoil left by early antiquarians, and it may be the site was originally flat topped.

If that were so, and the surface of area D is projected across the site, as in (35c), then the cist was just below the surface and its cap stone may have been visible; an arrangement which would allow access to the cist to be gained at various times. This interpretation is supported by the fact that it appears to have been built above the old ground surface (35d). Whilst this feature may simply have resulted from it being a secondary structure, one inserted into an earlier structure, it is apparent from (35d) and Taylor's plan that the lower part of the monument remains intact and was never excavated.

Three other features of the cist are worth noting. Firstly, that the cist was not central to the monument which may support the idea that it is secondary. Secondly, that the cist may have been intended to be orientated on midwinter sunrise/midsummer sunset. Thirdly, the single large slab, which Taylor said covered it, may be represented by two large pieces of limestone, and whilst the underlying geology of the site is limestone, the majority of the cairn material is not. White appears to have been a significant colour in prehistory,[11] and it is interesting to note here the actual name of the site.

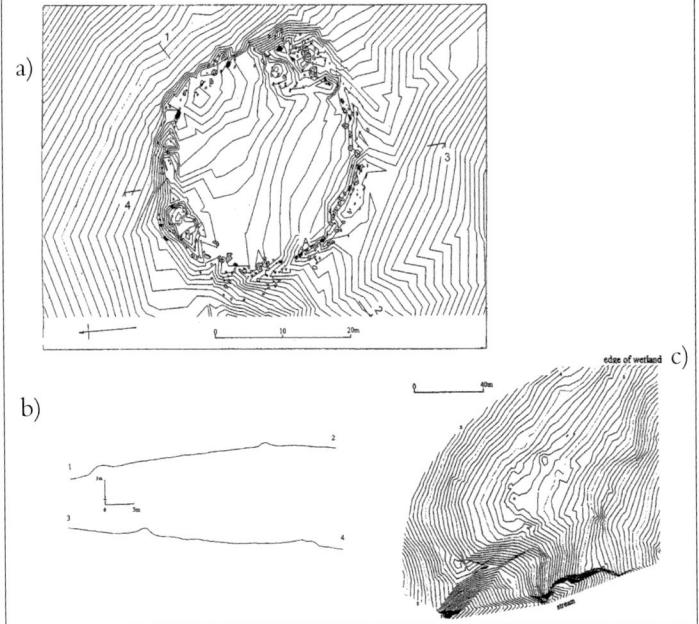

37a-c The Cockpit. (a) The plan of the stones is that of RCHME, 1936. (b) Profiles. (c) The location of the site; the form lines are based on readings excluding those of the bank

It is also necessary to note that whilst Taylor thought there might have been some kind of circular arrangement of stones, and there are large erratics nearby, there does not appear to have been a prominent, visible megalithic structure like those of The Standing Stones, or Site V. Rather, the location of the site may have been determined by the existence of at least one large boulder, such as that now visible.

THE COCKPIT, NY48272224

The perimeter of this monument is formed of two concentric circles of uprights; an arrangement which is similar to those of an 'orthostatic' wall. Here, however, the larger stones have been placed on the inside, and in places they both lean towards the 'inside' of the wall whilst also forming 'straight' lengths (*colour plate 18*). Both of those features appear to be original, but in two places the perimeter appears to be overlain by round cairns. In addition, there is the suggestion that the perimeter has been trenched; although there is no record of the site ever having been excavated.

The area enclosed by the 'wall' supports a better quality grass than that of the surrounding area, and this allows for the possibility that the centre is 'paved'. In addition, the impression gained by walking around the site is that it might be built as a platform. Both profile 3-4, and the form line survey, support this interpretation. However, the 'platform' may in part be a natural one (*37c*).

Figure *37c* also shows that the monument is located on a subtle spur between the steep sides of a small valley and the wetland/former tarn. Significantly, the monument appears to have been located at the western end of a dry 'corridor' between two areas of that wetland; drier ground utilised by the path from White Raise. Nevertheless, the stones are only visible on the skyline from a few small areas of the Moor, one being across the former tarn. Equally, the area of Moor visible from the site is restricted, and the only other large monument visible is that of White Raise. In contrast, the views northward are spectacular, at least on a clear day.

To the south there is an extensive cairnfield, a possible cist and modern circle some three meters in diameter. In the same area there are a number of larger stones which could have been used to build the Cockpit, raising questions about the meaning of the size of stones actually used.

THE COCKPIT TO HEUGHSCAR HILL

The path northwards from the Cockpit towards Heughscar Hill partly follows the Roman road, and there are linear banks of unknown date; one in uncertain relationship to a wetland area. Beyond that wetland, and strung out along the path at the base of the hill, are a number of mounds and a small mound is located on the summit of the hill.

RIDDINGLEY TOP, NY49332291

Despite its name,[12] this mound is not located on a hilltop but rather below a steep section of the hillside. For that reason it is not very visible and hardly worth a visit, except that tucked into the hillside behind it are some stones which may be the remains of a cist.

RIDDINGLEY TOP TO THE COPSTONE

From the last site, it is worth returning to the road by the path which leads towards Standing Stones and, then, from there to the Copstone. Note how the monuments are occasionally lost against the background, hidden in folds or briefly highlighted on the skyline.

SWARTHBECK GILL, NY45721925

This site was reported by the Geological Survey in 1877 and described as 'a ring of standing stones'. However, by 1936[13] only one stone was standing and today even that has fallen.

The site is located on a valley floor adjacent to a spring, or springs, which have eroded the ground and created at some time a small pool A (*38*). Northwards, and beyond the edge of the steeply falling valley, is the low and relatively flat land stretching from

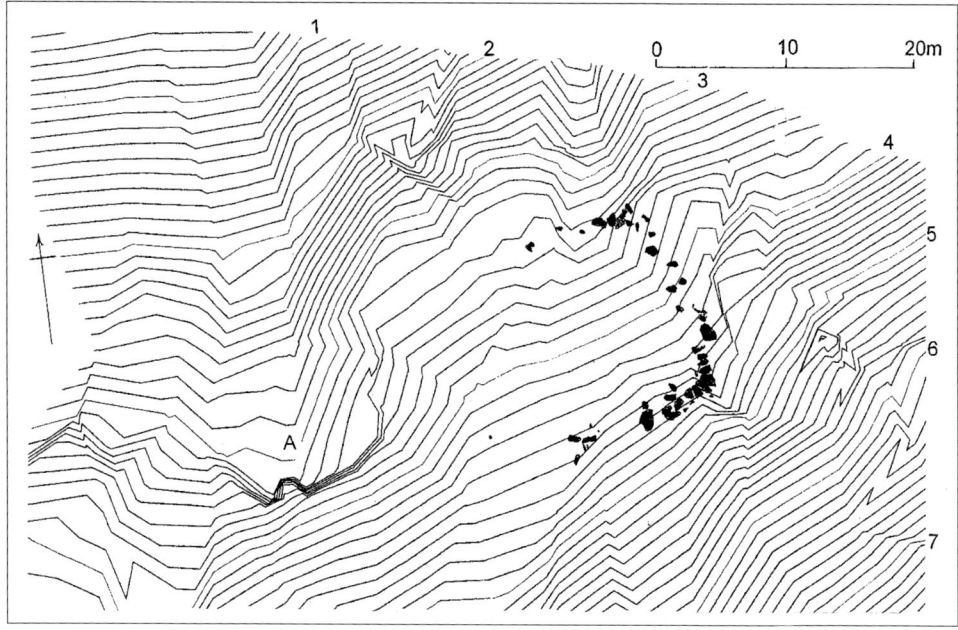

38 Swarthbeck Gill

Greystoke and Motherby to Carlisle. To the north-west are the high fells of Blencathra and, visible over Swarth Fell, the summit of Carrock Fell.

Whilst the midsummer sun must set over these peaks, the position of the site appears to have been determined, primarily, by the spring/pool and the phrase 'shrine' comes to mind. Another feature of the site is that it appears to have been composed of thin tabular slabs, which in places must have formed a continuous 'fence'. However, the most significant feature of the present monument, which has never been planned before, is that it does not appear to be a circle, rather an open-sided rectangle. As such, the site may actually be an old sheep pen. On the other hand, it is possible to believe that the stones may have been on the perimeter of a circle 18m or 16m in diameter. Interestingly, the pool A also appears to have a diameter of 16m and is most clearly defined in the south-east, just like the stone structure.

7

SHAP AND THE EASTERN LAKE DISTRICT

SHAP, NY 5614

Several groups of stones lie scattered across the landscape north and south of the village. Those visible from the highway or footpaths are shown in (*39*)[1] and some are decorated.[2] The distribution of these stones appears to echo the descriptions made by Camden and later antiquarians, and it may be that with the exception of the southern group, the evidence is not much different from that available to them. Certainly they, themselves, appear to have struggled to understand what they saw; whether the stones represented a single monument or there were several arrangements.

Camden's account, published in 1610, stated 'there be huge stones in the form of Pyramides, some 9 foote high and 14ft thick that ranged directly as it were in a rowe for a mile in length, with equall distance almost between'. About eighty years later, Thomas Machell, the local antiquarian, repeated Camden's description referring, in passing, to 12 stones. It is, however, William Stukeley, working some 30 years after Machell, who gives us the first detailed account of what was visible.[3]

Whilst Stukeley himself visited the site, he also employed a surveyor from Carlisle to make a plan. Unfortunately, that plan does not appear to have survived, and as Stukeley's published account is later than the survey, it is not clear whether his description is based on his own notes or the evidence of his surveyor. What is however certain is that Stukeley had formed the impression that there had been an avenue similar to that at Avebury, with his surveyor offering to alter his plan if it was not to the liking of his employer.

Whatever the basis of his description, Stukeley's account is worth quoting, in detail, as a reference point for what remains today and it should be compared with (*39a*). Stukeley thought there had been an avenue '70ft broad, composed of very large stones, set at equal intervals: it seems to be closed at this' (south) 'end which is on an eminence and near a long flattish barrow, with stone works upon it; hence it proceeds northward to the town, which intercepts the continuation of it … Though its journey be northward, yet it makes a very large curve, or arc of a circle, as those at Abury, and passes over a brook too. A spring likewise arises in it, near the Greyhound Inn. By the brook is a little round Sacellum, composed of twelve stones, but lesser ones, set by one great stone belonging to the side of the avenue; the interval of the stones is 35ft, half the breadth of the avenue; the stones no doubt did all stand upright, because 4 still do … it ascends the hill, crosses the common road to Penrith, and so goes into corn-fields on the other side of the way westwards, where some stones are left standing; one particularly remarkably called Guggleby stone'.

Pennant's description, published in 1776, may have drawn upon Stukely's account but includes other details and interpretations. 'On the common near the roadside about half a mile beyond the village are certain large circles and ovals formed of small stones: and parallel to the road commences a double row of granites of immense sizes, crossed at the end by another row …The space between the lines at the south end is 88ft; they converge towards each other for near Shap the distance decreases to 59ft; and it is probable that they met and concluded in a point forming a wedge'.

The drawing of Lady Lowther, published by Ferguson[4] (39b), and said to date (presumably coincidentally) to 1776, shows this wedge-shaped arrangement, but the fact that the stones appear to be angular rather than the rounded extant boulders, A (39a), allows the accuracy of the sketch to be questioned. Certainly it is difficult to reconcile that illustration with the one sent to the *Gentleman's Magazine* in 1844, where the southern end appears as a large diameter circle (39c).

39a-e Shap Avenue. (a) Location of the visible and accessible remains. (b) Drawing by Lady Lowther. (c) The southern circle from *The Gentleman's Magazine* of 1844. (d) The position and character of 'Karl lofts' on Hodgson's map of 1828. (e) The extant stones at the southern end. Note they are above a slight terrace B, which northwards becomes a short, linear hollow C with a depression D which might be the remains of a pond

The arrangement of the terminal shown in Lady Lowther's drawing is essentially the same as that of the present stones (39e), and it may be that her angular stones simply reflect a desire to depict the 'rude' nature of the monument. Equally, (39c) needs to be seen in the context of the accompanying letter objecting to the building of the Lancaster–Carlisle railway across the top of the monument; a letter which pointed out that the owner of the land, the then Earl of Lonsdale, was also a principal shareholder in the railway who could ask for the monument to be saved. Given that the letter was anonymous, we might infer that he was a local, perhaps even a tenant of the Earl, and the obvious person would be George Hall of Rosgill, who had described the monument in the *Gentleman's Magazine* twenty years earlier.

Hall's account, which may, in part, owe something to Pennant, states that the enclosing of the land after 1815 had led to the destruction of all the southern part 'excepting fourteen, which compose the turn at the south end'. Hall also reported that a cairn of granite and cobble stone, 20yds south-west of the southern end had been completely destroyed, as had a circle 18ft in diameter and with a central standing stone some 100 yards south of the avenue. Significantly, however, he does not state that the southern end was a circle, rather he refers to a 'turn'; a term which might be applied to the arrangements in (39b) and (39e). Could it be that the drawing (39c) employed licence in order to raise emotions and protests over the destruction of a perfect monument? What is certain is that the background detail of that drawing – the mountains of Wet Sleddale valley and the relationship of the low mound and field wall behind the circle – are those visible at the present time from the extant boulders.

Attention is drawn to ridge A (39e) which, when seen from the A6 to the south, appears to be a 'barrow'. This ridge is probably the 'long flattish barrow' of Stukeley, but whether it is glacial or human in origin is unclear. It may be that the higher, northern end is the remains of a round mound on a natural ridge; perhaps the remains of Hall's cairn said to be 20 yards south-west of the avenue. However, there appears to be no other evidence for the structures described by Hall.

In that context, it is necessary to note that if it were not for the fact that the present relationship of ridge A to the field wall appears to be that shown in (39c), the mountains in the background of that drawing best fit a location further south, near the junction of the A6 and B6261. Could it be that the circle in (39c) is one of the 'large circles' mentioned by Pennant or that reported by Hall to have stood 100 yards south of the avenue? The latter seems unlikely, as the road junction is more than 100 yards to the south and the circle is said to have been only 18ft in diameter. Pennant's sites remain a possibility, but it may be that he is referring, in part, to the putative circle on Hardendale Fell (below). However, Pennant's account is better interpreted as referring to the circular earthwork (B in 39a) and to the other earthworks, probably hut circles, further south and west of there.

Once such sites have been separated from the early accounts, then, as Pennant noted, 'parallel to the road commences a double row of granites of immense sizes', the 'Carl Lofts' of Hodgson's map (39d).

Clearly, without geophysical survey and/or excavation, it is now impossible to determine the original arrangements of all the stones. Indeed, without excavation, it is not certain whether some stones are *insitu* natural erratics or former erratics moved to form a monument; a situation which would have also faced early antiquarians and undoubtedly contributed to the idea that the 'avenue' had continued all the way to Moor Divock.

In 1978, the author suggested that there had been at least two avenues or rows; a single row to the west and north-west of Skellaw Hill, and a double row which may have been a continuation of Carl Lofts, south of that feature. More recently, Aubrey Burl[5] has suggested that the wide spacing of the rows, south of Skellaw Hill, is best explained by them being two separate rows of single stones rather than a double avenue, and whilst that is probable, the point this author was making in 1978 is that the round burial mound of Skellaw Hill appears to be the focal point for some of the stones. Here, however, the author would make one further observation. The former existence of separate monuments/lines can be inferred from the character/architecture of the surviving stones, for the upright 'pyramidal' and widely spaced monoliths, such as the Goggleby Stone, are quite different from the closer set boulders – of different geology – which may never have been upright, at the southern end.

The fact that some of the northern stones need to be considered in relation to a burial mound, whilst the southern end of the 'double row' appears to have been a mound, or mounds, requires us to think of the Shap monuments, not simply as standing stones, but as a complex of sites, equivalent to those in the vicinity of Mayburgh or Long Meg. Indeed, the (aggregate) labour needed to erect so many large stones at Shap must be comparable with that which created the monuments at Mayburgh and Long Meg. For that reason, the importance of the Shap complex lies in the apparent *absence* of a henge, or great circle. In particular, it requires us to accept that statements, such as 'large sites took on additional roles as focal points on communal and/or inter-communal levels',[6] refer to sites other than just stone circles. In short, Neolithic and Early Bronze Age societies cannot be understood by studying only stone circles. There is a need to study all sites within a region.

It is also necessary to note that whatever the precise arrangement of the stones, their location may have been, in part, influenced by topographical features. In particular, attention is drawn to three aspects of the topography. Firstly, that the high ground to the east restricted views, just as there are restricted views from some stone circles and megalithic tombs – although the mound on Hardendale Nab may just have been visible from the southern terminus. Secondly, that there may have been a former tarn, south of Green Farm. Thirdly, the double row of stones at the southern end appears to have ended at, or *deliberately* crossed the stream; an arrangement which can be compared with the ditched enclosure at Long Meg embracing a valley which connected it to the River Eden. Significantly, just as Long Meg appears to have been laid out with respect to a spring, so Stukeley noted at Shap, 'a spring likewise arises in it'.

HARDENDALE FELL, NY 57321240

This group of stones, which has not previously appeared in archaeological literature, was reported during a survey of one of the gas pipelines which cross the area. The stones, some of which appear to be upright, lie beyond the more massive boulders placed by highway engineers along the side of their road and appear to form a circle (*40a*).

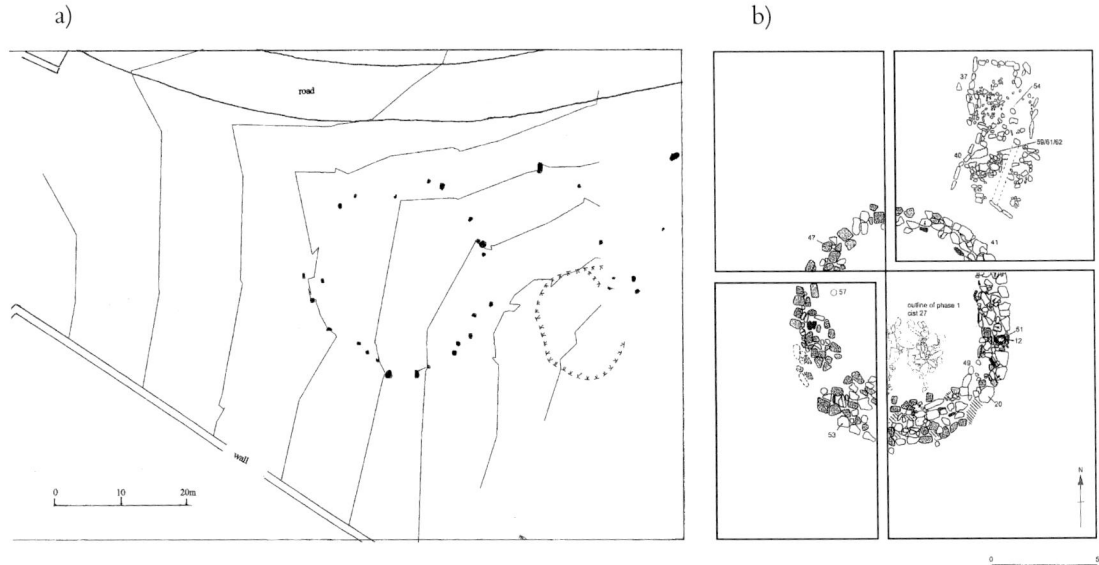

40a-b Hardendale. (a) The putative circle on Hardendale Fell (form lines at 0.5m intervals). (b) The second phase of the Hardendale Nab monument after Williams and Howard Davis

Whether this is a genuine stone circle, or not, a visit provides an introduction to the basic geography of this chapter, the previous one and that following; to the east is the corner of the great escarpment which is such a dominant feature of the next chapter, westward is an expanse of moorland (Rafland Forest) stretching towards Haweswater and the high ridges around High Street, and to the north-west the saddle of Moor Divock is partly obscured by the dramatic limestone slopes of Knipe Scar.

HARDENDALE NAB, NY 58141401

This site, a dished mound some 16.5m in diameter and 0.8m high, was excavated in advance of a quarry extension.[7] However, the latter never took place and the remains are well worth a visit.

The first phase consisted of a cist built on the old ground surface and protruding from a small supporting mound which contained a number of secondary burials. The cist possessed no capstone but contained the cremated remains of two individuals, possibly an adult and an infant, and small amounts of calcined animal bone, possibly the remains of feasting.

A limestone layer over the mound appears to have been kept deliberately clean so as to be visible as a white surface, and a number of cremations occurred nearby, one with fragmentary sherds of a collared urn. These were sealed by the building in phase two of a circular bank/wall, into which had been built a small cist with cremation. There was an entrance in the south-west quadrant and beyond the bank, and associated with it, or the earlier phase, were two rectangular areas (40b). These may have been excarnation platforms or for cremation pyres.

In the next phase, the area enclosed by the bank/wall was filled with rubble and the rectangular areas buried. This phase may have lasted some time, but within the body of the resulting cairn were 71 discrete groupings of human bone fragments and three other cremations associated with fragments of collared urns. The north-western quadrant appeared, however, not to have been filled, hence the dished top, and it may be that the central cist was still visible. However, the whole was finally buried (phase four) with more cremated and unburnt bones being included in the cairn material.

Though complicated, the sequence does provide a context in which to evaluate some of the earlier sites excavated in the area, most noticeably those of Greenwell. In particular, it provides analogous material for the bones he found scattered in cairn material and interpreted as evidence of previous disturbance, and the presence of water vole away from wetland habitats is again demonstrated.

Other palaeo-environmental evidence also shows that the cairn had been built within an area of grassland and not woodland and this, together with the attempt to create a white surface, suggest the monument would have been visible from afar. That being so, a noticeable feature of the site is that it was not built on the highest point; higher ground occurring immediately to the north and to the east. The site could not therefore be seen from those at Castlehowe or Harberwain Rigg but was visible from the north-west and south, where there is a possible standing stone. Whether the site was visible from the southern end of the Shap 'avenue' is, however, not clear; the view being currently obscured. Nor is the relationship of the cairn to the bank, which runs eastwards along the break of slope, known, but the latter was presumably aligned on both.

WHITE RAISE AND RAFLAND FOREST, NY 53431345

White Raise – not to be confused with the White Raise on Moor Divock – is best approached along a grassy track at the point where the unfenced road approaches the enclosed land of Tailbert farm. From here, it ascends southwards, and at NY 53561379 crosses a mound some five metres in diameter. This may, or may not be part of a small cairnfield but there is the remains of a boulder fringed terrace, probably a settlement site, against the nearby rock outcrop. Again, it is not clear whether some of the linear earthworks which can be discerned near here are former (and associated?) field boundaries, or simply the original ground between holloways. Certainly there are holloways running approximately north–south which provide a context in which to consider the location of White Raise itself.

Despite its name, the cairn is a pile of grey stones, nine metres in diameter and now over one metre high. It was excavated by Simpson in the nineteenth century[8] after it had been partly quarried, and at its centre he found ashes, portions of calcined bones and 'fragments of an urn scored with parallel lines'. Cobbles had been packed around the urn and a flagstone placed on top; an arrangement which could be explained by the urn being coeval with the building of the cairn, or by it having been inserted into the body of an existing cairn.

Although damaged, it is apparent the 'cairn' was originally just that – a heap of stones with little interstitial material. The significance of this is the relative paucity of stones on the moor at the present time, so that the collection of the stones must reflect a deliberate and meaningful decision, one which compares with the bank at Mayburgh.

BAMPTON COMMON AND FOURSTONES, NY49021626

A cairn, which has been dug into, is situated in a high col parallel to the main valley. At the western end of this col, 'a sort of defile',[9] are two standing stones (*colour plate 19*). The site name implies the existence of two more stones, and in 1901 these were described as being another pair, albeit prostrate, but today it is difficult to identify them.

One of the extant stones is tilted and the faces of both are at an angle to each other, resembling gateposts, although there is no evidence of any wall or former field boundary. Nevertheless, there are a number of other cairns nearby, some apparently the remains of 'field clearance' associated with enclosures, suggesting that in the past the area may have functioned like a 'saeter' or 'alp', a shoulder for summer pasture and hay. Their position is reasonably described by Noble:[10] 'If this has been a British homestead, as appears probable, they showed great taste in the selection, as the view from it is unsurpassed in the Lake District'.

LOW RAISE AND HIGH RAISE, NY45621374 AND NY44821345

Low Raise is a cairn nine meters in diameter and with an external height of one meter (the central hollow being some 1.4m deep). A modern marker cairn has been built in the north-east quadrant, and the antiquity of the main cairn is shown on the northern 'side' where the stones appear to be partly buried by blanket peat. Another noteworthy feature is its topographical position at the end of the ridge *but* just below the break of slope.

In contrast, High Raise, with its modern marker cairn and shelter, can be said to be located on the summit of the ridge. However, on the western side, the ancient cairn can be seen to have an upper surface like a platform, so that the site might be better described as being built against, rather than on, the summit.

KNIPE SCAR, NY529193

This site is located below and to the east of the highest point of the Scar, and is in an inconspicuous position. A little to the east, however, are the steep, forested slopes of a high glacial mound, which without its trees must have looked like a giant long barrow when seen from afar e.g., from Hardendale Fell. In short, the general location of the site within the broader landscape is a conspicuous one.

The site itself consists of limestone slabs within an area of limestone pavement. The slabs, together with smaller stones, appear to have been built as a bank (*41a*) with an internal diameter of 15m. In the centre is a limestone block, and this is shown on the plan of 1907[11] where a gap is shown in the south-eastern quadrant, together with a curious distortion of the overall circular shape. Miss Noble, who published that plan, argued that the site was one dug by Simpson.

Simpson does mention digging on Knipe Scar, but his description of a central stone, being found 0.5m. below the ground and within the centre of three concentric circles, hardly fits this site. Moreover, in another paper, quoted by Noble, Simpson's site is referred to as being on Shap Moor.[12] On Jeffrey's map,[13] 'Shap Moor' is to the east and south, whilst the excavator of Wilson Scar refers to that site (below) being 'below the crest of Knipe Scar'.[14] It seems reasonable to conclude, therefore, that Simpson's site was that described next.

SHAPBECK, NY553188

This circle, discovered during systematic field survey,[15] is located adjacent to a public footpath. Although dilapidated, it can be described as three concentric circles, and the diameters accord with those of Simpson's lost site (*41b*). According to Simpson,[16] in the centre of his site, and at depth of about 0.5m, was a 'flat-shaped stone' under which 'were evident traces of charcoal and burnt earth, but no bones'.

Simpson, however, also states that there was a second circle, the centre of which was *c*.29m from this one. Infuriatingly, he does not state in which direction the site lay, nor what its dimensions were; only that at the centre, and again about 0.5m down, there was 'a rude pavement of cobbles' under which was a 'similar deposit of charcoal'. The dimensions of the pavement are given as 1.8m x 1.2m, and whilst it is unclear whether the plan shape was rectangular or ovoid, it does appear that the feature did not extend across the whole interior of the circle. Simpson also refers to a third circle in the 'adjoining field', and this may, or may not be that destroyed on Wilson Scar.

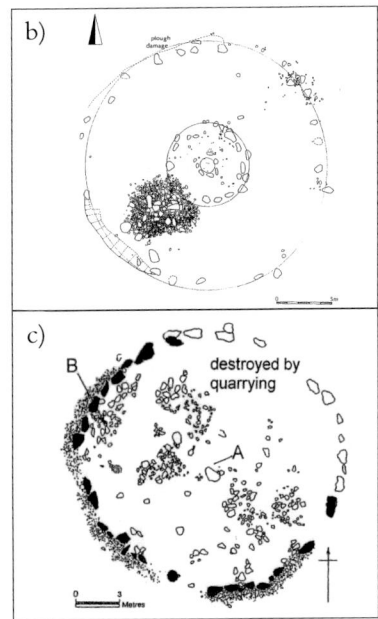

41a-c The circles on Knipe Scar. (a) Knipe Scar. (b) Shapbeck based on TCWAAS2 LXXXVI, 245, but overlain with the diameters of Simpson's lost site. (c) Wilson Scar based on TCWAAS2 LXXXXIV

WILSON SCAR, NY549182

This site was first described in 1935 and excavated in advance of destruction by quarrying in 1952,[17] and unless otherwise stated, the quotes are from the excavation account. The site lay on gently sloping ground 'below the crest of Knipe Scar', and thus, the view northwards must have been almost non existent. However, southwards, and towards Shap, there appears to have been a wetland, perhaps even a tarn at some time.

The circle was approximately 18.3m in diameter and composed of 35 unevenly spaced stones, although originally they might have been 'continuous', for the 'available supply of large erratics, up to 1.5m x 1.2m in horizontal dimensions, had been supplemented by packing smaller stones in between'. Significantly, for our understanding of the possible original arrangements at other sites, the excavations at Wilson Scar demonstrated that the stones had *not* been upright but simply placed 'on their longest sides in their natural resting positions'. In addition, they 'were provided with a low external retaining bank … to make a continuous circle', and it was this feature which led the site to be described in 1935 as being terraced into the hillside.

Nevertheless, the interior of the circle did appear to have been roughly levelled with slabs forming a discontinuous paved surface. At the approximate centre of the circle was an inhumation, and at A in *41c*, a charcoal patch contained fragments of human teeth and cranium. A second cremation, associated with a flint flake, black pebble split into three, a flat plaque of limestone with three holes and a mammalian skull (probably a water vole), may originally have been placed against one stone prior to its removal by quarrying. Near another stone B, however, there was an *in situ* and probably 'disarticulated' inhumation. The bones had been placed in a shallow grave surrounded by a setting of small boulders.

GUNNERWELL OR GUNNERKELD, NY56821777

Gunnerkeld lies within a small valley, the mouth of which is visible from the Shapbeck circle, and a number of features make the site worth greater academic consideration than previously given. Two have long been known:

1. Although the shapes of the stones make it difficult to determine whether they were all originally 'uprights', there appears to be a northern portal of two such stones (A in 42a). Is this chance or intentional?
2. As at Oddendale, further south there is a central mound with 'kerb', although the precise chronological relationship of the two is not known.

Simpson and Dymond[18] record the 'opening' of this mound at some unknown time, and it appears that spoil from the excavation was piled to the south, B, with the result that the central mound appears higher than it probably was originally.

In addition, it is necessary to note three other features. Firstly, that there is a small mound C which may be quite recent. Secondly, that the circle is located on the end of a small ridge within a broader valley and, thirdly, that the eastern side of the ridge has been steepened D by the erosion of a stream, although the valley also contains alluvium.

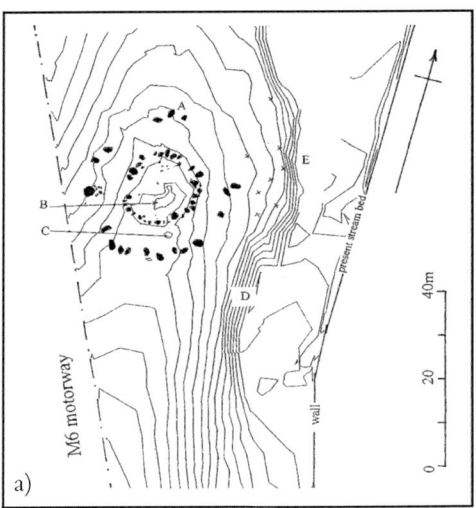

42a-c Gunnerkeld. Dymond's plan of the stones is superimposed on a form line survey. The form lines are at 25cm intervals and the crosses mark the centre of boulders/stones which appear to be natural. Note that practical considerations created by the steep slope made it impossible to record area E

Whilst the latter offers the potential for some environmental analysis, it is the position of the circle on the ridge which requires further consideration here. In particular, attention is drawn to the fact that because of the width of the ridge, and the diameter of the outer circle, the area enclosed is unusually far from horizontal. In reality, the ground below the eastern and western arcs of stones is lower than that below the northern and southern ones. As the ridge to the south almost certainly offered flatter land, the implication is that there was something else dictating the precise siting of the circle.

One possibility is that the outer circle was added to an existing feature and the most obvious one is the central mound. It is also possible to speculate that there was a post, stone or structure which that mound later covered. Against the mound being the earliest feature, however, is the fact that a north–south axis, passing through the 'portal stones', does not pass through the centre of the mound (*42b*). Rather, the latter appears to have been determined by the wish to have, as at Oddendale, a kind of 'platform', with the eastern arc lower than the western one (*42c*).

It may also be that the site was located where some astronomical event could be observed above a significant landscape feature. Whilst the M6 motorway has destroyed the view to the west, it is possible that midsummer sunrise would have occurred at the head of the small valley behind the farmhouse.

KEVERIGG, NY57211712

This site, located in the small valley in which Gunnerwell is situated, is also visible from the M6 motorway, but a more leisurely (and legal) view is to stop on the lane leading to Sleagill from the A6. It lies on private farmland with no public access, but the essential features are those visible from the road; a large erratic/boulder appears to sit on top of a mound. Without excavation, however, it is impossible to determine whether that was the case or whether the cairn had been built around the boulder. Indeed, the cairn may be nothing more than field clearance, for it sits at the junction of a number of ancient enclosure banks.

Only one antiquarian mentions the site, stating that on top of the mound had been 'erected a memorial or bauta stone commemorative of victory'.[19] The latter phrase is probably an interpretation, but the Ordnance Survey record a 'Cross Stone of Keverigg' nearby and at the bend in the parish boundary.

THREAPLANDS, NY59271743

Perhaps it was because this small stone circle was only mentioned in the Bland manuscript, which was not published until 1910,[20] that its existence has never been recognised before. Whilst the stones may be the remains of relatively recent field clearance, there are three pieces of evidence to suggest they are prehistoric:
1. There are other boulders in the field which have not been cleared, one of which A (*43a*) lies exactly south of the circle.
2. The site is on a break of slope like others,
3. and is located at the southern end of a ridge at the point where it merges with the hillside; a discrete locational feature which again compares with other sites.

Although the number of stones, seven, is the same as that stated by Bland, one is light bluish in colour and appears unweathered, as if moved recently. In addition, there are hollows around several of the stones, and the character of the ridge, on which the circle is located, is partly obscured by the massive, ruined field bank to the east, so that the original configuration of the ground is uncertain. Nevertheless, there may have been a low mound or pavement within the circle.

As noted above, the circle is located on the southern end of a ridge above a steep-sided valley; presumably Bland's Threaplands Gill, where he recorded the finding of the butt end of a stone axe. Across that valley, the mound on Windrigg Hill may originally have been visible, and northwards the valley opens into a magnificent panorama with the hills above Leacet Hill circle and Long Meg visible on a clear day. However, the slightly higher ground to the immediate south obscures the view in that direction. There too, is a mound, although it is unclear whether it is prehistoric, the remains of quarrying or of mining, like the bellpits nearer to Reagill. The site and its landscape setting are visible from a public footpath to the south.

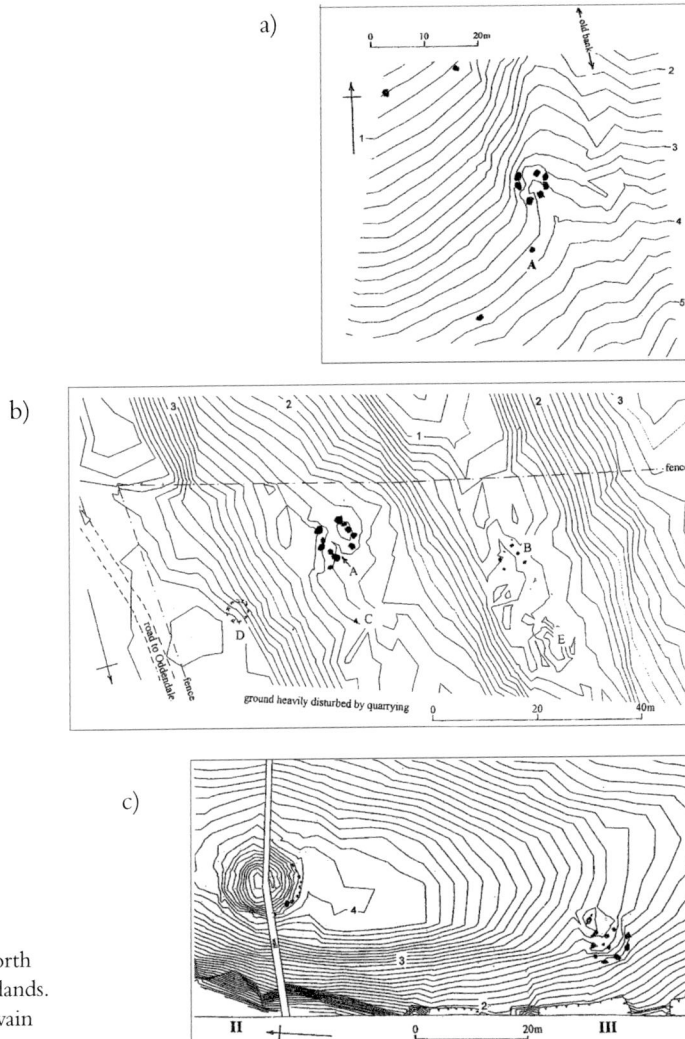

43a-c The smaller circles north and east of Shap. (a) Threaplands. (b) Castlehowe. (c) Harberwain Rigg II and III

CASTLEHOWE SCAR OR HARKELD, NY 587154

This small stone circle is located on private farmland but can be seen from the adjacent highway. From there, too, it can be seen that it is located on a terrace within a small valley and not on the more extensive flatter ground traversed by the road only 30m to the east. The plantation, also to the east, makes it, however, impossible now to know whether the monuments on Harberwain Rigg could be seen, but the distinct twin peaks of Long Scar Pike are visible on the southern horizon. Significantly, the mound on Hardendale Nab, to the south-west, would have been hidden by the high ground which forms an interesting feature of that site. Similarly, the mound on Windrigg Hill, to the north, may have been hidden, but Lowther long cairn may just have been visible.

At the present time, the Castlehowe Scar site might be best described as consisting of two arcs of boulders enclosing an area some 6m x 5m (43b). Both arcs have five stones, but there is an eleventh stone to the immediate north-east. However, the overall appearance suggests that not all of the stones may be in their original position. Certainly some of the stones in the north-eastern quadrant need to be seen in the context of the contiguous hollow A, which appears to be the product of an unreported antiquarian excavation.

In fact, nineteenth-century antiquarians do not mention a circle at Castlehowe Scar, although they do mention one at Harkeld, a place which is otherwise unknown. The area known as Harkeld is, however, shown as a small area of unenclosed common land on Hodgson's map of Westmorland, dated 1828, and the circle shown in (43b) is at the eastern end of that area. Moreover, Bland's description of the circle on Harkeld fits the present monument; 'Another on Harkeld is formed by ten stones and is six yards in diameter'.[21] The significance of this identification is that Bland goes on to state of Harkeld that 'in digging this one, a few inches deep was found a stratum of charred bones'.

South of the circle, the valley is littered with erratics, with some of the larger ones being in an approximate line reflecting a major break of slope rather than an avenue. There is a further group of stones at B, whilst that at C may, or may not have been an outlier to the circle. There is also a small mound, possibly from field clearance at D, and an embanked, rectilinear hollow at E, which may be the result of quarrying, like that on the common to the immediate south of the circle.

HARBERWAIN RIGG OR IRON HILL, NY596148

This small group of sites consists of a small mound north of the wall, a mound around the base of which are the remains of a circle of stones (Harberwain Rigg II), and a small circle of stones with possible outlier (Harberwain Rigg III); the last two being planned in (43c). Of these, site II is a prominent landscape feature, whilst the stones of site III are visible on the skyline when seen from the road to Oddendale. In addition, there is a prominent mound on the southern edge of the ridge which was not recorded in the nineteenth century and is probably top soil scraped from the rock surface prior to quarrying.

When Collingwood surveyed site II in 1933,[22] there were stones around the base of the mound north of the wall, like those to the south, but these have now been lost. However, the position of the missing stones accords well with the form line survey, suggesting that the monument was ovoid rather than round.

The ground within the circle of site III is slightly higher than the surrounding hillside and can be described as a 'low mound'.[23] However, the surface of the ground within the circle also appears to have been disturbed, or 'dug over', and the original form of the monument is further obscured by the hollows around many stones which may be the product of digging or of animal movement. What is also not clear is whether any of the stones 'stood upright', although Bland writing c.1860 asserted they had.

Nevertheless, it can be assumed, on the basis of the form line survey and Bland's comparison of this site with White Hag, that any internal mound here was no more than 10cm high. As such, it might also be compared with site B at Broomrigg, where there was a central pit (see 22a). Of Harberwain Rigg III, however, Bland notes 'three stones in the middle, but no traces of ashes'.

This last statement is important, for Collingwood suggested site III might be that referred to by Simpson,[24] when it was reported the bones 'of a man of great stature, a portion of the antler of deer, much larger than those of our days and bones of other animals' had been found. However, both Simpson and Bland (the latter writing about the same time as the former, but possibly using his published paper) are quite clear in ascribing the remains to site II, with Bland adding that they were 'in the south-west side'.

In addition to the above, a nearby stone appears to have cup marks,[25] and a number of flints and sherds of Peterborough and Grooved Ware have also been found in the vicinity of the extant sites.[26] One sherd of Peterborough Ware was found close to the kerbstones of site II, and amongst the flints nearby was a flake of volcanic tuff, again suggestive of Neolithic land use.

Bland also records the finding nearby and 'in a cleft of the rock' of a bronze blade. The implement does not appear to have survived, although Simpson exhibited it in London in 1866 and later reported that it was in his possession. According to Bland, it was 'a bronze dagger blade 13 inches long and four inches broad at the hilt', dimensions which suggest a halberd.[27]

Of greater interest here is, however, the fact that Bland said the find was made halfway between Harberwain Rigg and Harberwain Plantation, 'near' which there 'was formerly a circle of stones eight yards in diameter within which had been a mound'. No others mention this site and, like the site at Threaplands, it has been lost to the archaeological record, with its location awaiting rediscovery.

ODDENDALE, CENTRED NY592133

Site 1, NY59201290
In contrast to that of Harberwain Plantation, the stone circle at Oddendale is well known. It consists of two concentric circles of relatively small stones, the inner apparently the kerb of a mound which has evidently been dug, and between the two circles is single stone A (*44*a). Just to the north is another group of stones B which appear to be the remains of another 'concentric circle'. It is probably these which Simpson had in mind when he described 'a class formed of upright stones, much smaller in size, standing not more than 20 inches or two feet above ground, and … it is not unusual to find two of these circles adjoining, one of which is more perfect than the other. I have specially noted two instances in which the circles are concentric – in one of which most of the stones remain, in the other, the outer circle has either been partly destroyed or … never been completed'.[28] Certainly Simpson had the central mound here 'excavated', reporting that it had only contained burnt matter.

Close inspection of the central mound reveals, however, that the eastern side is higher than the western one, so that it can be described as a platform. It is a feature also evident in the whole monument, where the break of slope beyond the outer circle E may have been accentuated by another Holloway F, with a mound G similarly emphasised (*44*b). Is the latter artificial or simply a result of the holloway? Indeed, is F really a holloway or a deliberate creation reflected in the bank, like contours at H (*44*c).

Whatever their precise origins, the eastern break of slope and the platform-like mound of the centre, suggest that the monument is laid out to the cardinal points, and this conclusion is supported by the geology of the northern stone being very different from the others. In addition, the platform-like form demonstrates that the monument is not on the centre of the ridge, but to one side, the highest point of the ridge being at I in 44c. Equally, the holloways C, D and F show that the site is on a natural north–south routeway, one reflected in the M6 to the west.

In the context of the prehistoric landscape, two other features should be noted. Firstly, that some of the nearby erratics are larger than the stones used to build the monument. Secondly, that whilst the view to the south-east is dominated by the slopes and mound of Seal Howe, a number of other sites are visible: Windrigg Hill, Harberwain Rigg, Raise Howe, the three sites on Long Scar Pike, Moor Divock, Hardendale Fell, Hardendale Nab (over which the midsummer sun sets) and the site of the Oddendale ring cairn.

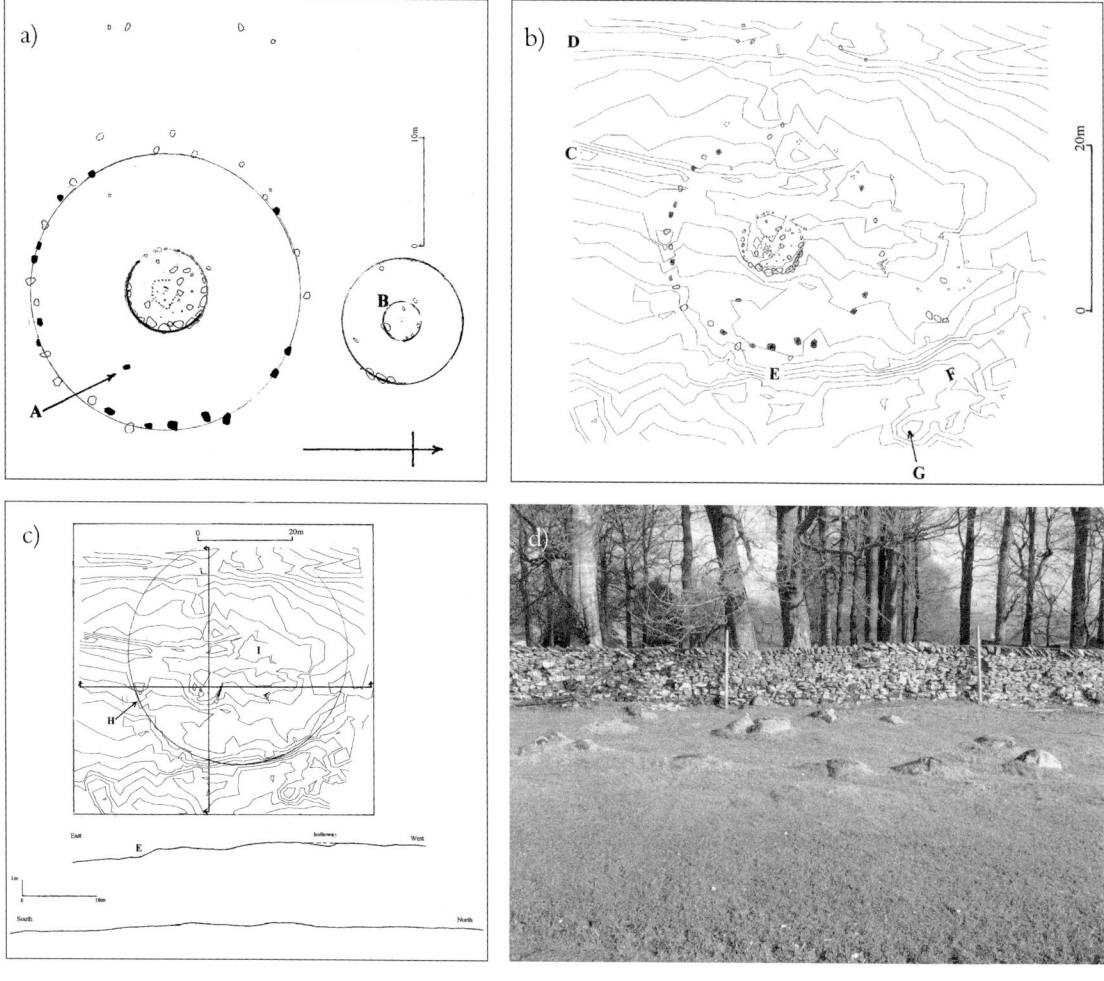

44a-d The visible Oddendale sites. (a) Plan of the stones showing two possible monuments. (b) form line survey showing holloways C, D & F. (c) profiles showing how the central cairn is a platform. (d) Site 3

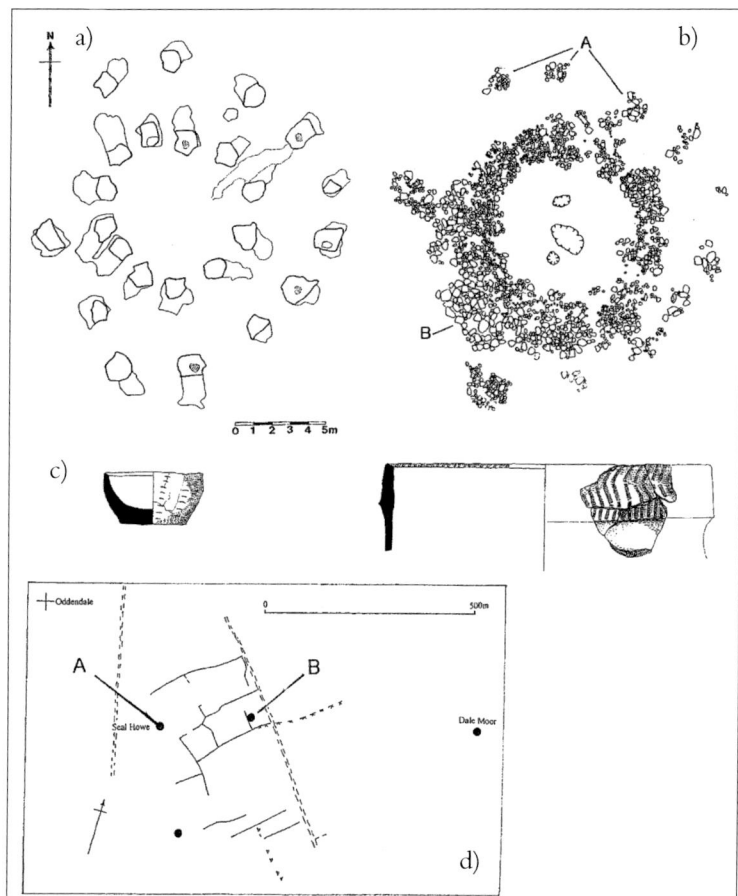

45a-c The structures and finds of the Oddendale ring cairn after Turnbull and Walsh. (d) The field system and mounds on Seal Howe and Dale Moor

Site 2, NY59031352

Having discovered the latter site as a research student, the author had mixed feelings when he had to arrange for its excavation in advance of destruction.[29] However, beneath it, and forming the first phase, there had been two concentric circles of posts (45a), the radio carbon dates of which (see Appendix, p.145) are Neolithic in date. At some stage, the posts were removed and the pits sealed and capped with boulders A (45b) so as to remain visible.[30] Later, and in the Early Bronze Age, the ring cairn was built to a height of approximately 0.3m, the southern edge being more pronounced than the northern one. It is also possible that the bank was emphasised by the addition of vivid yellow-white limestone, and in the final phase the southern quadrant was further emphasised by the addition of larger boulders. Similar large stones were used to construct an external platform B on which were fragments of unburnt human bone, but within the ring cairn were a number of *tiny* deposits of cremated bone, scraps of pottery of food vessel and collared urn type, two flint knives and an almost complete accessory vessel. A sherd of 'all over cord' beaker was also found but in uncertain stratigraphic relationship to the central shallow grave with its crouched inhumation.

Site 3, NY59031332

Just south of the surfaced road and against the farm wall is a small circle (*44d*), a miniature of the main one. This is not recorded anywhere else, but in 1972 the author was assured by a resident that he had not built it. However, thirty years later the story has changed.

SEAL HOWE AND DALE MOOR, NY59521273 AND 60221291

A number of burial mounds have been reported and excavated on Seal Howe. The most obvious is that visible from Oddendale 1 A (*45d*). Excavated by Greenwell,[31] it had already been dug. In the centre, and originally placed on the rock surface, was the remains of a male inhumation, whilst 2.9m south of the centre an urn held the cremated remains of a woman and infant. Unfortunately, the urn was too decayed to allow description.

Southwards from the summit is another mound, and beyond those, on the horizon, are the sites of Long Scar Pike, Howenook Pike and Wicker Street. Less visible are the earthwork remains of a rectilinear field system where one boundary passes to one side of another burial mound B, which also appears to have been excavated. Whilst the field system is undated, analogies would suggest it is prehistoric, and it is interesting to note that it appears to have been laid out from the lower ground, where it disappears.

Following the boundaries down slope allows Dale Moor to be more easily located. This is a mound some 6m in diameter and 0.75 m high. There are traces of a kerb in the northern and eastern quadrants, and on the south side, in a disturbed area, there is a boulder, probably that of 'red granite' found at the centre when the site was excavated in the nineteenth century.[32] On that occasion, an inhumation was found, together with an urn and disc beads of 'brownish lignite', finds which have not survived.

1 The Goggleby Stone at Shap being re-erected after it had fallen and after excavation by the author

2 The standing stone at Redhills

3 Carrock Fell, from near the motorway junction at Shap

4a and b The unweathered colour of two stones. (a) A white one next to the old A66 below Castlerigg.
(b) A blue one on the track to Swinside

5 A mound on the banks of Coniston Water

6 The standing stone at Colton, SD330886

7 The limestone structure – natural or artificial – at Urswick

8 A mound on Aughertree Fell

9 The paired stones at Kirksanton

10 The texture and colour of stone D at Swinside

13 The standing stone at Kitchenhill

Opposite above: *11* Little Meg prior to the growth of the present plantation. The Long Meg circle is visible in the middle distance

Opposite below: *12* The monolith at Grey Yauds. The large stones at the base of the wall are probably from the destroyed circle

16 The site of the Leacet Hill circle from the road at nearby Wetheriggs Pottery. The stones are arrowed

Opposite above: 14 The Clifton stones

Opposite below: 15 The long cairn at Lowther prior to being planted with trees

17 The site of the destroyed circle at Motherby (arrowed). Note the numerous erratics on the adjoining slopes

Opposite above: 18 One of several straight sections in the perimeter of the Cockpit, Moor Divock

Opposite below: 19 The paired stones of Fourstones Hill, high above Haweswater

20 The cairn of Long Scar Pike I

21 Rasett Hill

22 The carved surface of one boulder in Langdale

23 The structure on Stainton Ground

24 Skelmore Heads

25 The shapes of the stones in the south-eastern quadrant of the Long Meg circle

8

THE UPPER VALLEYS OF THE EDEN AND LUNE

HOWENOOK PIKE AND LONG SCAR PIKE, NY60320988 AND NY59331086

Approached from the south, Howenook Pike appears to be a microescarpment with modern marker cairn. Below the latter, however, is an earlier domed cairn, 6m in diameter and 1.1m high, which does not appear to have been dug. However, in favour of the site being ancient is the difference in colour between the stones of the two cairns.

Whatever its origins, this site, and that on Long Scar Pike I enjoy magnificent views, 'positions truly worthy as the resting places of some ancient chieftains or warriors'.[1] The sites visible include White Hag, Wicker Street, Harberwain Rigg, Gamelands and Raise Howe/Bank Moor. Particular attention is drawn to the difficulty of locating specific places within the vast expanse and sweep of the 'bare' escarpment, and to the fact that it is the isolated trees which enable specific places to be located. Here, therefore, it is possible to ponder what the prehistoric vegetation might have been; to ask what tree cover existed then and whether here, or elsewhere, sites may have been located by single trees visible from afar.

From Howenook Pike, the walk to Long Scar Pike I reveals two other aspects of the changing environment. Firstly, at NY59941058, the sink hole has collapsed into an underground system. Secondly, there are ephemeral streams, such as that which disappears into a crevice at NY59391095. Beneath the high escarpment there is another world.

The large cairn of Long Scar Pike I is 18.5m in diameter and some 2.2m high. As Bland noted, 'it has been opened but no record kept'. The centre is, however, dished, and whilst some of this must be the result of quarrying for the modern marker cairn, the original profile is likely to have been that of *colour plate 20*. The large blocks ringing the present hollow are, however, suggestive of a complex structure.

When viewed from the north, it also appears that the cairn is not built on the highest point. Did prehistoric people deliberately avoid the highest point, or did they wish the cairn to be seen from the east and below? Did they see the highest point – now carrying a modern concrete 'trig point' – as a barrow? Indeed, is it one? Whatever the explanation, both mounds are visible from many kilometres away.

Northwards there is another, small marker cairn on what might be a tiny older structure, and from there another marker cairn is visible at NY59731127. This appears to stand on another ancient cairn (*c.*12m diameter) located on the edge of the limestone pavement. Seen from the south-west, this cairn appears to be located in such a way that its eastern side is continuous with the natural slope, and it has a slightly dished centre, both features of Long Scar Pike I.

Given the difference in altitude between the two sites, it is somewhat surprising to find this site is also visible from a number of points in the wider landscape e.g., Seal Howe. One non-limestone boulder on the perimeter has a natural pattern of criss-crossing grooves, and on a fine day, Harberwain Rigg II is visible on the horizon above this stone when viewed from the centre.

WICKER STREET AND WHITE HAG, NY60401173 AND 60701162

The mound adjacent to the Roman road on Wicker Street is easily found, as it carries the remains of a notice board. Approximately 12m in diameter and 0.9m high, it is not located on the centre of the ridge and because the upper surface is relatively flat, the north-western quadrant is higher than that to the south-east. However, it is not clear what the original form may have been, as the site was probably wholly excavated by Greenwell[2] who reported that it was made 'entirely of earth' and contained no finds.

Unlike Wicker Street, the White Hag stone circle is easily missed. The easiest way to find it, whether from east or west, is to start at the enormous erratic alongside the Coast to Coast footpath. From there, a route, diagonally up the slope in a north-eastern direction, brings the visitor to the circle at NY60701162.

A significant feature of this site is, therefore, its location *below* a nearby limestone hilltop. However, whilst visibility is consequently restricted to the north-west, it enjoys magnificent panoramas in the other directions. In particular, the cairns of Longscar Pike, Howenhook Pike, Linglow Hill and Raise How are visible on the distant skylines, whilst a feature of the intermediate horizon is the rise in the escarpment on Orton Scar, beyond which lies the next site and the Gamelands stone circle.

The circle itself appears to be located on a step of a discrete spur and is formed of granite boulders/erratics with others nearby (*46*). Those at A, which have not previously been planned, are probably the small circle mentioned by Bland.[3] On close inspection, the form lines suggest that there may be a small rise of ground level within the main circle, and the possible existence of a low mound or 'pavement' of cobbles should be considered. There is, however, no record, nor appearance, of the site having been dug.

The form line survey also confirms the existence nearby of a long mound which appears to be that mentioned by Bland.[4] The topographical survey suggests, however, that the feature may be natural, even though it is orientated almost exactly east–west (*46*b) and the majority of the visible stones are granite erratics, suggestive of having been collected. Even if the feature is natural, its existence may have been one factor in the location of the circle. Another might be hollow B (*46*a) which may be a former, if ephemeral, spring.

The upper valleys of the Eden and Lune

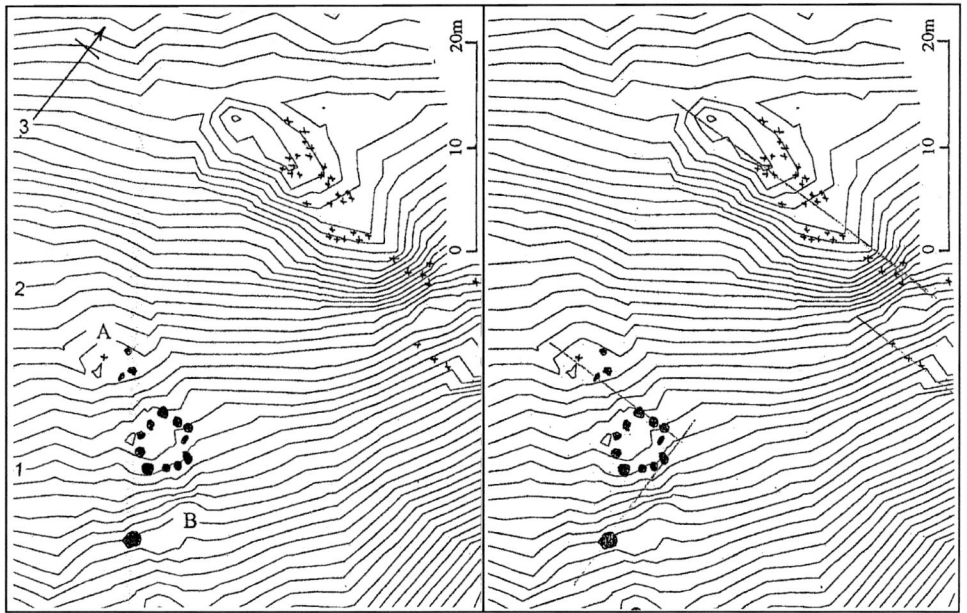

46 White Hag

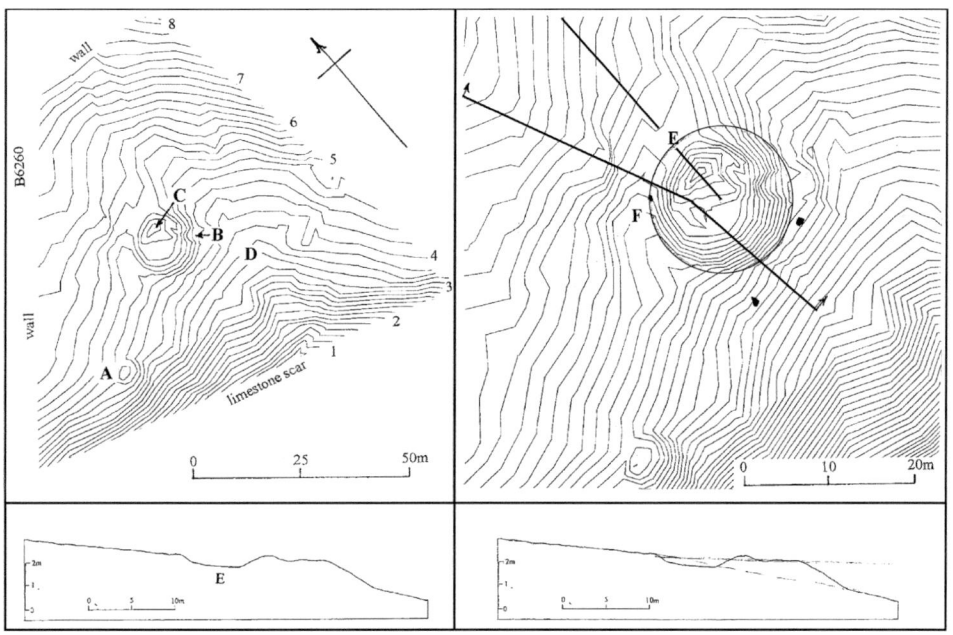

47 Orton Scar

ORTON SCAR, NY61790991

This mound appears on the first Ordnance Survey map and has no other history of archaeological investigation. Although it is near the Coast to Coast long-distance footpath, it is on private land, and the best views are those from the adjacent B2260. From there, several features can clearly be seen:
- The site is in a col with the principal viewshed being to the south, including the site of the Gamelands stone circle.
- The mound appears to have a 'dished' centre.
- There is a smaller, previously unrecorded mound at A (47).

Field survey, however, allows a number of other features to be added:
- An indentation B may be the remains of trenching by unknown antiquarians, and the dished centre may also result from such activity with the higher portion of the mound C being spoil from that work.
- Whilst the smaller mound A is directly above the sharp break of slope, the main mound is on a more gentle slope and adjacent to a slight valley D.
- As a result of being built on a slope and allowing for a possible excavation in the centre, the profile of the mound could be described as being that of a platform.
- In the profile, this platform effect is reduced by the fact that there is a hollow E which appears to be an area from which mound material has been scraped or quarried; indeed, the impression is that of a ditch F.

Despite being built on a slope, the mound may have been planned as a perfect circle, 16m in diameter, with the perimeter of such a circle passing through one of three 'largish' stones (47b). Moreover, the centre of this suggested circle is directly south of the highest point of C, and that line, when projected, divides hollow E roughly in half, providing the 'platform' with a north-south axis. Speculative and, perhaps fanciful, as these observations are, they do provide a basis for questioning further the origins of C and the central hollow; especially as the highest point C is juxtaposed with the hollow E. Of course early antiquarians may have dug their trench on a north south alignment!

PENHURROCK, NY62881045

Quarrying of this cairn below the putative causewayed enclosure of Howe Robin[5] led to the discovery of 'a great abundance of decayed human bones and a circle 12 yards over of rounded blocks of granite'.[6] Bland, writing some 50 years later, stated that the mound had a diameter of 'about twenty yards, having in the centre a cist surrounded by an irregular circle of stones about eleven yards across … A quantity of bones was found, some of them of gigantic proportions; and what is rather curious, in a small cavity on one side were found a quantity of ashes, remains of a fire by which the bodies had been consumed …'.[7] Bland's description implies there were no observed cremations, but what is less certain is whether the 'bones' were those of articulated skeletons.

Today the site consists of boulders, mostly Shap granite, located in and around a shallow quarry on a spur which has been partly quarried either side of the road (48a and c).

Some of the boulders appear to be grouped in arcs, others within the quarry pits. The base of the mound appears to have survived in a few place, and this interpretation accords with Hodgson's statement that 'a valuable remnant' had been saved. However, the highest part of the site, as revealed in the quarrying, appears to be solid limestone.

The mound may have had an external diameter of about 25m, with an internal ring some 14m across (*48c*); dimensions somewhat greater than those given by Hodgson and Bland. It is also possible that the mound had a kerb, for some boulders lie on the suggested perimeter with those at B corresponding to a possible bulge in the mound, due north of its centre.

Note:
- R.G. Collingwood[8] refers to this site as Robin Hood's Grave, which both the OS and Bland place at NY617107.
- There is no evidence that the site had an avenue, and this idea may have arisen from a wrong identification of sites.[9]

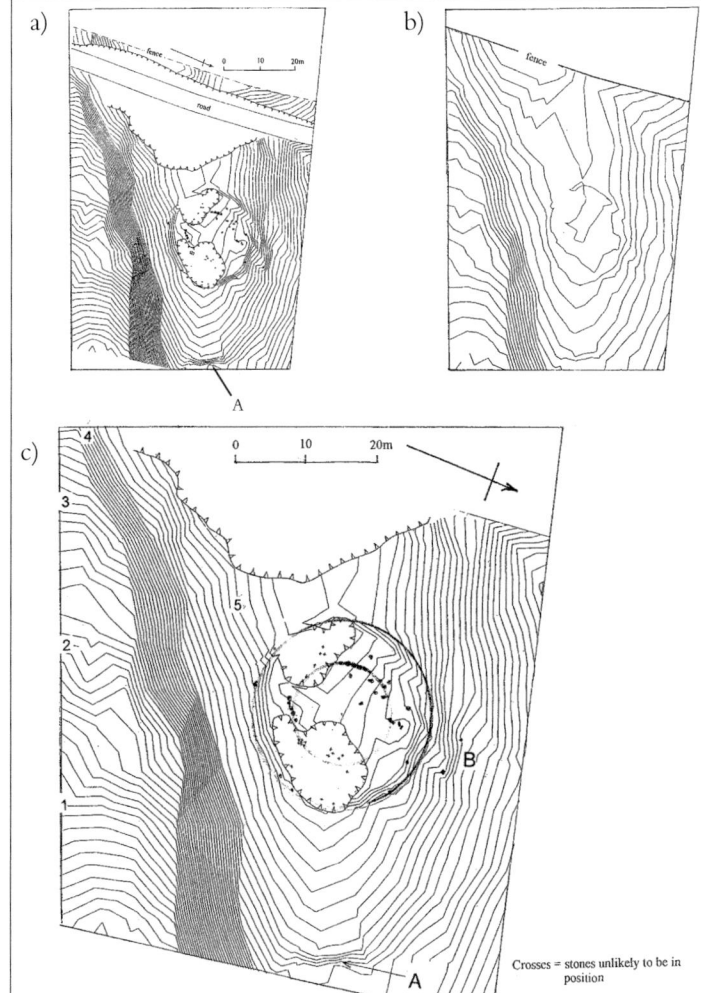

48a-c Penhurrock.
(a) The position of the site relative to the road and showing it is built on an asymmetrical spur. A is a sharp break of slope which appears to mark the upper edge of the limestone. (b) The possible original shape of the spur; the terrain modelling omitting readings within the quarried areas.
(c) Suggested diameters for both the mound and internal ring

RAISE HOWE, BANK MOOR, NY63721302

The remains of this mound, also partly quarried, lie on a prominent summit visible over great distances. Perhaps it was this fact which attracted Mesolithic people to the Moor and caused them to keep the area clear of trees.[10]

Little remains of the mound, which was some 13.5m in diameter, but Bland refers to a cist, skeleton and bronze spearhead being found here. However, these features were said by Hodgson to be those of a site one mile north of Penhurrock, a distance which does not fit this site well. Nevertheless, Hodgson provides two other details about the finds. Firstly, the skeleton was 'of more than ordinary stature' and, secondly, the spearhead had bronze 'nails through its sockets'.

GAYTHORN PLAIN 1, NY63851132

This low mound is in the right place to be the mound described by Hodgson as being one mile north of Penhurrock, but the details suggest it is not the one he was referring to. It is located on the north side of a dry valley and is built on a slope so that its surface might be described as a platform. More importantly, there is a small cist projecting above the surface of that platform (49a); an arrangement which would have allowed access at various times, not just on one occasion.

In addition, and despite its wholly inconspicuous position and structure, several aspects of its location appear deliberate and worth comment:

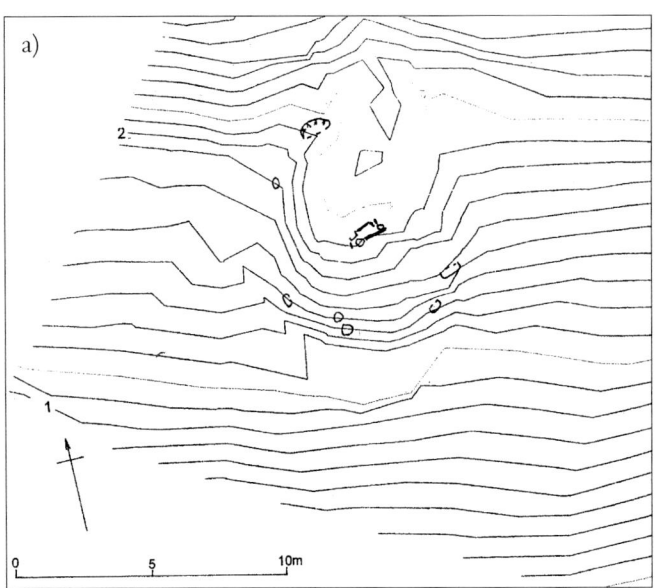

49a-b Gaythorne Plain 1. (a) although the cist appears to be on the edge of the platform, it is central to the overall monument. (b) the stones to the north-east showing the white upright slab with the erratic behind on the distant skyline

- It is located at the end of an area of outcropping limestone at a point where the relatively narrow and deep valley merges into the gentle slopes of the highest part of the common.
- It is above a fissure in the valley floor where water can occasionally be heard running underground.
- Its view northwards is almost non existent and essentially that of the hillside,
- where, to the north-east, there is a boulder on the skyline and, almost exactly halfway between the two, a small slab jammed upright (49b),
- whilst the midsummer sun sets over what appears to be a cairn (in fact natural outcrop) on the skyline to the northwest.

GAYTHORNE PLAIN 2, NY64651117

Eastwards from the previous site the valley broadens and becomes shallow, but as the walker ascends the slope above the valley head, a ring of stones becomes visible on a false skyline. The site appears to be one described in the nineteenth century as consisting of concentric circles and an avenue.[11]

If this is the same site, then the phrase 'concentric circles' needs to be abandoned, for the site consists of a stoney bank with a smaller grouping in the centre (50b) and a possible entrance at A. However, the character of the earthwork at A is confused by the contiguous bank B, the stones of which are probably the 'avenue'. The small group of stones C could also be interpreted as an avenue, but an alternative is to see them as something like the rectangular areas found beyond the early cairn at Hardendale Nab. Note the stones at D are due south of the circle's centre.

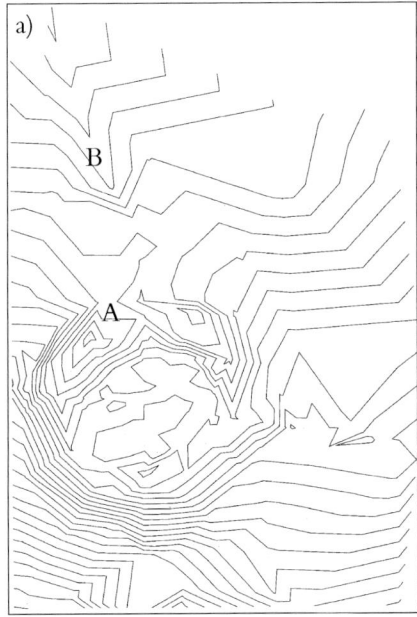
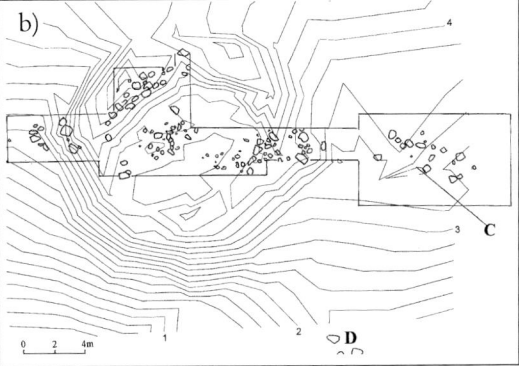

50a and b Gaythorne Plain 2. (a) form line survey showing the linear bank. (b) form line survey with some of the stones planned

Bank (B) leads towards a marked break of slope and area of sinkholes and possible coal pits. Note that the bank is constructed across relatively flat land which was not used by the cairn, rather the latter was sited on a break of slope with the result that it appears to be a platform with one side higher than the other.

GAYTHORNE PLAIN 3, NY648119

Two cairns are located on breaks of slope either side of a shallow dry valley. According to Bland, the larger one was opened by the Revd Holmes, who found an urn with 'rude zig zag' decoration at the centre. This appears to have been associated with 'ashes', and elsewhere in the mound were five different skeletons.

What is odd about Bland's description is that it was written about the time Greenwell was active, and so the good Canon's decision to dig *should* have been in the knowledge that someone had got there first. Moreover, what Greenwell found does not accord with what Bland says, Revd Holmes found. Are we missing a site or two?

According to Greenwell, the western site (his CLXXX) had been dug before, and this explained the scattered and broken bones of an adult that he found laid upon the natural surface at the centre of the mound. In the eastern one (his CLXXXI), he found, again, at the centre and upon a rock outcrop, similar broken and scattered remains of two bodies, again 'their condition being due to a previous opening'. However, about 2.5m from the centre and 0.5m above the surface of the ground, he found a cinerary urn – which does not appear to have survived – containing a cremation, and amongst the cairn material the bones of an ox.

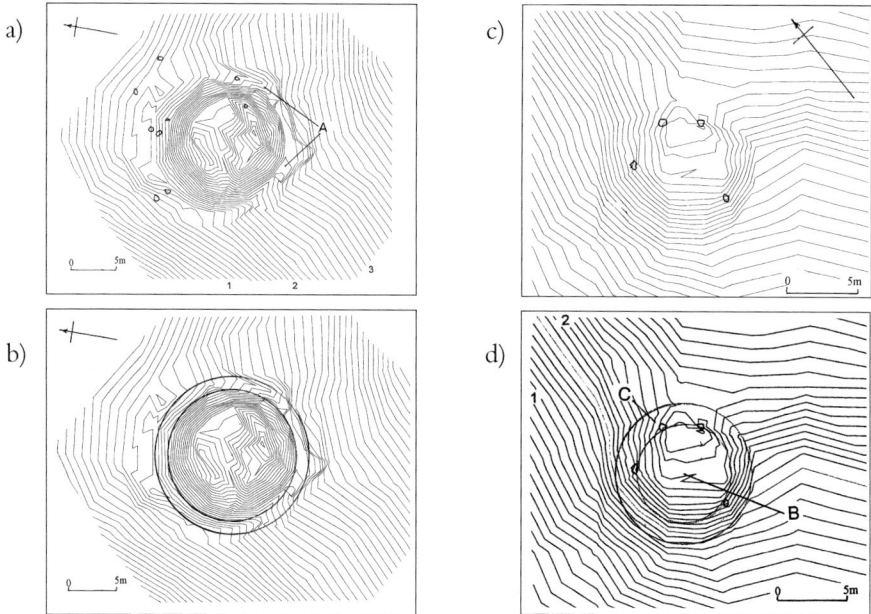

51a-d Gaythorne Plain 3: (a and b) are the eastern site, (c and d) the western one showing that despite being built over a break of slope it is still circular in plan

Greenwell also noted that the first site had three stones which appeared to form a kerb to its southern half, whilst there was a circle of stones around the base of the other. These can be seen in the present sites, but those in the eastern site (51a) appear to be some distance from the mound. Are they the stones referred to by Greenwell? Were they displaced by him or are they a separate feature, perhaps even belonging to a separate phase?

In that context, attention is drawn to what appears to be a ditch A. However, it does not continue around the whole mound, rather the same radius coincides with a slight mound on the northern side (51b). It appears, therefore, that the mound has been built on a platform, partly excavated into and partly built against the hillside. Interestingly, the putative centre of the western site B occurs at the edge of a break of slope so that mound, too, appears to be a platform-like structure. Stone C, to the south-west of that centre, is of different geology to the others.

One further feature of the mounds should be noted. Whilst the view southward is restricted, northward the view is of much of the Eden valley. Northwards, too, the valley leads to Gaythorne Hall, behind which Greenwell excavated another cairn (his site CLXXII). According to him, the cairn had a 'circle of stones' around the base, a burnt body in an oval hollow at the centre, and in the south-east quadrant 'several bones of two bodies, placed in the cairn without any order'. Again, ox bones were found amongst the cairn material.

GAMELANDS, NY64000818

One of the puzzles about this site is why it was never recorded before the middle of the nineteenth century. Indeed, Ferguson[12] railed that Dr Burns, one of the co-authors of the *History of Cumberland and Westmorland*, published in 1777, had lived 'within one mile' of the monument, yet never mentioned it. Access cannot have been a factor in the circle remaining unknown for so long, for roads – one of which is now part of the long-distance Coast to Coast footpath – passed close to the site.

Indeed, a principal feature of the circle is its location at a natural 'route centre'; a place where trackways along the foot of the limestone escarpment, leading to and from the area of Sunbiggin Tarn and Rayseat Pike long cairn, would intersect those climbing over or descending the escarpment. In particular, attention is drawn to the fact that the site is located at a prominent 'corner' in that escarpment, a point visible from some distance.

Flints and fragments of volcanic tuff, both polished and unpolished, and two sherds, one decorated found nearby,[13] suggest that the site was located in the vicinity of late Mesolithic and Neolithic activity. As such, the 'two bits of worked flint' found in Ferguson's dig may have been part of a 'background scatter' relating to such land use rather than to use of the monument.

The extent of Ferguson's excavations is not known, but he appears to have been concerned with demonstrating that there had been a cairn in the centre of the site and, consequently, the reported finding adjacent to one stone of 'a freestone slab, which possibly once formed part of a cist', should be noted with a little caution. Certainly the idea that the slab had been parked against the stone after being ploughed up in 'the centre' should be questioned in the light of cists being located against stones in some other circles.

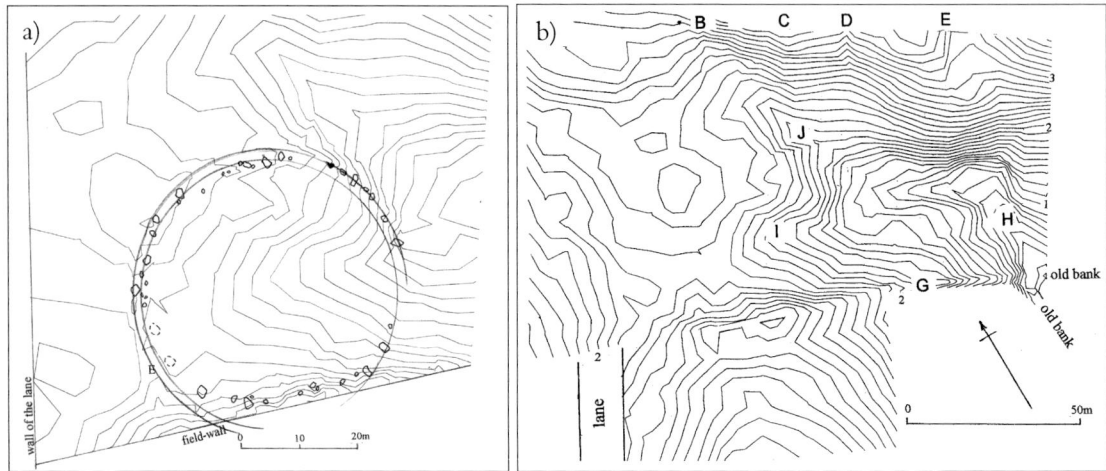

52a and b Gamelands. (a) Form line survey (at 5cm intervals) overlain by the plan of the stones published by Ferguson. (b) The wider landscape showing the land south of the wall F, the flatter ground traversed by the lane and the small valley to the east

According to Ferguson, ploughing had occurred eighteen years before, when the 'riggs' ran 'right through the circle', and that 'on that occasion two or three of the stones ... were buried by being rolled into holes dug under them; one or two others were blasted and the fragments are now lying about'. His published plan, used in (52), indicates the position of two missing stones A, presumably those buried.

Today there is no obvious sign of ploughing; there is certainly no prominent ridge and furrow. However, a low bank at B, and the slight lynchets or hollows at C, D and possibly E, suggest that the ground immediately to the north of the site was divided for ploughing at an earlier time. It is, therefore, interesting to note that the two buried stones of Ferguson lay 'inside' a low bank F. This bank can be considered to precede Ferguson's ploughing, if we assume that his buried stones indicate the ploughing 'right through' was roughly east–west. It is interesting to note that if the plan of the monument had been a proper circle, then the perimeter would have passed along this bank.

The possibility that the stones on the southern side of the site have been displaced by agricultural activity should, therefore, be considered. Certainly, ploughing provides a context in which to consider one of the most remarkable features of the site, the fact that the southern arc of stones abuts and appears to be partly enveloped in a low, but steep slope on top of which is the present wall (52a). This wall appears to have been preceded by a bank (most clearly visible at G in 52b), and it may be that the steep slope is simply the face of that bank i.e., that the latter was built over, or up against the circle and partly buried some of the stones. An alternative explanation is to view the steep slope as a lynchet. However, both interpretations, and the possibility that the stones have been displaced northwards from a more circular perimeter, still requires us to recognise that the ground to the immediate south of the stones was originally a half metre higher than the ground inside the monument. The monument appears, therefore, to have been located against a steep break of slope.

That slope may have been the side of a channel cut by melt water or equivalent at the end of the last ice age; a channel which is still evident to the east of the monument H. Closer inspection shows, however, that this channel has two small tributaries I and J, and that the stone circle surrounds the former. In short, and as Ferguson observed, there is a 'hollow' in the centre of the circle but this hollow is not a basin, rather it is a valley head. The possibility that there was originally a spring here enclosed by the circle should, therefore, be considered; as such it might be compared with the relationship of the Long Meg sites to the valley there.

That the relationship of the stone circle and valley head at Gamelands is not coincidence, is further demonstrated by the fact that the western perimeter of the site passes along the edge of relatively flat ground i.e., the monument is built adjacent to, but not utilising flat ground. Again, the same situation can be seen at Long Meg.

RAYSEAT PIKE, NY68380726

This site was excavated by Greenwell[14] who described it as a long cairn, and the details he found were indeed those of a typical long barrow of the kind he had excavated in eastern Yorkshire. He left no plan, but the position of the features he described are shown in the schematic plan (53a). There was a slab at A and a sandstone upright B six feet high and 'placed transversely to the line of the barrow, and apparently forming the termination of the primary burial deposits' C. These had been placed 'under a structure' just over a metre wide, composed of timber and stone 'piled in such a manner to facilitate the burning of the bones along the whole line of the deposit', and 'what may be regarded as flues had been formed, at close intervals'. There was also a transverse trench D which had also been the focus of fire and at its centre a pit; arrangements which suggests this was a timber façade with central, higher post. There was a similar pit at E, and again this can be interpreted as a burnt post.

The skeletal remains were those of six or seven disarticulated individuals; their bones sometimes 'laid on the surface, in others on flat stones, and in several instances small flat stones had been inserted between the bones'. A number of secondary burials, principally of children, had been inserted into the cairn, some on the original ground surface but all to the west of stone B; a stone which would not have been visible.

Also within the cairn material were the bones of ox, horse, goat or sheep, pig, foumart, watervole and grouse.

The only apparent differences between this site and those of eastern Yorkshire are the use of stone to construct the mound and the existence of standing stones, instead of posts. Consequently, the site has long been interpreted as evidence for the Neolithic farming 'package' spreading into the Eden valley from the east. However, Thomas Machell, writing c.1690, described the site as two round cairns, and even today, and after the work of Greenwell, the site appears much as in Machell's drawing (53b). There, it appears the eastern end had already been dug into and the flat rim which he depicts is still visible. However, the cairn at that point appears to have flat stones beneath what might be interpreted as spoil, raising the possibility that the arrangement is original and that Machell was assuming it had been dug.

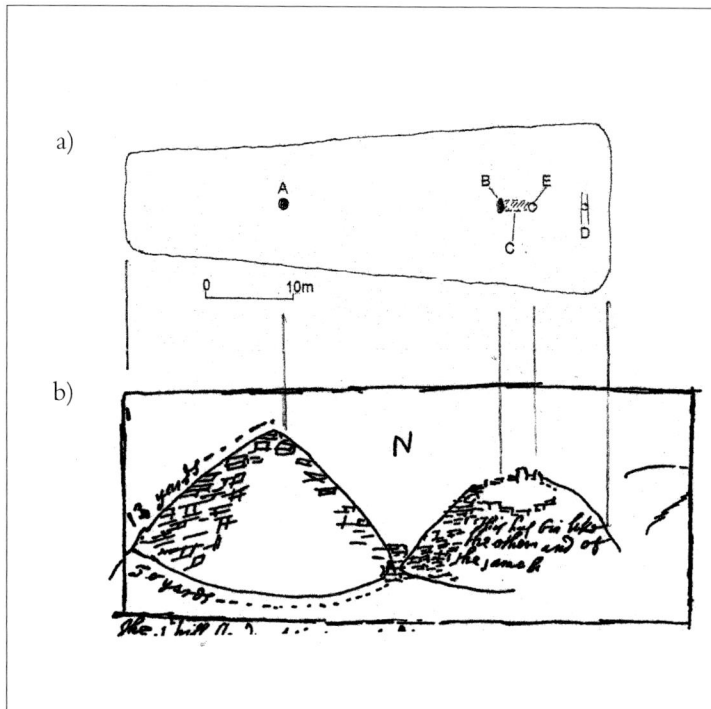

53 Rayseat Pike. (a) schematic plan based on Greenwell's account and (b) Machell's sketch. Note how the position of Greenwell's buried structures relate to the form recorded by Machell

Whatever the original profile, the possible existence of two contiguous round cairns provides a new context for the interpretation of the two standing stones (and other details) reported by Greenwell. Nor is the coalescing of two round cairns to form one long one unknown, and even round mounds are known in the Neolithic of eastern Yorkshire, and elsewhere. Consequently, even the interpretation of the site as two round cairns does not preclude it from being early Neolithic in date.

Significantly, a pollen diagram from Sunbiggin Tarn shows an almost classic early Neolithic story with grasses appearing and expanding at the expanse of woodland after a dramatic decline in elm. This, together with flint and pottery scatters, allow us to envisage the site being located in an area of early Neolithic settlement; albeit, the monument may not be a primary feature of that activity.

The artefactual evidence[15] also suggest that there was an expansion of land use and monument building away from places with early Neolithic activity. In particular, attention is drawn to the fact that:

- Areas of early Neolithic activity are below the highest ground and steep slopes, and the latter form a semi circular rim to a basin in which the centre is Sunbiggin Tarn.
- A number of other burial mounds are located within, and on that rim,
- and that the 'long cairn' stands on the edge of a small valley leading to Sunbiggin Tarn visible from the west and the road from Orton, but hidden from almost everywhere else.
- The oval mound at Mazonwath is not visible, but from that site many of the cairns on the 'rim' are.

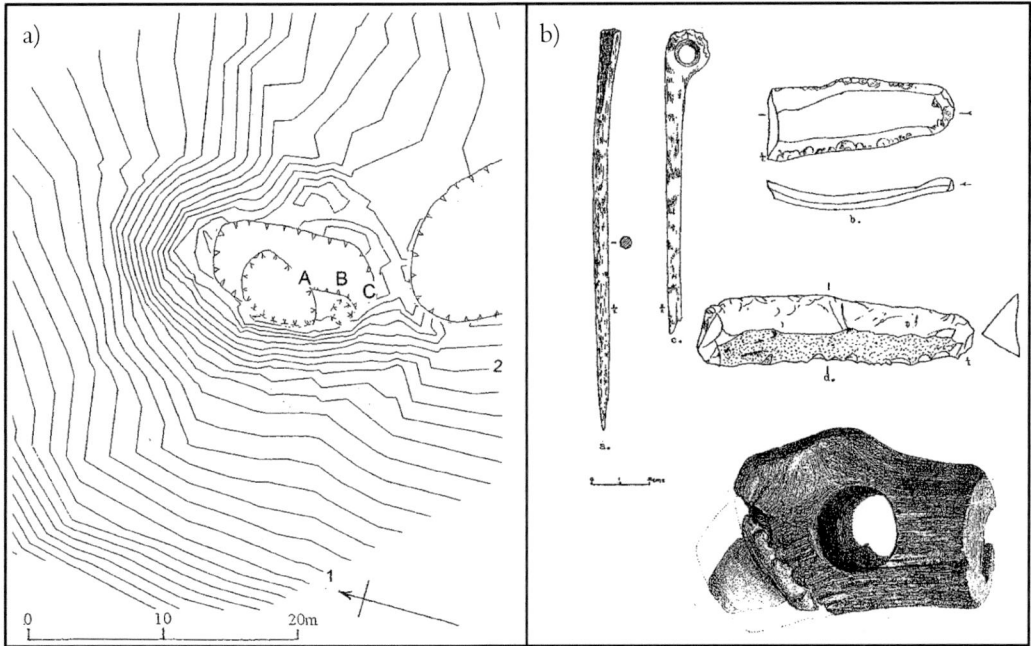

54 Mazonwath. (a) The mound today with the position of the principal burials recorded by Greenwell superimposed. (b) The finds, the macehead is as drawn by Greenwell

MAZONWATH, NY69350759

A number of other former tarns/wetlands within the basin, described above, can be identified. Amongst these is the valley floor at Mazonwath and, south of there, in a wholly inconspicuous position, are the remains of an oval mound (54a). This appears to be Greenwell's site CXXIV, the location of which is otherwise unknown.

Within the mound, Greenwell found artefacts of a late Neolithic date.[16] These were associated with a number of burials. At A was the complete skeleton of 'a strongly made' middle-aged man laid on his left side with his hands in front of his face, and nearby, the 'completely scattered' remains of three others: two adults and one child. At B, and also laid on the old ground surface, were the partially disturbed remains of a young man who had been laid on his right side with hands to face, and at C there was another similar, though complete, skeleton with a perforated antler macehead in front of the knees. Scattered elsewhere in the cairn were unburnt bones of an adult and two children, and teeth of ox, red deer and a small horse.[17]

LITTLE KINMOND, SUNBIGGIN AND ANOTHER LOST SITE[18]

As noted above, a number of cairns are visible from the sites at Rayseat Pike and Mazonwath, which means that they are *not* located on the highest point of the limestone escarpment but appear to be placed so as to be visible from the lower ground.

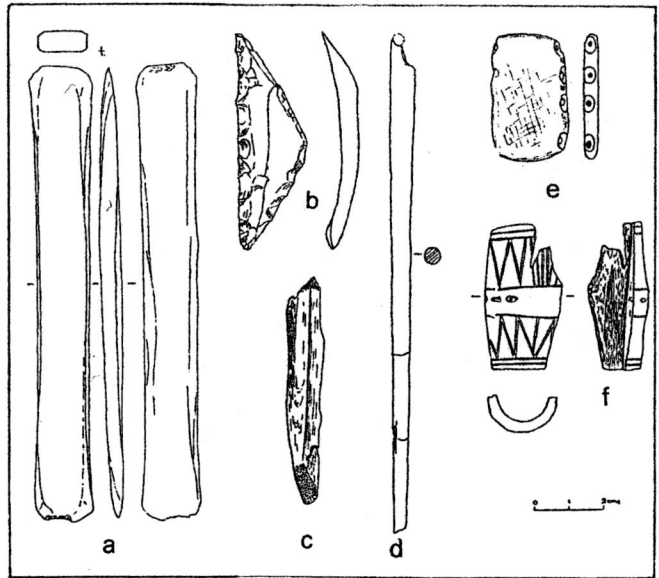

55 The finds from three other cairns dug by Greenwell

The round cairn of Little Kinmond NY66440901 contains the visible remains of a cist in which, and in close proximity, Greenwell found 'portions of three bodies'. He argued, however, that the site had been dug before and amongst the disturbed material were the remains of two more bodies, and near the cist, a 'chisel' of metamorphic rock (55a).

The round cairn at Sunbiggin NY65270897 had secondary burials which Greenwell thought 'Anglian'. At the centre, however, was a large rock-cut grave orientated north–south containing the skeleton of a young man who had been more than 1.8m tall. He had been placed on his left side with his hands drawn up to the face; a burial position reminiscent of Mazonwath. Near the head was a chert implement (55b).

Another site excavated by Greenwell, and which may have been on the lower ground, was his CLXXVI. It was some 7m in diameter and 0.3 high. South of the centre, the cairn 'was full of broken and scattered human bones' together with bones of ox and goat. At the centre, and laid upon the old ground surface, was the 'burnt' body of a woman. Overlying, and in contact with her bones, were those of two unburnt infants. All around were hundreds of bones of water vole, the head of a foumart and jaw bones from cat, dog and goat, and nearby, but within the cairn, the objects c-f in (55).

LITTLE ASBY COMMON, NY 6800834

This small group of sites, located on a spur overlooking Sunbiggin Tarn, was discovered during a systematic archaeological survey of the Common, and consists of a small stone circle and nearby mound which is seven meter in diameter, 0.3m high and flat topped.[19]

Detailed survey shows that 'the circle', which is composed of stones almost hidden by the grass, has a possible 'outlier' (A in 56) and an arrangement of stones in the centre. One of these stones appears to be tipped and the arrangement is suggestive of a cist. If this is

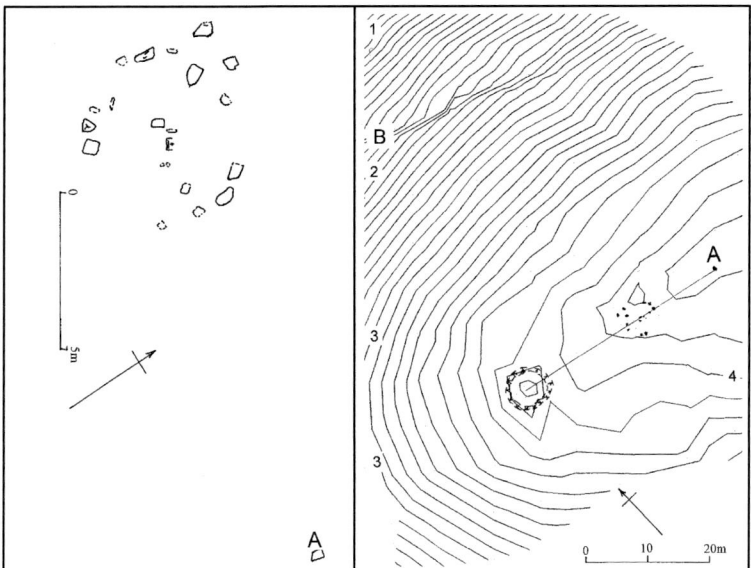

56 Little Asby Common. B is probably one of a number of old trackways

the case, and in the absence of any apparent mound, then the cist may have been accessible by removal of any 'capstone' or cover.

The topographical survey suggests that both the mound and circle are deliberately located on the central axis of the spur, and that the outlier A continues that line. There is, however, no certain astronomical alignment in the circle, although the inner face of the stone, which may have formed the southern end of the putative cist, is orientated about 308 degrees from north; an angle which, allowing for declination, may have been on the midsummer setting sun.

RASETT HILL, NY73790533

This mound, which is visible from the A685, is prominent on a hilltop (*colour plate 21*). Perhaps for that reason it looks larger than it is, being some 16m in diameter and 1.5m high. Greenwell[20] found it composed of 'clayey soil', and the only interment discovered, a cremation, was five meters east, south-east of the centre. This had been 'placed in a round heap' 0.3 m across, and whilst this may suggest a pit, or bag, it may also be indicative of a secondary burial.

Rasett Hill is part of Ash Fell, the eastern extension of the limestone escarpment, and east of the A685 a number of other burial mounds were excavated by Greenwell.

LORD'S TABLE, RAVENSTONEDALE, NY73740131

This site, located on a ridge on the valley floor south of Ash Fell,[21] consists of a low earthwork bisected by the farm track and appears to have consisted of a bank and central

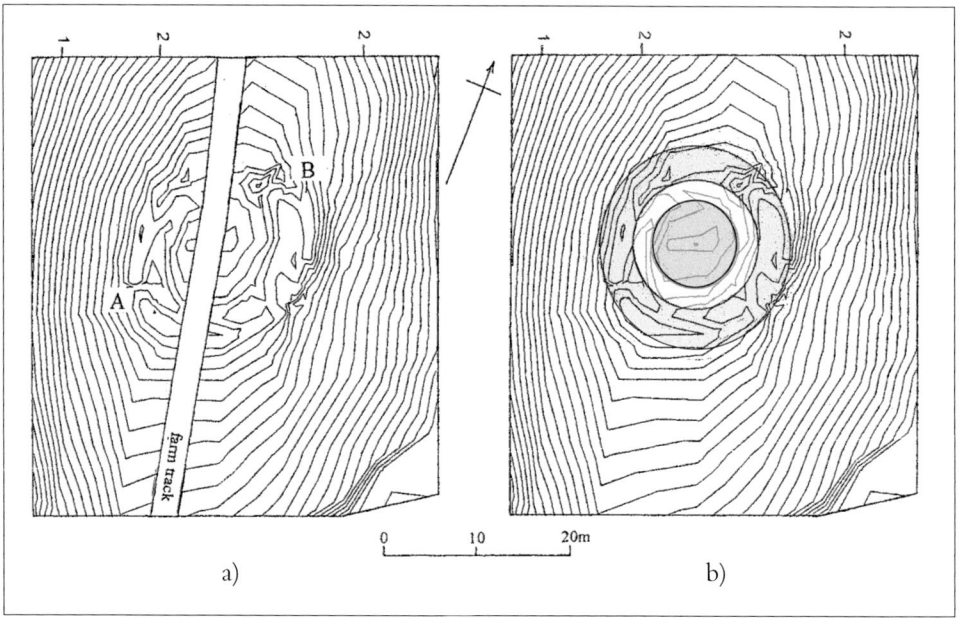

57 The Lord's Table. (a) The earthwork and its position on a low ridge. (b) The bank and central mound are shaded

mound. In the southern quadrant there is a narrow gap in the bank; probably a recent cutting A (57). Another cutting, but with a ridge between it and the central mound, exists in the northern quadrant at B. To the east, the form lines suggest that the top of the bank may have been intended to be level, and it is interesting to note that the northern arc of the bank appears to coincide with the highest point of the ridge (57b) i.e., the site is touching one side of the highest point. This is a feature found in some other sites, such as Oddendale, and is, therefore, consistent with the site being prehistoric in date. The antiquity of the name is unknown.

APPLEBY GOLF COURSE, NY709198

A number of mounds were identified here in the 1930s,[22] but accessing and finding them is now quite difficult. In addition, it is known that the local Yeomanry erected bell tents in the area about 1900 and dug trenches around them creating what might look like ring ditches. What makes the area interesting is, however, the discovery from the air of a circular ditched earthwork (58). Although originally interpreted as a Roman Signal Tower, it is located on the floor of a valley with restricted views. An alternative explanation is to see it as a small henge or hengiform structure, and nearby is a small subrectangular earthwork with rounded ends (arrowed).

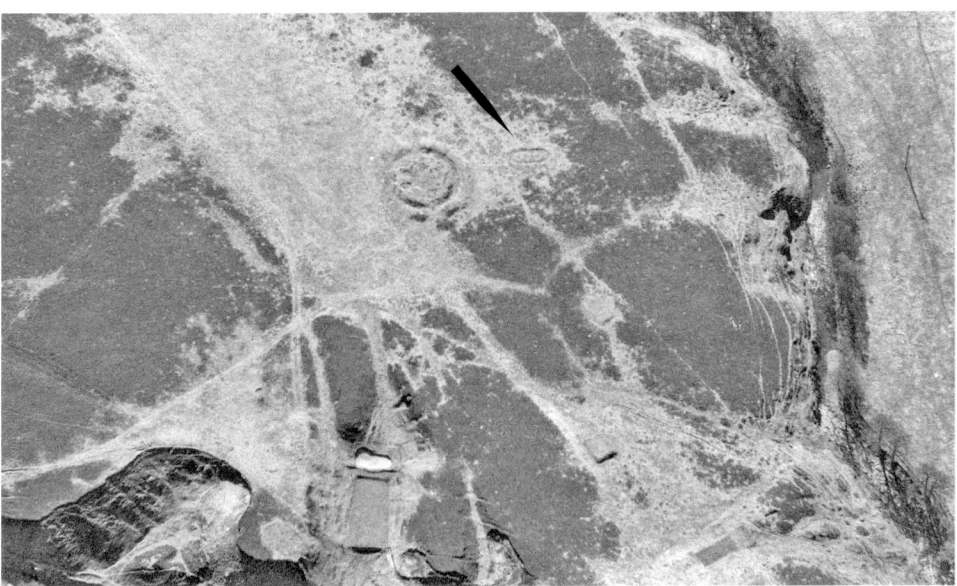

58 The two earthworks at the northern end of Appleby golf course. The photo is from the Cumbria SMR Reference MU CS 89, 24

SANDFORD AND BROUGH FAIR HILL, NY7317 AND NY7615

The existence of four burial mounds at Sandford was reported in 1776.[23] Their remains lie almost on the floor of the Eden valley on ground sloping down to what appears to have been a large tarn, but, truncated by the A66, dug into for a radio mast and with straw tipped on them, they form one of the saddest monuments in Cumbria.

What may be a denuded mound lies beneath one field boundary, but the most obvious feature is the humped profile of the field boundary alongside the busy (and dangerous) A66. This appears to be the remains of a second mound, but recent evaluation of the adjacent ground, at the time when the aerial was erected, found nothing.

One mound, excavated in 1776, was found to contain an iron 'urn', probably a shield boss, a broad two-edged sword and a spear. About 0.9m below this, the workmen found a cairn '7yds in diameter and above 6yds high'. This cairn, which is unlikely to have been six yards *high*, was covered with a thick layer of sand which had not fallen into the stones, leading the excavator to consider it the remains of inverted turf. Below the cairn were a few burnt bones in a fine black mould about seven centimeters deep and 1.8m square.

A second mound, almost 22m in diameter and *c.*1.8m high, was excavated by Greenwell.[24] He reported that the mound was of sand and that at the centre were unburnt human bones, probably of two bodies, 'juxtaposed' with a 'good deal of charcoal'.

Neither excavator left a plan, and it is now impossible to determine which of the remaining humps was excavated. However, a previously unpublished plan made by Machell, *c.*1690, exists (59)[25] and this shows two large mounds, probably those which attracted excavation. The most important detail of Machell's plan is, however, the previously unknown stone circle which he describes as being on the other side of the Roman Way, the present A66.

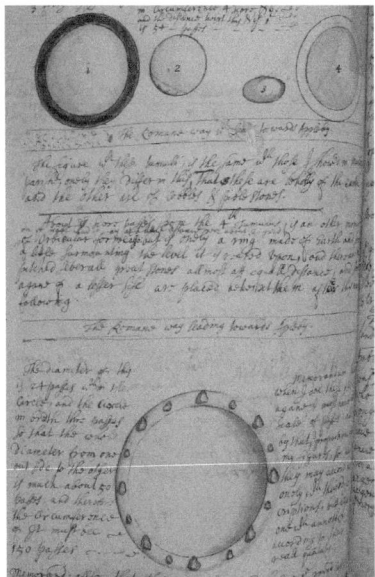

59 Machell's record of the Sandford sites

This circle is described as 'a ring made of earth and stone … surmounting the level it is raised upon, and there are pitched several great stones almost at equal distances, and some again of a lesser size are placed betwixt them … The diameter … is 24 paces within the circle, and the circle is' (?) paces so that the whole diameter from one side to the other is much about 50 paces …'. Clearly, these dimensions allow the site to be placed amongst the larger stone circles within Cumbria, and the stated ratio of bank to enclosed space echoes the ground plan of Mayburgh, although the sketch suggests an arrangement more akin to that postulated at Long Meg.

Unfortunately, the site appears to have disappeared entirely. No other writer is known to have described or been aware of the site, and nothing is visible at the location described. This is unfortunate, for the site could have contributed to our understanding of whether the banks visible at some extant sites, like Long Meg, are original or the product of later ploughing. In this particular case, the bank clearly existed prior to those centuries in which ploughing was characterised by 'narrow ridge and furrow', and that is consistent with the evidence from Long Meg. However, the Sandford circle appears to have been located on what was common land at the time of the tithe map award of c.1840, so that the area is unlikely to have been ploughed before that date. In short, the evidence is in favour of the bank being pre-medieval in date. Finally, it is necessary to note that the Machell manuscript, which is almost illegible in places, may hint at one further megalithic monument, for the text appears to refer to ' … two pair (?) one huge stone covered …'.

Edmund Gibson, who appears to have corresponded with Machell, does not mention these sites but says that there were 'some tumuli, barrows or ancient burying places' on Brough Fair Hill.[26] Again, there are no further references to the latter sites, but Brough Hill lies 3.5km further east than Sandford and is now partly covered by military installations.

Whatever their precise location, it follows we now have to recognize that there were significant numbers of burial mounds on the 'floor' of the Eden valley, as well as on the limestone uplands, and that some major monuments have not survived.

9

FURNESS AND SOUTH LAKELAND

COPT HOWE, LANGDALE, NY31390584

This group of decorated erratics (*colour plate 22*) visible from the road demonstrates the problems of understanding how prehistoric peoples perceived, and related, to built monuments and the world about them. Some of the questions posed are:
- Why were these particular erratics selected, and were they viewed as some kind of natural monument?
- Were they, for example, seen as being at the entrance to a valley and especially that leading to axe procurement sites, or were they seen as marking a place from which midsummer sun could be seen to descend over those procurement sites?
- But if their location was *the* significant factor, why was one surface decorated almost to the exclusion of all others?

In addition, it is important to note that some of the carvings occur at the very base of the stone and appear to be partly buried by the present ground surface. The significance of this is that some of the cravings on Long Meg occur low down and could be explained by having been made prior to erection of that stone, a scenario not possible here. Carving in difficult places may, therefore, have been seen as adding 'power' to the act. Indeed, the carving (or erecting) of stones – *the doing* – may have been as important as the actual motif, or final monument form.

DUNMAIL RAISE, NY32741170

According to tradition, this cairn was erected after a battle in 934 AD and is said to have been restored after damage by navvies building the Thirlmere aqueduct. The latter is consistent with the stones forming the conical top, having less lichen than those lower down, but the implication is that the lower part was not disturbed. The lower part, however, also appears as a platform; a structural form found elsewhere e.g., on Low and High Raise. It may, therefore, be that the site consisted of two parts, long before damage and restoration.

GRASMERE, CENTRED SD3408

According to Hodgson, 'where the road turns off from Keswick to the village of Grasmere, is an ancient monument, consisting of several huge stones, in circular form, but many of them displaced to make room for the roads'.[1]

Unfortunately, no other writers mention the site and it cannot be located with any certainty. Today, roads turn into the village at the bottom of Dunmail Raise and half way up at Town Head. The latter was the old, pre-turnpike road but both were in existence by the time Hodgson wrote.

BANNISIDE, SD28469670

This site is located below the steep slopes of Coniston Old Man and at the very edge of a wetland area which was once a tarn. It can also be said to be at the bottom of a small, shallow valley draining into that tarn. Today, the floor of the valley is also wetland, rather than an active stream, but a stream may have existed at the time of construction, and there is the hint of an associated debris cone contiguous with the monument on its northern side.

The monument itself is a hummocky platform with protruding stones, some upright, forming a ring which included an *insitu* erratic A (60a). The centre is a slight mound, but the uneven ground is the result of excavations by W.G. Collingwood in 1909[2] with the hollow in the south-eastern quadrant the result of earlier damage.

These excavations revealed that the outer ring was formed of 'large stones solidly packed together', but in the south-eastern quadrant the feature is built as a broad wall so that the whole site is 'raised on an artificially levelled platform on the gently sloping surface of a hill'. The excavations also revealed that there was black soil between the

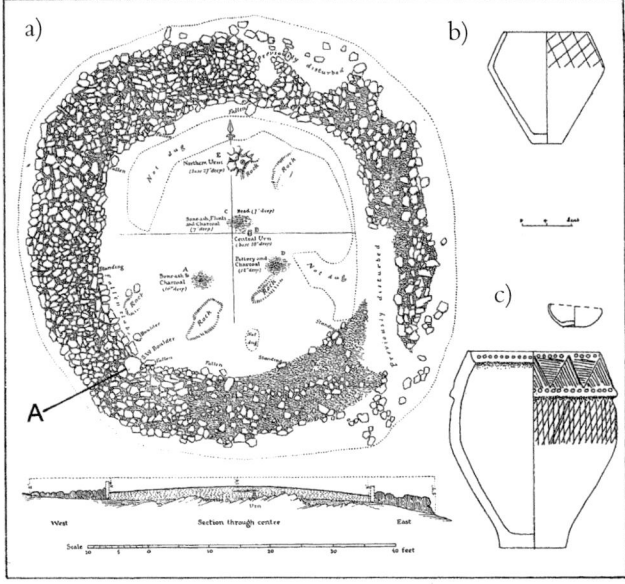

60 Banniside.
(a) Collingwood's published plan and section. (b) & (c) The surviving pots

stones, whilst yellow clay of glacial origin existed within the centre; an indication that the two had been built separately.

Near to the centre was a bipartite urn (60b), within which was 'bone ash' and a piece of white quartz, and, nearby were two small slate discs. More bone ash, charcoal and traces of fires were also found within the central area, together with some flints, a clay bead and sherds. North of the central urn was another (60c) placed against a rock outcrop and protected by slabs, and lying on its collar was the base of a pot, apparently the same as that of the sherds. The urn was half full of 'bone-ash', and on the top was the small cup, also containing a 'small quantity of bone-ash' amongst which were some teeth and bones of a two to three year old child. Within the larger vessel were fragments of a skull, apparently of a woman, and a 'cinder' to which 'was adhering a piece of woollen stuff'.

Collingwood believed his 'northern' urn was later than that found near the centre, but that does not explain how sherds from the same pot came to be associated with both. Were they really the same vessel? He called it a food vessel but his interpretation can be challenged, for the rim is similar to that of some early collared urns.

A prominent feature of the site today is the upright slab in the north-western quadrant, but the absence of lichen suggests it is a relatively new feature. Collingwood's plan shows only fallen stones in this area, but what may be the same stone is shown upright in his photograph of the work in progress. Perhaps, therefore, the stone was re-erected by him.

Collingwood records two upright stones in the south-eastern quadrant and one is diametrically opposite the present one. If one stands behind this and aligns the two, it will be seen that they seem to be orientated to the highest point of Coniston Old Man, the point at which the midsummer sun would set if the horizon had been horizontal – which it definitely isn't. Nevertheless, from the site, the midsummer sun should rise along the steep eastern slope of Yewdale Fells, whilst the midwinter setting sun would be over the cairn on the highest point of Bleaberry Haws (below).

Along the latter line, south of the present site, is a possible oval mound, some 7m x 4m, its long axis on the same alignment.

BLEABERRY HAWS, SD264946

There are a number of prehistoric monuments on this ridge but the most spectacular structure – of unknown date – is a linear dyke. This is best seen running straight up the hillside, across the valley to the south-east. On Bleaberry Haws itself it is less visible but can be seen just north of the summit where a modern marker cairn sits on an earlier mound.

The latter is one of several cairns on the ridge. Some appear to belong to a cairnfield and some were excavated in the nineteenth century by Swainson Cowper.[3] Unfortunately, the extant sites cannot now be matched to his published accounts. One, 11m across and 0.6m high, contained a scattering of burnt bones which he attributed to the disturbance of an earlier dig. In the centre of the site, and apparently surviving intact, was a pit covered with a slab; the pit containing a cremation, fragments of an urn – which could not be preserved - a serrated flint and perforated bone object (61a). Also, there was a cist, 2.45m to the south-west, again with cremation and nearby pieces of very decayed pottery.

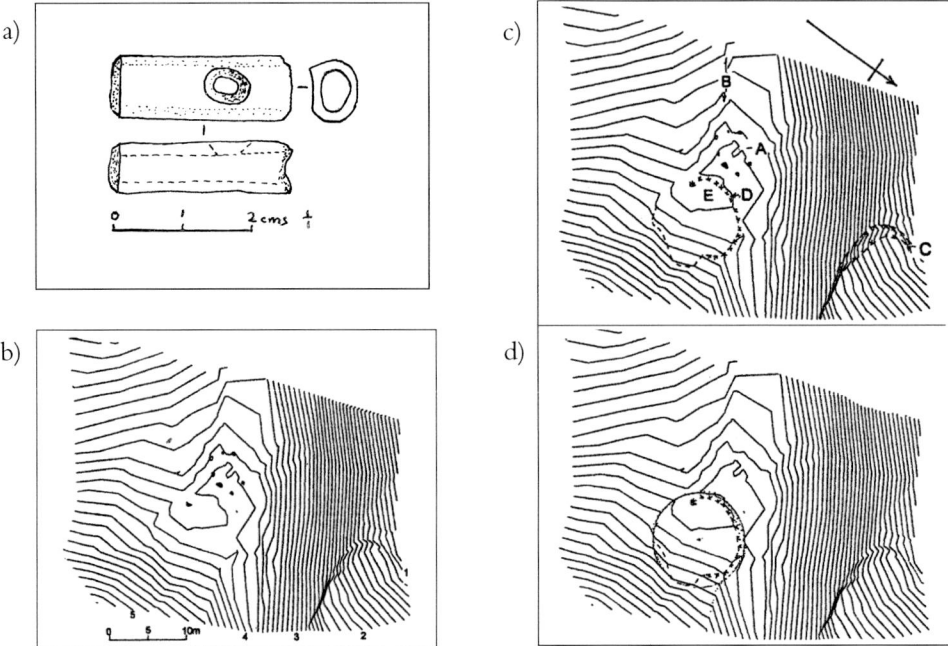

61a-d Bleaberry Haws

Cowper also began to excavate the small stone circle at SD26439466, reporting it was dug in his absence, and that there was a 'rough pavement of cobble stones' at a depth of 0.6-0.9m. There is, however, no prominent mound within the circle (61b), so the cobbles are likely to have been a natural feature or the bottom of a large pit.

Today, there appears to be a very, very low mound associated with the circle and, in the centre of that, a hollow A (61c) suggestive of early excavation. If the latter is the case, then Cowper did not excavate much. There is also a linear break of slope B, whilst below the site there is a faint curvilinear feature which, in part, is a bank C. A second curved break of slope can be seen at D and it appears to be associated with a hollow E. One possibility is that the feature results from an activity, such as turf stripping, but the contours suggest the upper break of slope is circular (61d), raising the alternative possibility that it relates to a prehistoric structure. There is, for example, a circular bank of uncertain date and purpose further along the ridge at SD26739501.

KNAPPERTHAW OR BEACON, SD28008423

This enigmatic site lies on private farmland and permission to visit must be obtained from the farm. From there, the track passes a previously unrecorded standing stone (62a), which may be a 'scratching post'. However, those are usually for cows and this one is surely too small for that purpose. From there, the track passes through an area of numerous erratics, so prehistoric peoples would have had no problem finding stones to build a freestanding circle if they wished.

 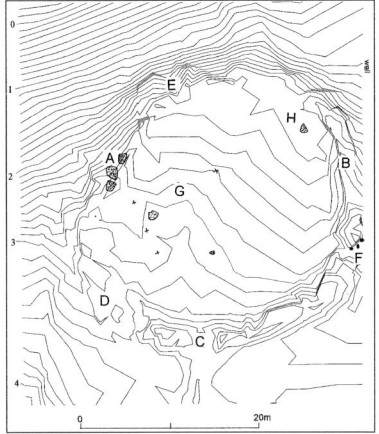

62 Knapperthaw

But this site is not a freestanding circle. It consists of an embanked area within, and from which stones protrude. To the north-west, the (apparently damaged/eroded) perimeter includes large slabs A (62b) but in other places, as at B, the bank appears to have been a wall of smaller stones 2m wide. At C, the bank is interrupted by what appears to be a track, and there are further possible disturbances and extraneous features at D and E. It will also be evident that whilst the northern arc of the site is a pronounced platform, the bank there is almost absent. In contrast, the bank is most evident in the south-eastern quadrant where it emphasises the level nature of the interior.

The overall impression is, therefore, that the site has been built as a platform, dug out on the south-eastern side and built up on the north. However, excavation is needed to test this because the ground to the south and east is also level. Nevertheless, the impression is that of a site deliberately built as a platform. That, and the character of the bank, allow the site to be considered as a settlement. However, there are no internal divisions or visible hut circles, as in the settlement to the south-east,[4] and possible entrance F is very narrow. This gap is to the south-east where any rising midwinter sun would be visible over the col in Lowick Beacon. It may also be significant that this putative entrance is central to the highest length of perimeter bank.

Other indicators of a possible ritual, rather than utilitarian purpose, are the location of the site due south of Coniston Old Man, the fact that the large slabs A are in the north-west where the midsummer sun would set and the possible existence of a low mound within the interior G. However, the possibility of alignments, of the kind described above, being included within the layout of a settlement should be allowed for. It is also worth noting that some of the stones, especially H, have natural cup marks.

STAINTON GROUND, SD22429332

This previously unpublished, but thought-provoking site (*colour plate 23*) is well worth a visit. However, the approach – from whatever direction – involves a somewhat strenuous hike of at least 20 minutes and walking boots are recommended. Limited parking is available at SD215933 and at the end of the track at SD216929. Note the block of woodland opposite the latter. Although composed primarily of conifers, it is indicative of what the crags and hillsides may have looked like at the time of the building and use of the monument.

The site consists of a subrectangular area of leaning slabs which rise from a low, flat topped mound. Within the enclosed space is a cist, the top of which is flush with the surface of the mound, suggesting that it would have been possible to gain access at any time.

The mound, itself, is located at the entrance to a small col, between and almost surrounded by rocky outcrops. Below and to the south-east is a wetland area across which are spectacular views with the flat top of Ingleborough, some 55kms away, being visible on a fine day. The peak to the north-east is The Caw, and beyond and to the east is White Pike which hides the summit of Coniston Old Man. The (possible) significance of this is that a line of 45 degrees from Swinside would pass through this site, and White Pike to the summit of Coniston Old Man.

In that context, it is worth noting two things. Firstly, that the col is to the north-west of this site – so that it is possible the midsummer sun appeared to set just within it and just beyond the immediate horizon. Secondly, that the proximity of the high horizon to the north and north-east would have meant the rising sun would have risen a little to the east of north, so that any calculation of north using the local position of the rising and setting sun would have produced an error. Interestingly, the long axis of the cist is some 13 degrees east of north, so it may be that the builders intended the orientation of the monument to be north–south/east–west.

The cist may also betray something else of prehistoric thinking, for the 'west' and 'south' sides are single, monolithic slabs, whilst the 'north' and 'east' are wholly of drystone walling. Given that there are plenty of slabs available in the area, this contrast must be intentional. Possibly also intentional, is the fact that the vertical slabs of the monument echo those of the adjacent rock outcrops.

Three other architectural details are worth noting. Firstly, there may be some small uprights within and against the southern face of the cist. Secondly, that white quartzite occurs in a number of stones and, thirdly, the uprights do not form a single 'wall' but consist of a succession of overlapping slabs suggestive of individual acts or placements, perhaps at different times.

THE KIRK, KIRKBY IN FURNESS, SD25068269

Two sites are located in this combe-like valley which is visible from and to the south-east of Swinside. The first is a cairn some 24m across and 1.6m high. The cist (possibly 1.5m x 0.9m and located in the south-west quadrant) is said to have contained 'calcined' bones.[5]

The second structure, located above the steep slopes of a stream, consists of a circular bank (63a). A number of stones protrude from this bank, and 'tradition related … many large stones were removed for building purposes'.[6] If this was the case, then it is possible

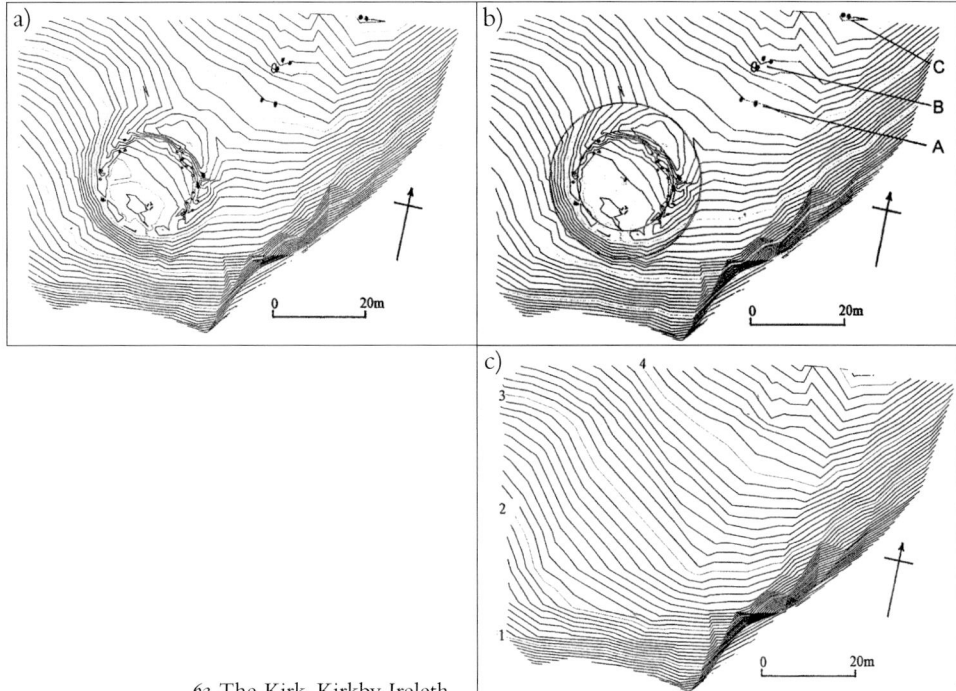

63 The Kirk, Kirkby Ireleth

they formed the inner face of the bank because one stone appears to remain in that position, and the inner face is steeper than the outer one. The bank also appears to have been laid out as a perfect circle (63b) with the central area being relatively level. The possible form of the hillside without this construction is shown in (63c).

North-eastwards from the enclosure are several small upright stones, and although some nineteenth-century antiquarians describe four as forming a square, it is also possible to see them as being paired A, B and C in (63a).

URSWICK AND SKELMORE HEADS, SD2775

A small 'long cairn' (arrowed in *colour plate 24*) is located at SD27437544, just north of the remains of a 'hillfort'. Less than 20m in length, from east to west, it appears to have had parallel sides but the eastern end is higher than the western one. There, and protruding from the mound, are two standing stones, but excavation revealed there had been two more at the western end. Although in a line, their axis is different from that of the mound. This might be because they belonged to two phases or simply the result of damage to the mound. Whatever the explanation, it is significant that the eastern stone is transverse to the others and echoes those which blocked some megalithic chambers. However, excavations beyond it failed to identify 'signs of a forecourt, or ritual area'.

No artefacts were found in the systematic excavation of 1957,[7] but it was reported that 'finds of bone and pottery' had been made in diggings some thirty years before. The reliability of this is clearly in doubt, but in 1959 a cache of four unpolished stone axes were found wedged in a crevice nearby. This led to the discovery that a fifth rough out had been ploughed up in a field to the north.

In the eastern wall, adjacent to the footpath at SD27577543, is a large boulder, possibly a former standing stone, and in the same field is a possible ring cairn (*colour plate 24*).

Another stone built into a wall is located on private land at SD267742. Having apparently stood upright, and served as a 'cow scratcher', it is possibly that 'which the inhabitants of Urswick were accustomed to dress as a figure of Priapus in Midsummer Day, besmearing it with Sheep Salve, Tar or Butter, and covering it with rags of various dyes, the head ornamented with flowers'.[8]

BIRKRIGG AND THE SUNBRICK CIRCLE, SD2974

The limestone hill of Birkrigg Common is intervisible with that of Skelmore Heads, and there are eight known sites here. They are, however, located on slopes which do not face Skelmore Heads, just as the long cairn there is hidden from Birkrigg.

Site 1, SD28157402

The most obvious monument is the Sunbrick circle, or 'Druid's circle'. It consists of a ring of uprights and beyond that a number of horizontal stones which appear to form a second circle (64a).

The North Lonsdale Field Club trenched the smaller circle[9] prior to it being 'turned over', finding two layers of cobbles separated by a thin band of soil. Beneath these

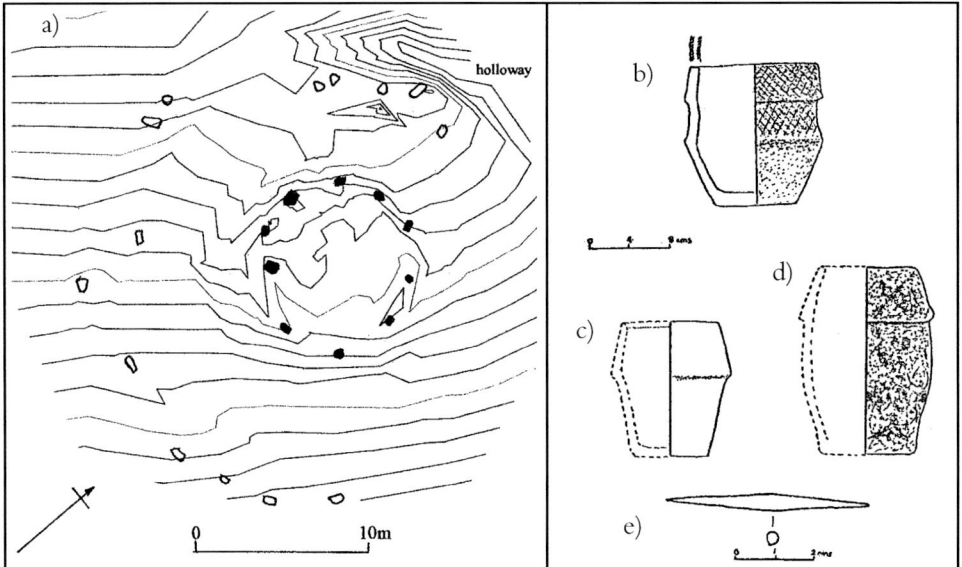

64 Birkrigg: a) the stone circle; b) the urn from the stone circle; c-d) the urns from site 3; e) the bronze awl from site 2

pavement(s) were a number of pits variously containing a few fragments of calcined bone, charcoal, burnt earth and the remains of vegetable matter. In one pit there was also a broken disc of sandstone, its edges ground until sharp, three contained spalls of stone amongst the bones, and in another there was a collared urn (64b).

In nearly every case, the excavators observed that the pit had been 'marked' by a flat stone or by stones larger than in the rest of the pavement, suggesting that they had been dug through the latter. In the case of pit 'a', that containing the disc, the flat stone marking it was observed to be 'lying lengthwise directly east and west'. This stone was in the lower pavement, and beneath that there was a third 'layer' of stones confined in an area to that of the pit. The implication is that here, and elsewhere, there was more than one phase of activity. Certainly, the pit containing the urn had been cut into an earlier one and the compaction of the fill of that pit appears to have caused the urn to tilt.

Today, the inner circle appears to be terraced and something like a bank appears to surround the stones, except in the south-eastern arc. Whilst it is difficult to believe that these represent the original character of the site, the excavators did note that around the uprights 'the paving was found to be of a different nature, being characterised by the presence of larger cobbles, many of which were flat and set up on end immediately around the boulders' to support them. In short, the site may indeed have possessed a bank-like feature. If that were the case, then the area inside and outside the smaller circle had been differentiated, and, significantly, the excavators found no pits and only a discontinuous 'pavement' between the two circles.

Site 2, 28937436
This cairn on Appleby Hill was an oval (*c*.12.5 x 10m) with a long axis, orientated ESE-WNW. Its eastern half covered a small stone circle, 3.6m to 3.9m across, the stones of which had an inward batter 'as if pressed out of the perpendicular by the materials of the barrow heaped around'. Whether this was a continuous ring of stones, or not, is unfortunately not stated, but within it were more than thirty deposits of dark earth, containing sherds or possibly 'broken down prehistoric pottery'.[10] Again, however, the details are vague and it is not clear whether these were in pits or the cairn.

Almost certainly within the cairn, and in a secondary position, was the remains of a skeleton accompanied by an awl (64e), and near the centre, and also above the original ground surface, was a rough vaulting containing a few pieces of skull.

Site 3, SD28837456
On the northern side of Appleby Hill, between two enclosures, was a mound of soil and stone, nine meters in diameter. All the deposits encountered in the excavations[11] were in the north-eastern quadrant. Amongst them, and placed on the old ground surface, were two urns (64c,d), with a third in a pit. There were five other pits containing only dark 'earthy matter' and charcoal, but one had been lined with thin, sharp flakes of stones. Three others had been covered by flat stones, inviting a comparison with the practices of the Sunbrick circle.

Site 4, 28187402
This site, 17m across and located on a natural ridge, is visible from the road. It appears as a platform with bank. The excavators[12] found the bank, four meters wide, to be constructed of slabs pitched against each other, and the enclosed area to consist of soil and stones. Beneath this was a 'pavement' of tightly wedged limestone blocks, and beneath that 13 deposits containing some human material. One was accompanied by a boar's tusk and strip of ornamented bronze. In another, a piece of human bone had been cut and one end 'rubbed smooth'. Subsequent analysis suggested that some of the bones from individual skeletons occurred in more than one deposit.

TROUTBECK, NY42480762

The remains of this cairn are located on the side of a ridge some distance from the public footpath. However, it is worth visiting the site because it has the remains of a large 'cist' (originally perhaps 2.4m x 1.2m), orientated north–south. The cairn has been damaged by the building of a shelter but it may have been oval in shape, approximately 7m x 12.5m.

HIRD WOOD AND WOUNDALE RAISE, NY4106

The cairn known as Woundale Raise is no longer visible but was probably located in the vicinity of NY40560675 where there is a natural mound in a col, visible from the Kirkstone Pass road. The site is said to have contained a cist of four stones, inside which were 'burnt bones' and a bronze spearhead.

To the south-east, the steep valley side is partly covered by Hird Wood, within which, and alongside the public footpath at NY41640588, there is a standing stone. The latter was first mentioned in 1901[13] when it was described as a 'ruined stone circle'. In addition to the obvious upright A (65a), there is a smaller one B, three orthostats within the wall C, D and E, and several other stones. The orthostats may not, however, be prehistoric, for a fourth smaller one at F suggests uprights were part of the wall building process. In favour of the stones being prehistoric is the fact that the wall bends as if to take in an existing feature, and they do in fact appear to lie on the arc of a circle about 17m across (65b). There it can be seen the circle would have included the natural mound on which the standing stone is located and its perimeter passes through the lowest point of the site. However, it will be seen that the stone is not central to the putative circle, raising doubts about the character of the site. Certainly it is difficult to agree with Cowper that the 'ground within had been artificially raised';[14] a view which may have been influenced by him, being told that the pile of stones, in which a rough-out axe had been found some 60yds away, came from this site.

Nevertheless, the position of stone A on a craggy shelf, on the steep valley side, suggests the present path is a very old routeway along the valley side.

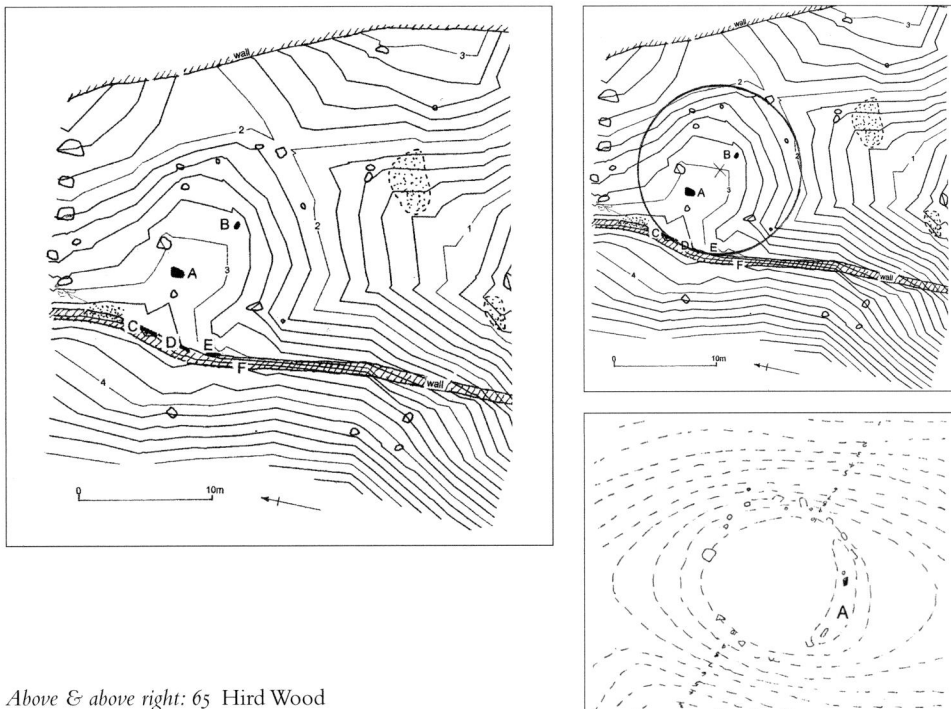

Above & above right: 65 Hird Wood

Below right: 66 Potter Fell, from Clare 1973

POTTER FELL, SD50349880

An almost overgrown circle of stones sited on a small natural ridge (66) appears to be the kerb of a mound 10-20cm high. How much of this mound is natural is unclear, but the bank at A appears to be an addition.

KENDAL

Two possible prehistoric monuments are located on the limestone scar to the west of the town.

Site 1, SD487938
The character and antiquity of the site recorded in (67a) is uncertain, and the most obvious feature is the arrangement of upright limestone slabs A which protrude a few centimeters above the turf. Whilst these might be the remains of a (water) trough at the junction of the field walls, the latter appear to overlie it. An alternative possibility is therefore that it is a cist (of uncertain dimensions) and that it was 'central' to a mound.

Nearby and to the east are the extensive remains of a native settlement first recorded from the air and now known to have produced Roman material. To the north-west and on the lower ground, two 'roughouts', one certainly Neolithic, were found in the vicinity of pillow mounds and other late prehistoric or Roman period settlements.

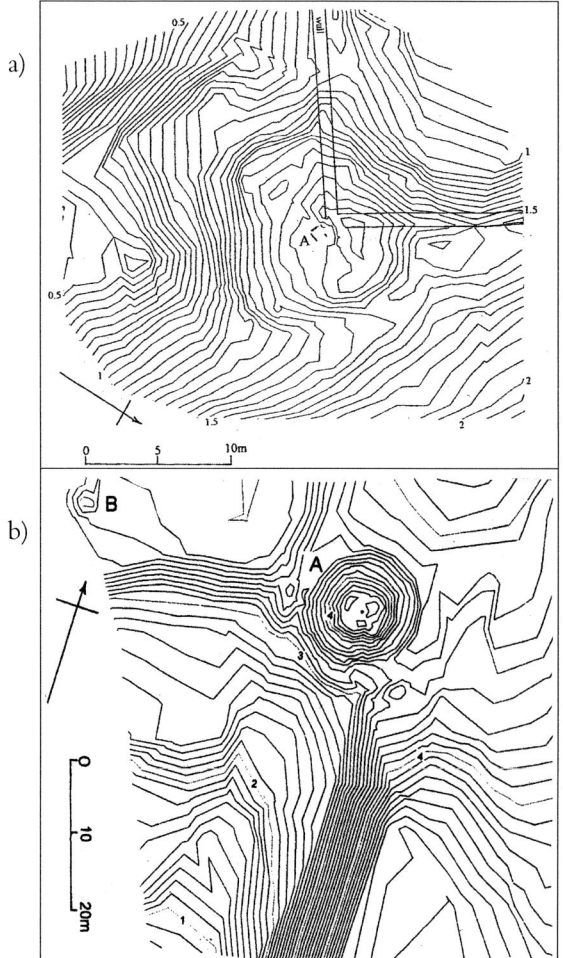

67a-b Two sites west of Kendal

Site 2, SD505915

This round cairn (67b) is located on the Old Racecourse. Given its size, it is surprising that it has never been noted before, and the possibility that it is somehow connected with the racetrack must be considered. However, a map of 1828[15] shows the northern side of the droveway into Kendal bending at this point, suggesting that it is an ancient landscape feature.

Certainly a number of features are worth comment:
- Its large size, both in diameter and height.
- It appears to be located at the head of a discrete, small valley.
- Some of the lower ground around the site, e.g., at A, suggests some of the cairn material was quarried or scraped up.
- There is a possible small cairn with cist like arrangement at B,
- and a small cairnfield in the north-west 'corner' of the racecourse beyond the public footpath.

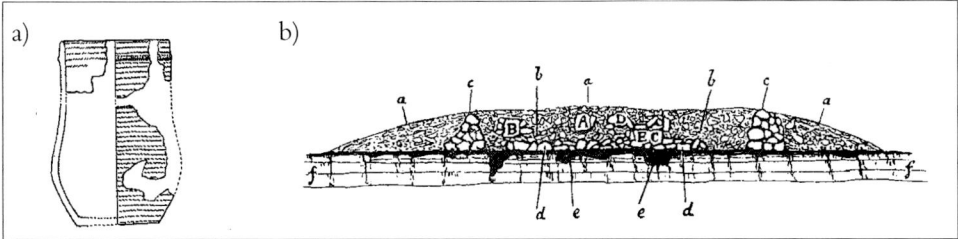

68 Sizergh Fell from TCWAAS2, LIII, 1-5 and TCWAAS2, IV, 200

SIZERGH FELL, SD49488684

This is the southern end of the limestone ridge, west of Kendal, which separates what would have been raised bog in the Lyth valley from the fast flowing River Kent. At this point, however, the ridge becomes a separate hilltop, a feature best appreciated from the A6 just south of Kendal.

In the centre of the hilltop is a large round mound, but despite its regular shape, all the evidence is that it is natural. Nevertheless, it was a focus for prehistoric activity, with a reworked stone axe being wedged against a rock outcrop and nearby, but separate, flakes of polished stone tools and a polissoir, or portable polishing stone.

There are other lesser mounds on the hilltop and lower slopes and those tested recently have been shown to be natural,[16] although at the beginning of the twentieth century a beaker (68a) was found in a 'stone heap with larger stones around the base'.[17]

The cairn at SD49488684 is artificial and was excavated in 1903, and recently. The section, published in 1904 (68b), is useful in showing that, prior to excavation, the mound was essentially flat topped. It was found to cover an embanked enclosure within which was a platform. The human remains A-E were on, or above, this platform, and the recent work suggest a minimum of 13 individuals had been interred with a significant number foetal or infant burials. The radio carbon dates (Appendix) show that the burials on the platform are Neolithic, whilst those from the body of the cairn are late prehistoric.[18]

LEVENS PARK, SD505862

This Park, originally created in the fourteenth century and remodelled into its present form in the late seventeenth, demonstrates how archaeological ideas change with time. Now recognised as being an important part of our heritage and as part of the famed topiary gardens of the Hall, it was not mentioned by the Royal Commission on Historical Monuments inventory of sites in Westmorland, published in 1936. Perhaps a lack of interest in the Park, itself, may explain why the Commission failed to describe any of the earthworks that exist within the area.

These include the remains of a 'native' farmstead, known as Diana's Temple, or more prosaically, as Kirksteads. There are also areas of what appear to be ridge and furrow,

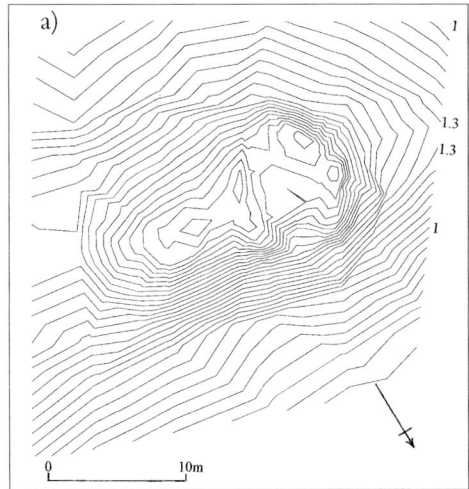 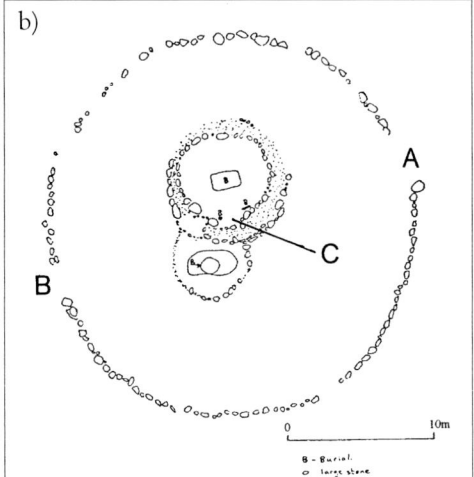

69a and b Levens Park a) the mound near Diana's Temple b) the ring cairn based on Scottish Archaeological Forum 1972, 4, 53

small rectangular 'pillow mounds' and some round mounds, most no more than five or six meters in diameter. One of the exceptions, visible from the public footpath, occurs north-west of Diana's Temple at SD505328594 and is a large oval mound on the western end of which is what appears to be a circular earthwork (69a). Could the latter be the circular structure alluded to by Nicholson and Burn in their account of Kirksteads?[19] And does their reference to a ruin imply they saw walls, or could it be that the earthwork is a variant ring bank?

Equally, although it is probable that the oval mound is glacial in origin, the possibility of it being man made should be considered. In particular, a number of features can be paralleled in known prehistoric sites described elsewhere in this book; its location at the edge of a slight valley, its platform-like surface projecting beyond the break of slope and its east–west orientation.

Another mound away from the public footpath, but just visible from the previous site at SD50568621, was excavated in advance of the construction of the nearby dual carriageway. Unfortunately, no full excavation report was published, so that the description given here is based on the short note published by the excavator, the notes made by this author after a visit to the excavations and on museum/archival material recovered later.[20]

In its final form, the prehistoric structure was a round cairn, 25m in diameter and with a boulder kerb (69b). This cairn, and the structures beneath it, appear to have been subject to half-hearted excavations on a number of occasions. The two large gaps in the kerb A and B might be the result of such digging but they can also be compared with those in the perimeters of the circles at Swinside and Gamelands. The possibility that the kerb was built prior to the cairn, as at Borwick,[21] some 13kms to the south, should therefore be considered.

At Borwick, the equivalent structure was described as a bank, as was that at Levens; an interpretation which allowed it to be viewed as the perimeter of a farmyard/settlement within which there had been a hut (below). Unfortunately, the excavation archive

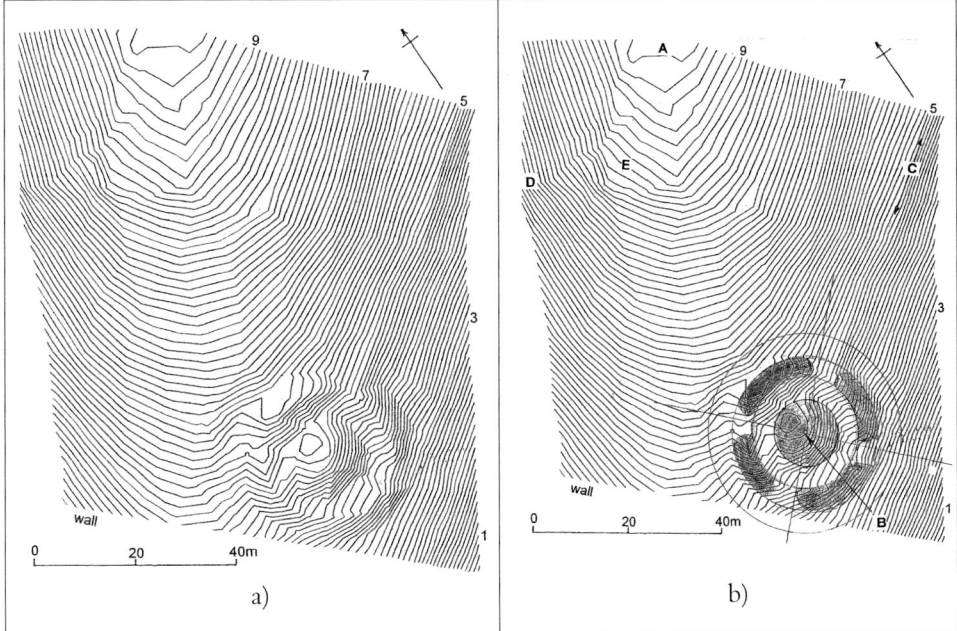

70 Middleton Hall

does not allow for these interpretations to be checked, nor does it provide any clear stratigraphic evidence for the relationship of the cairn to the kiln found to the south of the centre. The latter was assumed to be a post-Medieval and inserted into the mound, but it is worth noting that a similar kiln was found at Ewanrigg.

A number of structures were, however, clearly earlier than the cairn. 'Central' to the monument was a small circular structure in the centre, of which was a beaker grave. The structure was essentially a wall with a gap or entrance flanked by two larger boulders and, consequently, the excavator considered it to be a hut for the living. However, the gap was so small that anyone wishing to enter the centre would have had to turn sideways, so that the structure is best described as being built for the dead.

The 'entrance' to this primary structure was subsequently blocked and the centre infilled. Then, and in uncertain sequence, two inhumations were inserted into the southern quadrant of this fill. Outside the structure was another inhumation, within a grave covered first by a large boulder and then by a small kerbed cairn. The central, and presumably primary grave, 2m x 1m, was orientated east–west and contained much charcoal, leading the excavator to suggest that it had been plank lined.[22] Within this grave was a disturbed inhumation and fragments of two beakers.[23]

Several other aspects of this site are worth noting:
- The plan shows the two secondary inhumations in the central structure flanking a rectilinear 'cell' C of the kind recorded elsewhere.
- This rectilinear area appears to be the 'centre' of the later cairn, as defined by the outer 'kerb'. If so, then it can be postulated that the main cairn was built after deposition of these two inhumations which were themselves later than that under the boulder.

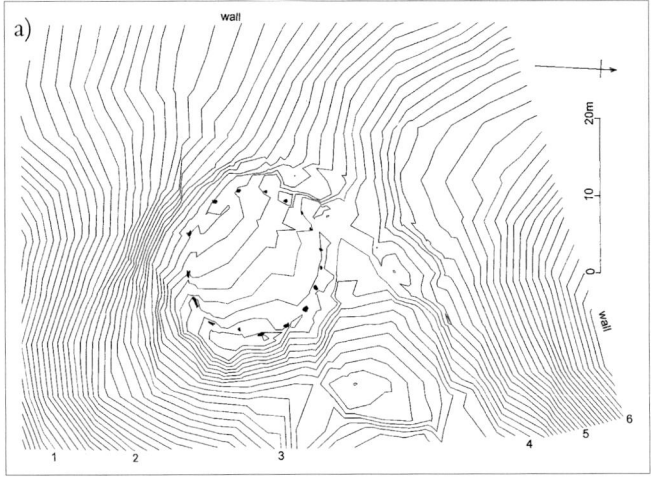

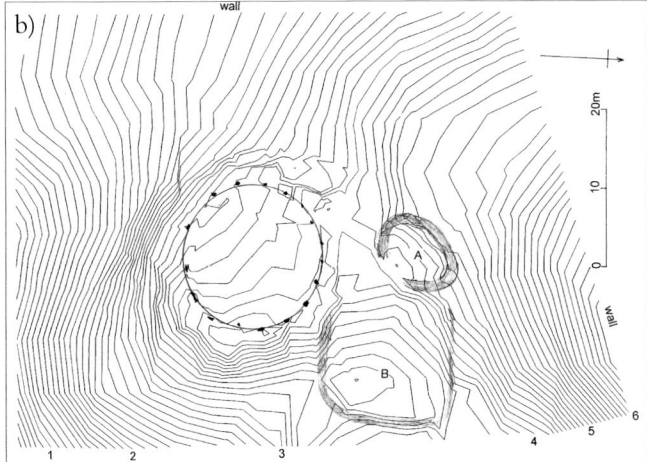

71a and b Casterton

- The recovery of some later, Roman material from the cairn can be explained by agricultural activity associated with the site, now known as 'Diana's Temple,' but the finding of two small pieces of Anglo-Scandinavian silver suggests the site may also have attracted reverence or superstition at a later time.

In contrast, the ground beneath and around the cairn contained numerous flints and, in uncertain stratigraphic relationship, charcoal.[24]

RAWTHEY BRIDGE LOST CIRCLE, SD7198

Early antiquarians reported a circle of large stones near Rawthey Bridge. Hodgson thought the site 'probably a sepulchre; but vulgarly called a druidical temple'.[25] Today, the site cannot be identified, but a cave within the valley has produced evidence of Bronze Age and Roman period burial together with later activity, including denning by wolves.[26]

MIDDLETON HALL, SD63088749

This site has sometimes been considered a Roman signal tower but its location, below the highest point of a ridge A (70b) and on a slope facing away from the Roman road, is against such an interpretation. Nevertheless, the view to the south-west is that of the whole of the middle and lower Lune valley, with Morecambe Bay in the far distance.

The site consists of a central mound surrounded by a ditch and bank with four gaps, beyond which is another hollow or ditch. Although the latter is most visible in the field on the uphill side, aerial photographs show it encompassing the whole site.

Two further features of the layout are its circular plan form, despite being constructed on a slope, and the putative centre B, being at the 'edge of the mound's top. It would appear that the form of the mound reflects the wish to retain a circular plan form in the horizontal plain whilst building on a slope. In addition, the gaps in the banks relative to that centre correspond roughly to the settings and risings of the sun at midsummer and midwinter.

Apparently, also aligned on that centre or break of slope is a faint lynchet, C. This is one of several visible on aerial photographs and together they form, with low bank D, a field system which extends over hilltop A. However, when seen from the south-west corner of the field, the hilltop at E appears to carry a low, circular earthwork; a feature not visible on the aerial photographs. Whilst, therefore, it is unlikely to exist, it is interesting to note that centre B would be due south of its centre.

CASTERTON, SD63938000

Although on private land, this site is visible from the footpath to the east and from there all the main features are visible:
- The stones forming the circle are not high.
- They stand on a platform with a low bank on the outside, with the eastern arc being the highest (71).
- The monument is located on the side of a ridge above a small valley.
- Although the top of the ridge is flatter to the north and west, the structure is built as a platform protruding beyond the ridge.
- Had it been built to the west, it would have enjoyed spectacular views across the Lune valley but instead looks across to a rising hillside.
- The area enclosed by the bank is almost perfectly flat
- and the stones form an almost perfect circle (71b).

In places, however, the bank appears to have been quarried and there is what appears to be a hut-like structure at A (71b), and an embanked hollow B reminiscent of the stockyards in some early farmsteads. There is in fact an early, subcircular farmstead in the field to the south.

There is no physical evidence to suggest that the site has been dug.[27]

10

THINKING ABOUT THE EVIDENCE

Those familiar with the landscapes around southern monuments, such as Stonehenge, Avebury and Stanton Drew – the latter with 'avenues' reminiscent of the portals of Long Meg and Swinside – will have noticed the absence from the Lake District of some familiar site types. There are apparently no barrow cemeteries on skylines, no paired long barrows and few bowl barrows. Perhaps the latter did exist, associated with the ring ditches identifiable in the lowlands, but if that is the case then some, such as those at Brougham, must have been almost imperceptible by Roman times when they appear not to have been a constraint on *vicus* development. The monuments of the Lake District, it would seem, are similar to but different from those of contemporary Wessex; sites so long held to be archetypes of, and the basis for, our understanding of the Neolithic and Bronze Age.

The monuments of the Lake District, and indeed of other areas, such as that north of the Solway, require us to recognise regional variations and that, in turn, means research and conservation polices based on southern England might be less appropriate than those of *southern* Scotland.[1] On the other hand, KART appears to be exactly the same as monuments in the north of Scotland and Wessex, so that regional variation has to be seen against a background of contemporary awareness of a wider world.[2]

One regional monument type appears to be paired stones, such as those at Kiksanton,[3] Similarly, the structures at Plasketlands, north-east of Maryport, have no known parallels in England, although they may be related to those across the Solway in Scotland.[4] It follows that any discussions of the evidence might best begin with a consideration of the types of site *known* or *recognised* within the area.

TYPES OF SITE

Without adequate excavation of all sites, however, any typologies must be based, firstly, on the present appearance of the site, accepting that the latter may reflect re-modelling of the site in prehistory.[5] And, for the same reason, any discussions of distributions and sequences of types may be skewed. Nevertheless, it is possible to recognise within the Lake District a number of distinct monument forms.

One easily recognised type appears to be the small stone circle, such as White Hag, which has a diameter of less than 6m and no internal mound. Excavation of the example at Broomrigg, however, revealed a central pit, almost certainly for burial, and a 'pavement' of cobble stones; a feature which might also exist at the similar, but unexcavated sites of Harberwain Rigg III and Bleaberry Haws. Here, then, the process of classifying monuments is based partly on the visible characteristics of the site, and a comparison with excavated sites of similar appearance with the caveat that such comparisons cause us to think we can see evidence which may not actually be there.

Equally, features which appear to relate directly to the purpose and thinking of prehistoric peoples may occur in more than one monument type. At Banniside, for example, a circular open space was created by a bank or wall, and subsequently infilled in a sequence paralleled on Sizergh Fell, nearby Levens and at Hackthorpe, although in all four cases the final monument form was different.

Consequently, it is useful to think of the *present* form of a monument as consisting of two elements – a perimeter and a central area, each of which reflected or involved separate processes – and to recognise that in plan form, the perimeter might be rectangular, circular, oval or irregular. This can be expressed as a matrix (72),[6] which can include buried and excavated structures. However, recognition that the later may exist means that unexcavated sites can only be placed in *generic* classes, and for purposes of discussion here these are called, stone circle, ring cairn, hengiform, mound and sites with no perimeter. Interestingly, Stukeley toyed with a similar scheme, recognising at least ten perimeter types, calling a penannular wall, 'parietal', and a ditched perimeter, 'cesspititous'.[7]

As already noted, however, it is important to recognise that the present form of the monument may only represent a final phase, and there may have been complex sequences of development, as at Hardendale Nab. Moreover, such sequences raise the possibility that we should envisage some of the structures found beneath mounds as having originally stood and functioned as separate monuments. In particular, attention is drawn to the fact that paired stones, like those at Kirksanton, are best paralleled in the paired stones below the Skelmore Head 'long cairn'. The latter, in turn, appear to reflect the arrangements beneath the eastern end of Rayseat Pike long cairn where they can be interpreted as forming a chamber-like area and façade of the kind familiar in Eastern Yorkshire. There, the structures appear to have been freestanding until sealed by a mound, and it follows that we need to consider recognising the two as separate monument types. Consequently, the single standing stone, beneath the western end of Rayseat Pike, might be compared with that on Moor Divock, whilst the putative ring bank there might have been, if it existed, a later addition; a separate structure incorporating an earlier feature, just like the mound at Rayseat Pike.

Similarly, there is a need to consider the possibility that Harberwain Rigg II is a mound built within an existing stone circle and not a simple 'kerbed cairn'; a sequence which can be postulated at Grey Croft where a low mound appears to have buried the central cairn, which might, itself, now be seen as added to an existing structure. Certainly, there is a need to accept that the cairns within the circles at Gunnerkeld, Oddendale and elsewhere may belong to a separate phase to the rest of the monument, and may even be infill of an existing, concentric circle. Equally, it is necessary to ask whether the circle beneath the cairn at Penhurrock was not originally freestanding because its size was that of some 'freestanding' circles, such as those on Burnmoor.

Such sequences have been discussed, in general, by Bradley[8] and he argues that burying, or 'closure' of once open sites – here by mounds, such as those at Rayseat Pike and Hackthorpe, or by the construction of mounds over a perimeter, as at the Cockpit – represent a distinct change in the way the monuments were perceived and utilised. However, the observations made above about paired stones, and the possibility of early Neolithic monuments being buried, suggest that 'closure' was part of the tradition of monument building rather than a feature of one particular period. Nevertheless, recognition of such sequences requires us to think of the monuments, not as single structures, but as evolving ones (below), and to accept that some dateable material, such as the urn from the Sunbrick circle, may not relate to the building or primary use of the site.

PURPOSE/FUNCTION

Clearly some monument forms, including perhaps stone circles like Castlehowe, were simply burial monuments, and the contrast between those and larger diameter sites, such

72 Table illustrating the variety of circular monument forms in the Lake District

as Long Meg and Swinside, has allowed the latter to be seen as places where people came together, probably at certain times of the year. Amongst activities at such times, we might envisage ritual, social exchange and trade.

One particular aspect of such activities, which has often been emphasised in connection with stone circles, is that connected with the movement of stone axes away from procurement sites in the Lake District.[9] However, it is necessary to recognise that:
- Some circles, such as Swinside, are not on direct routeways away from the main sites of procurement.
- There are no known stone circles to the south-east of the Langdales, from where the main area of procurement was visible.[10]
- Axe finds are no more concentrated around Long Meg or Castlerigg than in some other areas, such as Furness.
- There is doubt over the number and context of the axes said to have been found at Castlerigg.
- Whilst one was definitely found buried in the entrance to Mayburgh, similar burials can occur in other contexts e.g., on Sizergh Fell and a *bronze* axe was also associated with Mayburgh.

It follows that the trade/exchange of stone axes was part of wider Neolithic social discourse and engagement, and there is evidence that the axe itself, whether of stone or bronze, had its own significance. As such, the occurrence of axes in connection with stone circles appears to be simply part of the wider Neolithic landscape and one which included deposition of similar materials in tarns, bogs and crevices.[11]

The idea that monuments, like Long Meg, were places where a number of communities came together, for a variety of purposes, has led to the direct association of the size of the monument with the size of the population using it.[12] This seems to imply that the diameter might be dictated by the number of people to be accommodated, yet a number of writers have suggested that the perimeter of some sites, and those of the henges, in particular, were designed to 'exclude'. If this were the case, and only a select few were to enter the monuments, then the diameter of a site serving 1,000 people would not need to be any different from one serving one hundred.

What we are probably seeing in the construction of large diameter sites is the same process behind cathedral churches, namely that size and elaboration reflects status and what is considered appropriate. But analogies, such as that of the cathedral, imply the existence of a hierachy of sites and, significantly, the large monuments appear to be 'spaced' approximately 10kms apart[13] in a manner echoing that of later market towns and *their* associated hierarchy of settlements. Consequently, implicit in such comparisons is the possibility that there were smaller circles/monuments used at the local level; a situation which has implications for our interpretation of typologies based on size and elaboration because it would require some 'different' monuments to have functioned in similar ways, and at similar times.

CONSTRUCTION

Nevertheless, the size of some stones can *only* be explained by people coming together to share and/or contribute to monuments, like Long Meg and Her Daughters. For that reason, the size of stones might be a better indicator than diameter of the number of people building and using a site. In this context, and with some of the comments above, it may be significant that Oddendale 1, almost the same diameter as Castlerigg, has stones no larger than those in the tiny, nearby sites of Harberwain Rigg III and Castlehowe.

Whilst the possibility that diameters may have reflected some other factors (below), estimates of the number of people required to move a particular sized stone tend to make assumptions. Firstly, that shape did not affect the ease of transport, and here it is necessary to note the comments of the excavator at Grey Croft, namely that they found it impossible to use sheer legs to re-erect the stones because of their shapes. Secondly, that draught animals were not used. In commenting upon the re-erection of the Goggleby Stone (*colour plate 1*), this author postulated that both may have been used.[14] Whether that was the case, or not, the comments of the farmer at the time when we struggled to re-erect the stone are almost certainly true; prehistoric peoples must have developed an expertise which we have lost.

The 12-ton weight of the Goggleby Stone, and the bulk of the stone at Kitchen Hill, also require us to recognize that the communal efforts utilised in such monuments was no less than that in a stone circle, like Long Meg. What distinguished Long Meg and Shap from Kitchen Hill was the continued aggregation of that community involvement over many years and not just on one occasion.

SIZE AND LAYOUT

As noted above, diameter size may be one way of subdividing stone circles but (73a) shows that the diameters of 'small' circles, like Threaplands and White Hag, are not actually statistically different from Potter Fell or the inner circle at Sunbrick, although two other groups – with diameters of 40m – 50m and more than 100m – can be easily distinguished. If the majority are to be divided on the basis of size, then it is into two more groups; those with diameters of 3m – 20m, and 23 – 35m.[15] However, it is also apparent (73b) that similar diameters occur amongst the ring cairns and hengiform monuments, and indeed amongst mounds. It follows that caution is needed in interpreting as a freestanding stone circle some sites described in the early literature. For example, the phrase 'discovered' used to describe the 'circle of rude stones … about 30yards in circumference'[16] near Dalston is suggestive of a structure beneath a mound.

Another implication already noted is that diameter size is not simply related to the size of the population building the monument but to what was felt appropriate for purpose. Implicit in this, too, is the possibility that simple units of measurement might have been used, whether that unit was a 'megalithic yard', cubit, outstretched arms or something else.[17] This is not a new suggestion, and several early workers drew attention to the similarity in size of Castelrigg, Swinside and Gunnerkeld, and to the fact that their

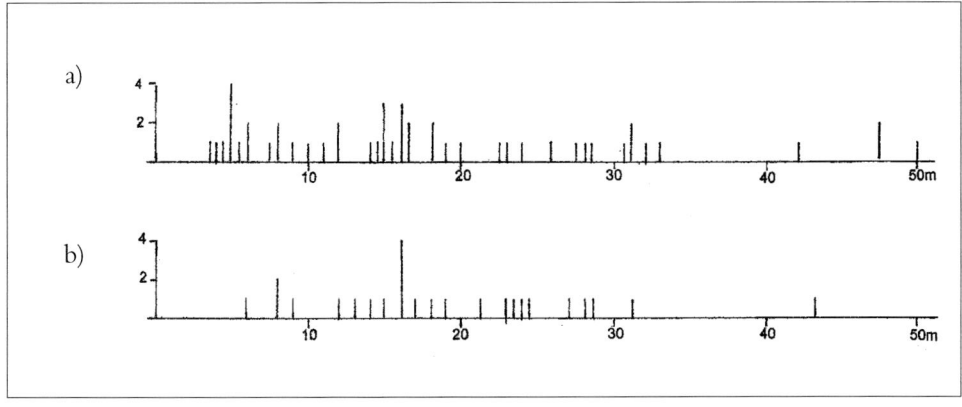

73 The average diameters (in metres) of (a) the stone circles and (b) ring cairns and hengiform sites, below 55m. Note the stone circles include those around and under mounds

diameters of 100ft, or thereabouts, might imply the unit of measurement was a 'foot'. Whilst those sites are not exactly the same size (73), it is worth noting that the use of '100 units' might have derived from the fact we have 10 digits, or toes.

Burl, and others, have highlighted other possible examples of preferred numbers in the construction of stone circles. However, the present numbers of stones in the sites (TABLE 3) do not support the suggestion that 12 was of particular importance, although three may have had some interest.[18] The diameter of the outer Shapbeck circle, for example, is three times that of the inner one, and the width of the entrance at Castlerigg could be said to be three megalithic yards. However, such examples are rare and it is interesting that three 'megalithic yards' is about ten feet.

TABLE 3

The number of *recorded* uprights

★ plus an outlier			Lacra B	?	
Annaside	20		Lamplugh	?	
Ash House	?		Leacet hill	10	
Banniside		continuous	Levens inner		continuous
Birkrigg 4 circle		continuous	Little Meg	11	
Bleaberry Haws	7		Long Meg	68★	
Brats hill	37		Long Meg lost	20	
Broadfield	6	paired	Low Longrigg east	8	
Broomrigg		portal stones?	Low longrigg west	9	

Broomrigg B	7		Little Asby	12	
Broomrigg C	11+		Mayburgh inner	4	
Casterton	16		Mayburgh outer		portal stones
Castlehowe	10★		Moor Divock V		line
Castlerigg	38	in perimeter	Motherby	?	
Cockpit		continuous	Oddendale inner	24	
Egremont Common	10		Oddendale outer	32-34	
Elva Plain	14+?		Oddendale timber inner	12	
Gamelands	40		Oddendale timber outer	12	
Grayson lands	30	continuous	Penhurrock circle	?	continuous?
Grey Croft	10		Potter Fell		
Grey Yauds	88		Sandford lost	?	
Gunnerkeld inner	31?		Shapbeck inner	14?	
Gunnerkeld outer	18?		Shapbeck outer	23?	
Gutterby circles	30		Standing stones	10	
Hackthorpe		continuous	Studfoldgate	?	
Hall Foss	8		Sunbrick inner	10	
Harberwain Rigg 3	9		Sunbrick outer	16	
Harberwain Rigg 2	19?		Swarthbeck Gill		
Hardendale Fell	22		Swinside	57	
Hird wood	?		Threaplands	7★	
KART outer		portal stones	White Hag	11★	
Kirkby Ireleth	?		White Moss west	12	
Knapperthaw	?		White Moss east	11	
Lacra A	?		Wilson Scar		continuous

Perhaps more significantly, the width of the entrance at Castlerigg is the same as the diameter of the visible ring ditch within the interior and that of the width of the rectangular arrangement. In fact, many of the stones also appear to be spaced at that distance, and multiples of the unit appear to lie behind much of the present arrangements (74a). A similar situation also exists at Long Meg and Her Daughters (74b) where the distance from the monolith to the portal is roughly three times the width of the latter.

Nevertheless, it is also necessary to recognize that there is one other group of sites which appear to have similar diameters to the monuments recorded in (73) and they are the prehistoric settlement sites. For example, the subcircular bank enclosing a single hut south of the Casterton ring cairn has a diameter of c20m, so that it strongly resembles the site in Levens Park (see 69b). Indeed, the excavator of the latter site did argue that it may originally have been a settlement, as might Knapperthaw.

ORIGINS

A further linkage between the world of the living and that of the dead/otherworld is suggested by the fact that some hut circles, such as that at Woodhead, have entrances facing south-east,[19] in the way that monuments like Swinside do.[20] It is sometimes difficult to distinguish a hut circle from a ring cairn. Indeed, it is probable that prehistoric peoples, unlike ourselves, did not differentiate between this world and the next. Certainly, the changing forms of 'domestic' and 'ceremonial' sites appear intertwined so that a change from rectangular houses to round ones is, in some areas at least, paralleled by a change from long mounds to round ones.

Again, the plans of Long Meg and Her Daughters, and Swinside, can be compared with domestic buildings, with their portals the equivalent of porches. Similarly, the two larger stones, flanking the entrance to Castlerigg, have parallels in the 'doorposts' of some hut circles and 'henges' (75a). However, the latter are also paralleled in the posts at the entrance of the Bleasdale palisade (75b), and in that context, the close set tabular stones around the Swinside portal are reminiscent of a palisade. Significantly, since 1973, when this author first suggested Swinside might have had its origins in a timber monument, like Bleasdale, a number of middle Neolithic palisaded monuments with portals or passageway entrances have been identified (75c,d). In short, it is possible to suggest that some of our stone circles may have had their origins in such sites, and the recognition of some 'timber henges' in the vicinity of Kirksanton adds to such a hypothesis.

DATES

Such a hypothesis is in line with the suggestion of Burl, that some Cumbrian circles, such as Castlerigg, are amongst the earliest in the British Isles but it is important to note that there are no dates available from the region to support this argument. It may, therefore, be significant that Bleasdale, north-east of Preston, and in an embayment of hills, just like Swinside, appears to be Bronze Age in date.[21] Consequently, it is necessary to accept that within north-west England some palisaded monuments existed alongside stone circles.

On the other hand, the timber circles at Oddendale, erected about the time when it is postulated Castlerigg might have been built (see Appendix), were not palisades, rather they were open rings, much like that inside the ditched area at Bleasdale. This suggests that the distinction drawn between those stone circles with regularly spaced uprights and those with larger numbers of irregularly placed stones[22] is one which existed amongst contemporary timber monuments; both of the later Neolithic and Bronze Age.

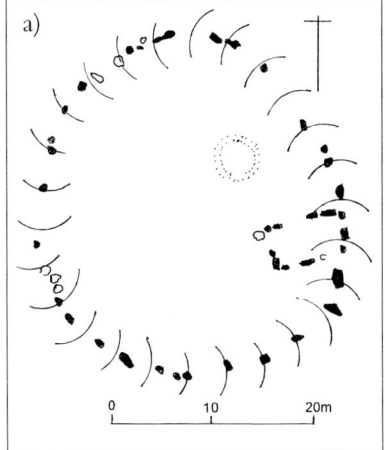 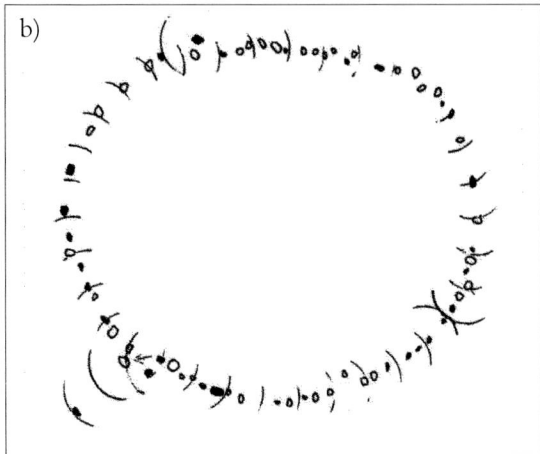

74a and b The spacing of stones at Castlerigg and Long Meg

Again, therefore, it is necessary to revisit the idea that those circles with regularly spaced stones are typologically later than sites like Swinside.

Nevertheless, it is the case that sites like Swinside and Castlerigg are distinguished by their portals, and it may be significant that Brat's Moss, which has no such arrangement, may have been remodelled.[23] Similarly, and as noted above, the urn used to date the Sunbrick circle may not have been a primary event. Indeed, it is possible to speculate that the 'fallen' stones of the outer circle there belong to an earlier monument.[24] It follows that some stone circles may have had a longer sequence of usage than the 'finds' imply. Equally, the evidence (see Appendix) suggests that some ring cairns, such as that on Sizergh Fell, were also contemporary, with the earliest stone circles and the timber ones at Oddendale.

For that reason, and given the similarity in size between many stone circles and ring cairns, the fundamental question is, why was one monument type preferred to another and did they perform different functions?[25] Clearly, the majority of ring cairns appear to be burial – at least in their final form – just as many of the stone circles less than 20m in diameter might be, but the question remains when we compare the Penrith henges with the Long Meg complex of sites. Is the difference of form one of chronology, purpose, or of different social groupings expressing their identity in different monument forms? And do the answers to these questions explain the existence of avenues rather than a large circle at Shap?

Leaving aside the latter question, Richard Bradley has argued that the difference of perimeter form between the stone circle and the henge should be seen from two perspectives – that of the people observing what was taking place inside the two monument forms and that of those participating in the central area.[26] In connection with the latter, he has suggested that the bank of a henge hid the outside world to the 'participant', whilst the stone circle allowed them to see the distant horizon, which, in a sense, was circular and echoed in the stones. Attractive as this theory is, and the bank at Mayburgh does largely (but not entirely) close off the world outside, that would not have been the case at KART

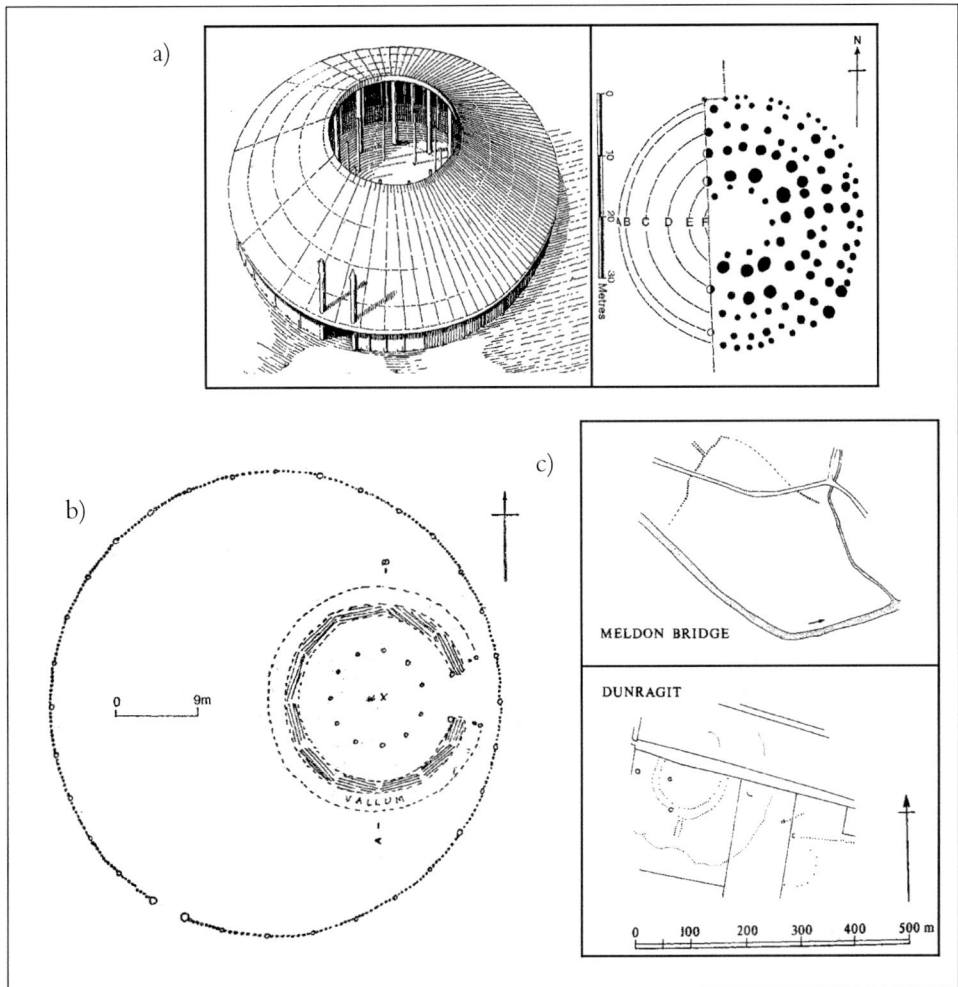

75 Timber monuments. (a and b) Durrington Walls southern circle after Wainwright and Longworth; note that in the plan the posts of the outer circle diminish in size away from the entrance and that it faces south east. (c) Bleasdale based on *Trans. Lancashire and Cheshire Antiquarian Society* 17, 254-257; note the large posts appear to be the same distance apart as those of the entrance at 3m, or 10ft, whilst the inner monument lies to the east. (d) two large dimater monuments, after Gibson

and, as already noted, there appears to be no correspondence between the height or shapes of the stones at Castlerigg and the surrounding mountains. Moreover, it is possible that the nearby forest precluded those participating in the monuments from seeing the horizon, which is now visible. Significantly, however, those standing within a clearing might well see and be enclosed by a ring of upright posts – the trunks of living trees.

Whatever the explanation for differences in perimeter form, the early date for the Sizergh Fell site implies that alongside the large monuments there were smaller ones. This is consistent with the idea of a hierachy of monuments suggested above, and it is worth restating the possibility that the differences between stone circles and between them, and other monuments, may be functional and hierachical rather than just chronological; that

Swinside and Castlerigg are distinctive, not merely because they are earlier but because they had a different role to that of Gunnerkeld or Grey Croft. Significantly, therefore, no known later sites cluster around Swinside, Castlerigg or Elva Plain as they do around Long Meg or Mayburgh/KART, as if they functioned at an earlier period at a different level to the largest monuments.

EVERY ONE IS DIFFERENT…

In the context of some of the questions posed above, it is necessary to note the observation of Thomas, partly based on his work at the timber complex at Dun Ragit on the other side of the Solway (75d), that the monuments 'can be seen as a project, or work in progress, in which contrasting or even conflicting materials and constructional devices were deployed in successive phases … in order to transform the use and meaning of location … Our problem is that we tend to isolate particular diagnostic traits from within such sequences, and use them as the basis for a classification which flattens temporal variability'.[27] Richards, working in Orkney, reached a similar conclusion; ' … perhaps we should consider a situation where instead of architecture being built to be used, its actual use lies in the building'.[28]

Here is an explanation or framework within which to consider the earthwork enclosure at Long Meg with the contrasting, but contiguous, stone circle and the apparent opposites between Mayburgh and KART. Moreover, on Moor Divock, and in the area of Oddendale and Seal Howe, it appears that every monument is different, as if successive or contemporary groups had deliberately built to assert their own identity. Again, we might see the possible remodelling of some sites, such as Grey Croft, Sunbrick, Leven's Park and Brat's Hill as part of the same process. But above all, Thomas' observation allows us to rethink the nature of the bank at Mayburgh and to envisage there, and at some cairns like White Raise and Stainton Ground, the addition of materials whenever the site was visited, so that the monument was indeed 'work in progress'.

Now, too, it is possible to suggest that the pattern of stones noted in (74) may be of two successive and different processes. Firstly, the pattern may be a construction phase involving a large community effort or 'social process' with regularly spaced stones, and then an 'infilling' by smaller groups over time, perhaps in competition rather than collaboration; a situation which would help explain Shap. If this were the case, then it is also possible to envisage particular parts of the perimeter 'belonging' to a particular group; the equivalent of the individual (ditch) sections in the earlier causewayed monuments or some henge monuments.[29] At Long Meg there is certainly one arc (*colour plate 25*) where the stone shapes are remarkably similar, but this does not necessarily mean they were erected by one particular group, rather they require us to recognize that shape, as well as colour, was a possible factor in the selection and arrangement of stones.

...YET THEY HAVE COMMON FEATURES

Not only do ring cairns and other monument forms appear to be of similar date to the stone circles, there appear to be a number of common features.[30] These include:
- A proximity to springs and tarns e.g., at Samson's Bratful, Long Meg, Gamelands, Rayseat Pike and Banniside.
- Building the site as a 'platform' or creating a level surface e.g., at Mayburgh, Swinside, Oddendale, Sunbrick, Knapperthaw, Banniside, Middleton, Casterton, all four sites on Gaythorn Plain, Mazonwath and perhaps, even, Rayseat Pike.
- The incorporation or reflection of cardinal points e.g., Castlerigg, Mayburgh, Oddendale 1, Moor Divock V and Orton Scar.
- Orientation in the direction of the rising and setting points of the midwinter and midsummer suns e.g., the entrances of Swinside, Long Meg and Hardendale Nab, the external platforms at Hackthorpe and Oddendale 2, and the concentration of burials in one quadrant at Hackthorpe and elsewhere.
- The laying out of a perfect circle regardless of topography e.g., Swinside, Moor Divock V, Orton Scar, Gaythorne Plain 3 and Casterton.

In addition, it is necessary to note that at several sites, such as Shiel Knowe, Stainton Ground, Hardendale Nab, Gaythorn Plain 1 and White Raise – monuments of very different form – there were cists which could be opened at any time. These, together with the platforms at sites like Oddendale 2, Hackthorpe and Hardendale Nab, suggest the practice of excarnation, and/or access to and the circulation of human bone after 'burial' – practices normally thought of in the context of early Neolithic monuments – continued into, or was present at a later date within the Lake District.

Such features and practices provide a context for the interpretation of the rectangle at Castlerigg and, indeed, to see one of the functions of such a stone circle as being connected with the dead. Equally, the circulation of skeletal material implies that the building of some monuments did not necessarily create a barrier between the living and the dead.[31] Nevertheless, we might note that the 'closure' phase, discussed by Bradley, occurs across a variety of monument forms, such as Rayseat pike, Old Parks, Gunnerkeld, Hackthorpe and Sizergh Fell, and perhaps in the mounds of Castlerigg, Swinside, Long Meg and KART. The implication of closure, presumably in the Bronze Age, is however, that the large circles had continued as focal points in the landscape until that time; a conclusion consistent with the idea that they operated alongside the smaller monuments.

Four final comments need to be made here:
- In a number of places, such as Stainton Ground, the sites appear to be located in straight lines, the most spectacular being that of Riddingley Top–Knipe Scar–Hardendale Nab–Oddendale 1–Seal Howe–White Hag–Gamelands.
- Although the final form of Stainton Ground and The Standing Stones was similar, the actual burial practices were very different; the latter, it would seem, did not go hand-in-hand with monument 'type', a situation consistent with the fact that multiple burials of the type encountered under a mound at Aughertree might be 'unenclosed' at some places, such as Ewanrigg, Allithwaite and Aglionby.

- The time span of usage at unenclosed sites, like Ewanrigg and Aglionby[32] might also extend to sites like Hackthorpe and Leacet Hill.
- The 'small' stone circles, such as The Standing Stones, Castlehowe and White Hag are not perfect circles, and of course Stainton Ground is subrectangular.

BEYOND THE CIRCLE

The types of site described above and in (see 72) are those with a circular perimeter, and it is necessary to emphasise that other types existed. Some of these, such as the arrangement of posts at Plasketlands, might relate to monuments recognized across the Solway, whilst others, such as single or paired standing stones, appear to relate to structures also encountered below the long cairns; as indeed do the walls below Old Parks and at Moor Divock V.

Taken together, they are a reminder that there were other foci than round monuments within the landscape, and that some of these preceded the stone circles, henges and ring cairns. Significantly, the distance between such sites, between the putative long mounds at Sewborrens and Lowther, and Lowther and Shap, is 8 and 9m, respectively, whilst that from the Copstone to Lowther is five kilometers; distances which compare with the 10 kilometres between Grey Yauds, Long Meg and Mayburgh. It would appear, therefore, that the social, exchange and settlement networks, served by the large circular monuments, had already been established in the preceding centuries, if not millennium.

All the sites need, therefore, to be considered in the context of contemporary land use, and three observations can be made. Firstly, that at a number of locations, such as Long Meg, Moor Divock, Burnmoor, Bleaberry Haws, Lacra, Birkrigg, Sizergh, Oddendale and Casterton, there is evidence of later prehistoric farming and settlement. Secondly, that on the limestone escarpment between Rayseat Pike and Shap, the distribution of late Neolithic and Bronze Age monuments appear to represent expansion into the landscape from core areas of earlier Neolithic settlement.[33] Thirdly, that many of the larger monuments, such as the Penrith henges, Long Meg, Elva Plain, Swinside and Gamelands, appear to have been located near springs. Whilst the water/spring may itself have been imbued with magical properties and regarded with awe, the occurrence of other sites, such as Rayseat Pike, Lacra, Gutterby and Banniside, adjacent to tarns and or springs,[34] suggest that water was, itself, a resource. Certainly, such places would have been natural focal points in a heavily forested landscape, and such locales are likely to have seen continuity of use from the Mesolithic onwards. This is perhaps well illustrated by the position of the Grey Croft circle; a monument overlooking the meeting place of a stream and the beach, which is an ideal location for Mesolithic settlement. The prehistoric structures visible in our landscape are not, therefore, simply monuments articulating and reflecting the beliefs and social engagement of prehistoric peoples, but monuments to prehistoric land use and land taking, the making of our own landscape.

APPENDIX

Radiocarbon dates

Site	Context	Uncal.	Cal. BC
Allithwaite	Fill of urn 1023	3570+/-50	2107-1747
	Ditto	3470+/-55	1922-1637
	Fill of urn 1049	3545+/-50	2027-1741
Ewanrigg	Beaker		3350-2980
	Collared Urn		2290-1750
Hardendale Nab	Phase 1 inhumation	3430+/-80	1940-1525
	Phase 1 Watervole	3290+/-100	1880-1400
	Phase 1 Frog/toad	4190+/-90	3030-2500
	Phase 4 charred bone	3360+/-60	1870-1520
Leacet Hill	Primary silt of ditch		1880-1730
	Cremation, context 86		1920-1755
Oddendale	Phase 1	4009+/-36	2852-2464
		4077+/-37	2869-2498
		4018+/-74	2872-2350
Plasketlands	Postholes	4940+/-90	3970-3610 or 3580-3525
		4810+/-60	3775-3750 or 3710-3500 or 3420-3380
		5090+/-60	4030-4025 or 400-3780 or 3735-3720
Rawthey Cave	Human skull	3167+/-55	1520-1395
Sizergh Fell	Secondary inhumation	2410+/-40	760-640
	On platform	4950+/-40	3790-3650

NOTES

Note: *TCWAAS* = Transactions of the Cumberland and Westmorland Antiquarian and Archaeological Society.
PSAL = Proceedings of the Society of Antiquaries of London.

CHAPTER 1: PREHISTORIC MONUMENTS AND THE LANDSCAPE OF THE TWENTY-FIRST CENTURY

1. *PSAL2*, **x**, 311.
2. *TCWAAS1*, **x**, 272.
3. Site F. in Soffe and Clare 1988.

CHAPTER 2: THE PRINCIPAL TYPES OF EVIDENCE

1. *TCWAAS3*, **III**, 208.
2. Ordnance Survey record card.
3. *TCWAAS2*, **IV**, 71-76.
4. Soffe and Clare 1988.
5. *TCWAAS3* **II**, 21-27; Beckensall 2002, 84; CCC/06/H/034, copyright Tim Gates, includes a previously unrecorded ring ditch.
6. *TCWAAS2*, **LXXII**, 37.
7. *TCWAAS2*, **LXVII**, 17.
8. Kendal Mercury 15 Aug., 1868, p5. col.1.
9. *TCWAAS3*, **III**, 23-50.
10. *TCWAAS1*, **VIII**, 330-332.
11. *TCWAAS1*, **I**, 167. The existence of a site here must be questioned.
12. Dugdale, 113.
13. *TCWAAS2*, **XIV**, 473.
14. *TCWAAS2*, **XL**, 169-206.
15. Williams and Howard-Davis, 2004.
16. *Proceedings of the Prehistoric Society* **53**, 129-186.
17. Gibson 1695, 831.
18. Philemon Holland 1610, 4.
19. Gibson 1695, 810.
20. Philemon Holland 1610, 4.
21. Pennant 1776, 256.
22. Williams and Howard-Davis 2004, 19.

23. *TCWAAS3*, **III**, 98.
24. But see Cummings 2002 for the other side of the Solway.
25. Gibson 1695, 811, for 'subterraneous trees' at Orton.
26. Pennington 1970.
27. *New Phytologist*, **62**, 53-66.
28. Rackham 1993 for this term.
29. Conolly, A. and Dahl, 1970.
30. eg. *Salix herbacea* in Halliday 1997.
31. *Journal of Biogeography* **26**, 45-54.
32. Clare 1996.
33. A view shared by a correspondent of the *Gentleman's Magazine* in 1752, as quoted in *PSAL2* **X**, 311.
34. *TCWAAS2*, **L**, 31.
35. Interim Report, Carlisle Archaeology Unit, 1993.
36. *TCWAAS3*, **III**, 23-50.
37. Hodgson 1811, 152.
38. *Archaeologia* **44**, 273-292 for Ehenside Tarn; a bronze spearhead was found in Whinfell Tarn between Kendal and Tebay and, one mile to the east a stone axe and quern were found in draining another tarn (*Antiquaries Journal* **12**, 225).
39. *Journal of Wetland Archaeology* **1**, 83-105.
40. Cummings 2002.

CHAPTER 3: NORTH AND WEST

1. Clare 1973, site 4.
2. *TCWAAS2* **XL**, 154-162.
3. Greenwell 1877, 379; sites CLXIII and CLXIV.
4. *Archaeologia* **10**, 106-108.
5. Britton and Brayley 1802, 177.
6. *TCWAAS2* **XXXVIII**, 32-41.
7. Fell and Davis 1988, 74.
8. Oswald *et al.* 2001.
9. *TCWAAS1* **VI**, 190.
10. Hutchinson 1794, **II**, 159-161. The less stylised plan in Pennant 1772 (**II**, 38) shows a fallen stone immediately outside the SW quadrant at point C, but this might simply be his depiction of the three extant stones there.
11. Stukeley 1776, **II**, 47-48.
12. *TCWAAS1* **VI**, 505.
13. Burl (2000, 119) thought at least one of these gaps was created to allow eighteenth-century farmwagons into the circle during harvesting.
14. *TCWAAS2* **XV**, 111.
15. *TCWAAS2* **XV**, 99-112; *TCWAAS3* **IV**, 1-26; see Burl 1988, 178-179 for a wider discussion.
16. *Journal of Archaeological Science* **33**, 1580-1587.
17. *TCWAAS2* **LII**, 178.
18. Burl 2000.
19. *TCWAAS3* **II**, 21-28.
20. *Proceedings of the Prehistoric Society* **58**, 325-354.
21. *TCWAAS1*, **IX**, 436 and *TCWAAS2*, **IV**, 250 for decorated stones; *TCWAAS2*, **LVI**, 1-6 for the urns.
22. *TCWAAS3* **V**, 1-10 for new material and other references.
23. Thom 1967 for references.
24. Ordnance Survey Record Card.
25. *TCWAAS2*, **LVIII**, 4.

26. see plate 4 in Clare 1988
27. *TCWAAS1*, **v**, 55-56; Burl (2000, 108) does not refer to the idea of an outer circle but accepts the former existence of the rectangle, stating that 'The two rings' (this one and Castlerigg) 'are an astonishing likeness in situation and architecture'.
28. Pennington 1970.
29. *TCWAAS2*, **LVII**, 1-8.
30. Burl 2000, 50-52 for discussion. In particular, he points out that numerous sight lines can be constructed for a circle like this one.
31. *TCWAAS2*, **LXI**, 1-6.
32. Hutchinson 1794, **I**, 553.
33. *Journal of Wetland Archaeology*, I, (2001) 83-105.
34. The farm of Hall Foss is located due east of Barfield Tarn at SD117870.
35. Whellan 1847, 499.
36. Hutchinson 1794, **I**, 529.
37. The large boulder A appears to be that referred to by Waterhouse (1985) as belonging to the circle. Like the OS (p. 10 here), this author thinks it natural and uncovered by quarrying.
38. Whellan 1847, 499.
39. *TCWAAS2*, **XLVIII**, 1-22.
40. Hutchinson 1794, **I**, 529.
41. *TCWAAS2*, **II**, 53-76.
42. See Ruggles 1999, 131-132 for discussion of imprecision in alignments with respect to Cumbrian sites …
43. *TCWAAS2*, **LXXII**, 324-325 for the original reference and possible explanation.
44. Housman 1821, 47-50.
45. *TCWAAS2*, **XXIX**, 257-8.
46. Housman 1821, 47-50.
47. *TCWAAS2*, **II**, 64-74.
48. *TCWAAS2*, **LXXII**, 325.

CHAPTER 4: THE LONG MEG AREA

1. Soffe and Clare 1988.
2. For Dugdale illustration, Bodleian Library R.Top.505 (1), 115; Burl 1988, 177-178 for the idea that they were simply clearance cairns and 'in a waste corner of the field'.
3. Stukeley 1776, **II**, 47.
4. *PSAL2*, **x**, 312.
5. Stukeley 1776, **II**, 47
6. *Journal of Archaeological Sciences* **33**, 1580-1587 for this and earlier references.
7. Beckensall 2002, 59-70.
8. Clare 1973; Burl 2000.
9. Soffe and Clare 1988.
10. Stukeley 1776, **II**, 47.
11. For gypsum on the Thornborough banks *Yorkshire Archaeological Journal*, **38**, 441-442.
12. *TCWAAS1*, **x**, 272. Stukeley was the first to note the different geologies and that some made of 'square crystallisations' were 'the same sort as those at Shap'. Two stones are of Shap granite and two of another granite (Vin Davis pers. comm). These would sparkle but there are a number of other distinctive stones (*16b*)
13. *PSAL2*, **3**, 258 but see *TCWAAS1*, **VI**, 492 and Thompson **1**, 11, for a sketch purported to be of the urn.
14. *TCWAAS2*, **II**, 381-382.
15. Ferguson writing of Old Parks (*PSAL2*, **xv**, 259-261) says the carvings extended into the ground and so must have been made first.
16. *PSAL2*, **x**, 313.

17. Gale and Evelyn, 115.
18. *TCWAAS2*, I, 295-299; includes earlier references.
19. Beckensall 2002, 84.
20. *TCWAAS1*, VIII, 389-394.
21. *TCWAAS2*, IV, 351.
22. *TCWAAS2*, XXXV, 77-79; L, **30-42;** and LII, 1-8.
23. See Appendix A of Hodgson's 1950 report.
24. Graham in *TCWAAS2*, VII, 67 follows Hutchinson in saying the outlier was to the north-west and not as Waterhouse says, to the north-east.
25. Hutchinson 1794, I, 175.
26. *TCWAAS2*, XXXV, 78.

CHAPTER 5: THE PENRITH AREA

1. Topping 1992.
2. Pennant 1776, 276.
3. Housman 1821, 68-69.
4. *TCWAAS1*, VI, 451.
5. *Proceedings of the Royal Irish Academy* **91C**, 254-84.
6. Note 'Holme' meant island.
7. Topping 1992, Fig. 4.
8. *TCWAAS3*, III, 210.
9. eg Bradley 1998, 116-131.
10. Stukeley 1776, II, 43.
11. *TCWAAS2*, XL,188.
12. Collingwood (*TCWAAS2*, XXXVIII) for the latter term; compare the low dome in the centre of Mayburgh.
13. Bersu (*TCWAAS2*, XL) for the date of re-cutting of KART's ditch and the bank having a flat top.
14. Topping 1992, Fig.6.
15. Stukeley 1776, II, 43.
16. *TCWAAS2*, XL, 202-205.
17. Topping 1992, 260.
18. Stukeley 1776, II, 44.
19. Pennant 1776, 277; Hutchinson 1794, I, 312
20. This is consistent with it being in Cumberland but Waterhouse follows Burl in calling the site Brougham, a parish south of the river and in Westmorland.
21. *TCWAAS1*, VI, 447.
22. Thompson **2**, 164.
23. *TCWAAS2*, LXXII, 37.
24. *PSAL2*, VI, 270.
25. *TCWAAS1*, V, 91.
26. Stukeley 1766, II, 44.
27. Could this be Leacet Hill?
28. *TCWAAS2*, LXXIX, 1-4.
29. *TCWAAS1*, V, 79-97.
30. RCHM(E) 1936, xxx.
31. The author has deposited a contour plan with the Lowther Estate Office.
32. *PSAL2*, VIII, 389-391; *TCWAAS1*, V, 76-78.
33. *TCWAAS3*, VI, 27-44.
34. Clarke 1789, 50.
35. *PSAL1,* **3**, 225.
36. There is a thumb nail sketch in *TCWAAS1*, III, 242; for the reliability of Williams see Dymond in *TCWAAS1*, V, 55-56.

37. Beckensall 2002,128-133; *TCWAAS3*, **IV**, 245-247 for Penrith churchyard.
38. *TCWAAS1*, **VI**, 110-118.
39. Clarke 1789, 22.

CHAPTER 6: MOOR DIVOCK AND SWARTHBECK GILL

1. *TCWAAS3*, **VI**, 1-16.
2. Greenwell 1870, 24; for a sketch plan see *TCWAAS1*, **VIII**, 323.
3. It appears to be first recorded as 'Helton Copstone' on Hodgson's map of Westmorland in 1828.
4. *TCWAAS1*, **VIII**, 330-332.
5. RCHM(E) 1936, 26.
6. Beckensall 2002, 101-104.
7. *TCWAAS1*, **I**, 24.
8. *TCWAAS1*, **VIII**, 332; RCHM(E) 1936, 28; Waterhouse 1985.
9. *TCWAAS1*, **VI**, 180.
10. *TCWAAS1*, **I**, 24; *TCWAAS1*, **VI**, 180-181.
11. Lynch 1998; see also Long Meg and Hardendale Nab here.
12. RCHM(E) 1936, 28.
13. RCHM(E) 1936, 40.

CHAPTER 7: SHAP AND THE EASTERN LAKE DISTRICT

1. *TCWAAS2*, **LXXVIII**, 1-15 for a more detailed map by the author.
2. Beckensall 2003, 107-111.
3. Stukeley 1776, **II**, 42.
4. *TCWAAS1*, **XV**, 27-34.
5. Burl 1993, 100-101.
6. Barnatt 1989, 4.
7. Williams and Howard Davis 2004.
8. *Archaeological Journal* **XVIII**, 33.
9. Noble 1901, 16.
10. *TCWAAS2*, **VII**, 211-214.
11. *TCWAAS1*, **VI**, 176-182.
12. *TCWAAS2*, **VII**, 213.
13. Jeffrey's map of Westmorland 1770.
14. *TCWAAS2*, **LXXXIV**, 31.
15. *TCWAAS2*, **LXXXVI**, 248-250.
16. *TCWAAS1*, **VI**, 177-178.
17. *TCWAAS2*, **LXXXIV**, 31-40 for the excavations and references to earlier work.
18. *TCWAAS1*, **IV**, 537-540; *TCWAAS1*, **VI**, 176-178.
19. Bland, 22.
20. Bland, 8.
21. Bland, 15.
22. *TCWAAS2*, **XXXV**, 219-221.
23. RCHM(E) 1936, 90.
24. *Archaeological Journal* **XVIII**, 36.
25. Beckensall 2002, 105-106.
26. *TCWAAS2*, **LXXXIV**, 19-20.
27. Ferguson 1894, 10 for a similar view; Simpson in *PSAL2* **III**, 258 says there were 4 rivet holes.
28. *TCWAAS1*, **VI**, 178-179.
29. Turnbull and Walsh 1997.
30. Note that the position of the former palisade of the Street House Wossit in Cleveland received similar treatment. *Proceedings of the Prehistoric Society*, **54**, 173-202.

31. Greenwell 1877, CLXXXII.
32. *PSAL2*, VII, 214.

CHAPTER 8: THE UPPER VALLEYS OF THE EDEN AND LUNE

1. Bland, 15 for both sites.
2. Greenwell 1877, 398.
3. Bland, 8.
4. Bland, 15.
5. Oswald *et al.* 2001.
6. Hodgson 1811, 147.
7. Bland, 15.
8. *TCWAAS2*, XXXIII, 220.
9. See *TCWAAS2*, LXXIX, 144 and Gaythorn Plain 2 here.
10. *Journal of Biogeography* **26**, 45-54.
11. *Archaeological Journal.* XXVII, 200-203.
12. *TCWAAS1*, VI, 183-185.
13. Cherry and Cherry 1987, 34-36.
14. Greenwell 1877, 510-513.
15. Clare *submitted*; for the pollen diagram see Webster 1969.
16. Kinnes 1979.
17. Recent work (Clare, O'Regan and Wilkinson submitted) recovered small fragments of human material from the upper part of the cairn but their relationship to Greenwell's bodies is unclear.
18. Greenwell 1877, 394-396 and 389-390.
19. Sites 77 and 78 of Oxford Archaeology North.
20. Greenwell 1877, 382.
21. *TCWAAS* 1971, 2.
22. RCHM(E) 1936, 178-179.
23. *Archaeologia* **3**, 273.
24. Greenwell 1877, 385.
25. Machell, I, 318.
26. Gibson 1695, 815.

CHAPTER 9: FURNESS AND SOUTH LAKELAND

1. Hodgson 1814, 223.
2. *TCWAAS2*, X, 342-353.
3. *TCWAAS1*, IX, 497-504.
4. For the settlement above Knapperthaw see Plate 5 in Clare 1988.
5. Barber 1894, 36.
6. *Archaeologia* **31**, 450-451.
7. *TCWAAS2*, LXIII, 1-30.
8. *TCWAAS2*, LVIII, 185-6.
9. *TCWAAS2*, XII, 262-274 and XXII, 346-352.
10. *TCWAAS2*, XIV, 468-472.
11. *TCWAAS2*, XIV, 472-479.
12. *TCWAAS2*, XXVII, 100-109.
13. *TCWAAS2*, I, 135.
14. *TCWAAS2*, XXXIV, 92.
15. Hodgson's map of Westmorland, 1828.
16. *Archaeology North* **20**, Summer 2002, 13-15.
17. *TCWAAS2*, IV, 76-79.

18. Information from Jamie Lund of the National Trust.
19. Nicholson and Burn, I, 208.
20. *Scottish Archaeological Forum,* **4**, 52-61; Clare 1973; *TCWAAS2*, XCVI, 13-26.
21. *Proceedings of the Prehistoric Society* **53**, 129-186.
22. *TCWAAS2*, XCVI, 19, for discussion of possible alternatives
23. At the time of excavation it was thought there were three.
24. *TCWAAS2*, C, 25-32.
25. Hodgson 1811, 180.
26 *Archaeology North* **14**, 11-20.
27. It has been suggested it might be the 'Druid's circle' reported to have been dug in 1828 (*TCWAAS2*, LIII, 3). This is unlikely as it can hardly be described as being on the road from Lancaster to Richmond.

CHAPTER 10: THINKING ABOUT THE EVIDENCE

1. *Proceedings of the Prehistoric Society* **67**, 1-19 for a discussion of regional variations and research strategies.
2. Such awareness need not necessarily have involved direct contact. See Clare Forthcoming 155-157.
3. This type of monument did not appear in the Monument Protection Progamme list of site types.
4. For Plasketlands *TCWAAS2*, XCIII, 1-18. Although considered to be part of the ditched enclosure the posts might be better seen as a 'pit-defined enclosure' of the kind described by Barclay (1997).
5. Bradley 1998, 136 for discussion of the idea that some monuments need to be thought of not as one type but as several successive ones.
6. This matrix is essentially an extension of that used to describe 'fancy barrows' in the material issued by the Monument Protection Programme. Note the matrix could be extended to include details of burial practice and as such is a simple form of multivariate analysis.
7. Stukeley; unpublished Ms. Top. Gen.b. 53 in the Bodleian Library.
8. Bradley 1998, chapter 9.
9. eg Burl 1988, 183-184.
10. Clare Forthcoming.
11. For those in the vicinity of Castlerigg see *The Archaeological Journal*, **159**, 2002, 242-248.
12. eg. Burl 1988, 189; Bradley 1998, 121.
13. Burl 2000, 101 for the regular spacing of sites.
14. *TCWAAS2*, LXXVIII, 9-15 for re-erection of the Goggleby stone; Clare 1981, 16 for draught animals and sheer legs.
15. This suggests the idea that diameters of 27m+ are an 'early' trait (Burl 2000, 109) needs to be modified.
16. Nicholson and Burn 1777, II, 323.
17. Thom 1967 for a general overview and reference to earlier work. He suggested that the spacing of stones was so similar that a standard 'rod' of Megalithic Yards must have been used. However the length of the megalithic yard is very similar to half the length between an adult's outstretched arms so that something like a standard unit would be created if several individuals had linked hands. By chance, many years ago this author had just enough students at Bleasdale for us to stand on the markers of the inner circle and we found that our linked arms were the distances between the former posts.
18. Burl 1988, 186.
19. Bradley 1998 for a summary of some evidence for doors facing SE.
20. Woodhead, Bewcastle, (*TCWAAS2*, XL, 162-166) was considered by the excavator to be a hut containing a V-perforated jet button and jet pulley ring but Ritchie and MacLaren (*Scottish Archaeological Forum* 1972, 7) suggested it may have been a ring cairn.

21. But see Clare 1973, Appendix C for the case that Bleasdale was multiperiod and the urns belong to the last phase of 'closure'. Note the regular spacing of large posts in the Bleasdale palisade and that the entrance is about 3m or 10ft wide, as at Castlerigg.
22. eg Barnatt 1989.
23. Burl (2000, 109) does place Brat's Moss later than some of the other large diameter sites.
24. Compare the suggestion made in this book that the central mound might have been added at Gunnerkeld and see Bradley 1998, Chapter 9 for discussion of similar sequences elsewhere.
25. *Proceedings of the Prehistoric Society* **25**, 153-172, for the idea that some ring cairns were for ceremonial, albeit mortuary ritual, rather than burial; a view compatible with the similar size of such monuments to 'stone circles' (**73**) here.
26. Bradley 1998, 124-6.
27. Thomas 2001, 141. Compare too the view of Bradley (1998, 316) that the re-modelling of monuments means that an individual site 'might have to be characterized not as one "type" of monument, but as successive ones'.
28. Richards 2004, 105.
29. Richards 2004, 103-4 for a brief discussion with references.
30. This is consistent with, and perhaps explains why, amongst the sites analysed by Burl (2000, 109) in his discussion of the date of stone circles, there are a number of ring cairns.
31. Bradley 1998, 134, for the idea that the monuments separated the living from the dead.
32. At Aglionby there is a rim sherd of Peterborough Ware, an encrusted urn, fragments of what might be a beaker and food vessel together with a collared urn. (Clare 1973, Fig.14).
33. Fig. 5 in Clare Forthcoming.
34. Whellan 1847, 449 for a spa at Gutterby.

BIBLIOGRAPHY

Note: *TCWAAS* = Transactions of the Cumberland and Westmorland Antiquarian and Archaeological Society.

Barber, H., 1894, *Furness and Cartmel Notes*. (Ulverston and London).
Barclay, G.J., 1997, The Neolithic, in Edwards, K.J. and Ralston, I.B.M (eds), *Scotland: Environment and archaeology, 8000 BC-AD 1000*. (Chichester: Wiley and Sons) 127-150.
Barnatt, J., 1989, *Stone Circles of Britain*. British Archaeological Reports British Series 215. (Oxford).
Beckensall, S., 2002, *Prehistoric Rock Art in Cumbria*. (Stroud: Tempus).
Bland, J.S., *c*.1860, *The Vale of Lyvennett*. Parker, F.H.M. (ed.), 1910. (Kendal: Titus Wilson).
Bradley, R., 1998, *The Significance of Monuments*. (Routledge).
Britton, J. and Brayley, E.W., 1802, Cumberland, in *The Beauties of England and Wales* (vol. III). (London).
Burl, A., 1988, Without sharp north….Alexander Thom and the great stone circles of Cumbria, in Ruggles, C.L.N. (ed.) *Records in stone. Papers in Memory of Alexander Thom.*. (Cambridge) 175-205.
Burl, A., 1993, *From Carnac to Callanish: the prehistoric stone rows and avenues of Britain*. (Newhaven and London).
Burl, A., 2000, *The Stone Circles of Britain, Ireland and Brittany*. (Yale University Press).
Cherry, J. and Cherry, P.J., 1987, *Prehistoric habitation sites on the limestone uplands of eastern Cumbria*. TCWAAS Research Series, Vol II. (Kendal: Titus Wilson).
Clare 1973, *Aspects of the stone circles and kindred monuments of North West England*. Unpublished thesis, University of Liverpool.
Clare, T., 1981, *Archaeological sites of the Lake District*. (Ashbourne: Moorland Publishing Co.).
Clare, T., 1988, The Prehistoric Landscape, in Rollinson, W., *The Lake District; landscape Heritage*. (David and Charles) 9-27.
Clare, T., 1996, Landholding and fashion as explanations for the arboreal population: two case studies in Cumbria, in Simpson, I.A. and Dennis, P., *The Spatial Dynamics of Biodiversity*, 123-130. UK region of the International association for Landscape Ecology 1996.
Clare, T., forthcoming, The view from Friar Cote, aborigines and the phenomenology of the Lake District axe production sites.
Clare, T., submitted, No man's land revisited: some patterns in the Neolithic of Cumbria.
Clarke, J., 1789, *A survey of the lakes of Cumberland, Westmorland and Lancashire*. 2nd ed. (London).
Conolly, A.P. and Dahl, E., 1970, Maximum summer temperature in relation to the modern and quaternary distributions of certain arctic-montane species in the British Isles, in Walker, D. and West, R.G., *Studies in the vegetational history of the British Isles*. (Cambridge University Press) 159-223.
Cummins, V., 2002, Between Mountains and Sea: a Reconsideration of the Neolithic Monuments of South-west Scotland, *Proceedings of the Prehistoric Society* 68, 125-146.
Dugdale; version of John Aubrey's *Monumenta Britannica* in the Bodleian Library R.Top.505
Fell, C.I. and Davis, R.V., 1988, The petrological identification of stone implements from Cumbria in Clough, T.H. McK., and Cummins, W.A., (eds) *Stone Axe Studies Volume 2*. (CBA Research Report 67) 71-77.
Ferguson, R., 1894, *History of Westmorland*. (London).

Gale, T. and Evelyn, J., version of John Aubrey's *Monumenta Britannica* illustrated sometime between 1665 and 1693.

Gibson, A., 1998, Hindwell and the Neolithic Palisaded Sites of Britain and Ireland. In Gibson, A. and Simpson, D. (eds), *Prehistoric Ritual and Religion*. (Sutton) 68-79.

Gibson, E., 1695, *Camden's Britannia*, newly translated by E. Gibson.

Greenwell, W., 1877, *British Barrows*.

Halliday, G., 1997, *A Flora of Cumbria*. (University of Lancaster).

Hodgson, (Rev), 1811, *A topographical and historical description of the County of Westmorland*. (London).

Housman, J., 1821, *A descriptive tour and guide to the lakes, mountains and other curiosities in Cumberland, Westmorland etc.* (Carlisle).

Hutchinson, W., 1794, *The History of the County of Cumberland*. (Carlisle).

Kinnes, I., 1979, *Round barrows and Ring-ditches in the British Neolithic*. (London: British Museum Occasional Paper 7).

Lynch, F., 1998, Colour in Prehistoric Architecture, in Gibson, A. and Simpson, D. (eds) *Prehistoric Ritual and Religion*. (Sutton) 62-67.

Machell, T., *c.*1690, manuscript history of Westmorland. Six volumes in the Carlisle Record Office courtesy of the Dean and Chapter, Carlisle Cathedral.

Noble, M.F., 1901, *A history of Bampton*. (Kendal: Titus Wilson).

Nicholson, J. and Burn, R., 1777, *History and antiquities of Westmorland and Cumberland*. (London).

Oswald, A., Dyer, C. and Barber, M., 2001, *The creation of monument,, Neolithic causewayed enclosures in the British Isles*. (English Heritage).

Pennant, T., 1772, *A tour in Scotland and voyage to the Hebrides*. (Warrington).

Pennant, T., 1776, *Tours in Scotland* (3rd ed.). (Warrington).

Pennington, W., 1970, Vegetation history in the north-west of England: a regional synthesis, in Walker, D. and West, R.G. (eds), *Studies in the Vegetational History of the British Isles*. (London: Cambridge University Press).

Philemon Holland, 1610, translation of William Camden's *Britain, or, a chronological description of.... England, Scotland and Ireland*.

Rackham, O., 1993 (and various eds), *The History of the Countryside*. (Dent).

Richards, C., 2004, A Choreography of Construction: Monuments, Mobilization and Social Organization in Neolithic Orkney. In Cherr, J. Scarre, C. and Shennan, S., *Explaining social change*. (Cambridge, McDonald Institute) 103-113.

RCHM(E), 1936, *Westmorland*. (HMSO).

Ruggles, C., 1999, *Astronomy in Prehistoric Britain and Ireland*. (Yale University Press).

Soffe, G. and Clare, T., 1988, New evidence of ritual monuments at Long Meg and Her Daughters, Cumbria, *Antiquity* **62**, 552-557.

Stukeley, W., 1776, *Iter Curiosum*. (London).

Thom, A., 1967, *Megalithic sites in Britain*. (Oxford: Oxford University Press).

Thomas, J., 2001, Neolithic enclosures: reflections on excavation in Wales and Scotland, in Darvill, T. & Thomas, J. (eds), Neolithic Enclosures in Atlantic Northwest Europe, 123-43. (Oxford: Oxbow).

Thompson, J., undated Mss, *Old Penrith and environs*.

Topping, P., 1992, The Penrith henges: a survey by the Royal Commission on the Historical Monuments of England, *Proceedings of the Prehistoric Society* **58**, 249-264.

Turnbull, P. and Walsh, D., 1977, A Prehistoric ritual sequence at Oddendale, near Shap, *TCWAAS*2, **XCVII**, 11-44.

Waterhouse, J., 1985, *The Stone Circles of Cumbria*. (Phillimore).

Webster, R.A., 1969, *The Romano-British Settlements of Westmorland*. Unpublished Ph.D. thesis, University of Reading.

Whellan, W., 1847, *History, gazetteer and directory of Cumberland*.

Wainwright, G.J. and Longworth, I.H., 1971, *Durrington Walls: Excavations 1966-1968*. Reports of the Research Committee of the Society of Antiquaries of London No. XXIX. (Dorking: the Society of Antiquaries).

Williams, J.H. and Howard-Davis, C., 2004, Excavations on a Bronze Age Cairn at Hardendale Nab, Shap, Cumbria, *Archaeological Journal* **161**, 11-53.

INDEX

Aglionby 131, 143
alignments/orientation 10, 11, 20, 24, 28, 29, 32, 33, 34, 39, 41, 42, 43, 50, 52, 58, 66, 72, 76, 79, 89, 94, 98, 100, 103, 110, 111, 115,117, 118, 120, 121, 123, 124, 129, 131, 140, 143
Annaside 10, 37, 137
Appleby Golf Course 12, 112
artefact
    boar's tusk 109, 124
    bone 110, 117-18, 124
    bronze 57, 93, 102, 123, 124
    jet/lignite 35, 52, 53, 96, 110
    stone disc 117, 123
Ash Fell 111
Ash House *42-3*, 137
Aughertree Fell 16, 26, 143, *colour plate 8*
Avebui-y 80, 132
avenues 16, 25, 39, 65, 72, 75, 80-3, 101, 103, 133, 140
axe
    bronze 13, 57, 135
    stone 13, 22, 25, 28, 31, 35, 58, 90, 93, 105, 121-2, 124, 125, 127, 135
    trade in 135

Bampton Common 86, *colour plate 19*
Bank Moor 21, 97, 102
Banniside *116-17*, 132, 137, 143, 144
Barfield Tarn 21
Baron's Pike 25
beads 50, 52, 53
Bewcastle Fells 7, 24
Birkrigg 19, *122-4*, 137 (see Sunbrick circle)
Blakeley Raise 32
Bleaberry Haws *117-18*, 133, 137, 144
Bleasdale 139, *141*, 142

blockfield/felsenmere 80, 94, 118 (see boulders)
bloomery 9, 43
boar's tusk 109, 124
bonepin 66, 109, 110
Borwick 17, 128
boulder/erratic 10, 25, 37, 42, 49, 54, 63, 66, 69, 72, 75, 77, 82, 90, 94, 96, 98, 103, 115, 116, 122, 129
Branthwaite 31
Brats Moss (see Burnmoor)
Broadfield 25, 137
Broomrigg 10, 22, *53-4*, 92, 133, 137-8
Brough Fair Hill 114
Brougham *12-13*, *64-5*, 69, 132
Burnmoor *32-4*, 133, 135, 137, 138, 140, 142, 144

cairnfield 32-4, 67, 69, 77, 85-6, 117-18, 126, 128
cardinal points 38-9, 58, 65, 67, 74, 94, 144
Cardurnock Pike 25
Carrock Fell 25-26, 79, *colour plate 3*
Casterton *130-1*, 138-9, 143-4
Castlehowe Scar 22, 85, *91-2*, 134, 136, 138, 144
Castlerigg 7, 19, 21-2, *26-29*, 30, 33-4, 41, 135-43
causewayed enclosure 25, 26, 100, 142
caves 7, 8, 11, 97, 103, 122, 130, 135
chance finds 11, 13, 16, 64, 65
cist(s) 13, 20, 24-5, 30-1, 48-9, 50, 53, 64-7, 69-70, 75-8, 84-85, 100, 102, 105, 110-11, 118, 120, 124-6
clava cairns 40
clearance cairn 75, 90, 92

Clifton 64, 65-6, *colour plate 14*
colour 29, 41, 48, 50, 76, 142, *colour plate 4* (see also white)
Colton 10, *colour plate 6*
Coniston Water 9, *colour plate 5*
construction/layout 8, 34, 51, 58, 60, 83, 118, 133, 136-9, 142-4
continuity 7-8, 23, 130, 144, 145 (see dating, sequences)
Copt Howe 115, *colour plate 22*
Crevices (see caves)
cropmarks 8, 11-13, 30, 36-7, 67
crossridge dyke 30
cup and ring (see decorated stone)
cursus 11, 12

Dale Moor 95, 96
Dalston 136
dating 11, 18-20, 34, 139-42, 145 (see sequences)
Dean 31
decorated stone 11, 28, 30-1, 36, 41, 43-4, 48-51, 53, 69-70, 80, 93, 115, 118
diameters, significance of *135-7*
distribution of sites 21-2, 132 (see survival and spacing)
doing/participation, importance of 115, 120, 142
druids/druidical name 19-20, 39, 67, 72, 130
Dunmail Raise 115
Dunragit *141*, 142
Durrington Walls 28, *141*

Eamont Bridge 56, 62-63
Eastern Yorkshire 107-8, 133
Egremont Common 32, 138
Ehenside Tarn 22
Elva Plain *29-30*, 43, 138, 144
evolving monuments 134, 142-3
Ewanrigg 30, 129, 143, 145 (see Maryport)

fauna 22, 32, 85, 88, 93, 104, 105, 107, 109
fieldsystem 12, 26, 90, 96, 131
flints/flint artefact 25, 36, 93, 95, 105, 109, 110, 117
folklore/tradition 8, 15, 17-18, 122, 130
Fourstones (see Bampton Common)
Furness 116-24, 135

Gamelands 64, 97, 98, 100, *105-7*, 128, 138, 143, 144
Garlands 13

Gaythorne Nail 105
Gaythorne Plain *102-5*, 143
geology 48, 50, 61, 75, 83, 94, 96, 100, 105
Goggleby Stone 7, 81, 83, 136, *colour plate 1* (see Shap)
Grasmere 116
Grayson Lands 28, 29, *50-1*, 138
Great Mell Fell 28-9
Green How (see Aughertree Fell)
Gretigate 36
Grey Croft 22, *34-6*, 133, 136, 138, 142, 144
Grey Yauds 22, *54-5*, 138, 144, *colour plate 12*
Gunnerkeld 7, *88-89*, 90, 133, 136, 138, 142, 143
Gutterby 22, *37*, 138, 144
gypsum 47

Hackthorpe *66-7*, 133, 134, 138, 143, 144
Hall Foss 37, 138
Harberwain Plantation 93
Harberwain Rigg 21, 85, 91, *92-3*, 94, 97, 98, 133, 136, 138
Hardendale Fell 82, *83-4*, 86, 94, 138
Hardendale Nab 17, 20, 21, 83, *84-5*, 91, 94, 103, 133, 143, 145
Harkeld (see Castiehowe Scar)
Heivellyn 21
henge/hengiform 14-15, 20, 37, 48, 57-62, 83, 111-12, 131, 133, 134, 136, 139, 142, 144
Hesket Newmarket 19
Heughscar Hill 77
hierachy 135, 141, 143
High Crosby 22
High Raise 86, 115
High Street 70, 84
Hird Wood *124-5*, 138
How Hill 10, 13
Howe Robin 100
Howenook Pike 96, 97, 98
hut circles 82, 119, 128-9, 131, 139

interpretation, general problems of 8-17, 19-20, 22, 132-3, 139
interpretation, weathering 115, 117
Irish monuments 56, 58
Iron Hill (see Harberwain Rigg)

Kendal *125-6*
Keverigg 90
King Arthur's Round Table 8, *14-15*, 17, 22, 56, *59-61*, 85, 132, 138, 140, 142, 143
Kirkby Ireleth 41, *120-1*, 138
Kirkby Moor (see Kirkby Ireleth)

Kirksanton *36-7*, 38, 133, 135, 139, *colour plate 9*
Kirkstones 37
Kitchenhill 63-64, 136, *colour plate 13*
Knapperthaw *118-19*, 138, 139, 143
Knipe Scar 85, *86-7*, 88, 143

Lacra *38-9*, 137, 138, 144
Lamb Crag 25
Lamplugh 31
Landscape 7, 10, 12, 23, 34, 36, 39, 86, 97, 103, 105, 115, 127, 135, 143, 144
Langdales 11, 13, 115, 136
Le Whales 32
Leacet Hill 67, 68, 90, 137, 145, *colour plate 16*
Leafy Hill 25
Legend (see folklore)
Levens 20
Levens Park 14, *127-30*, 133, 137, 139, 142
limestone escarpment 21, 84, 97, 108-10, 111, 144
Linglow 98
Little Asby Common *110-11*, 138
Little Kinmond 110
Little Meg (see Maughanby)
Little Mell Fell 29
Little Round Table 14-15, 56
Long Meg 7, 8, 11, 12, 21, 28, 30, 41, *44-8*, 50, 58, 83, 90, 107, 114-15, 133, 135-9, 140, 142, 144, *colour plate 25*
long mound 19, 24, 51-2, 63, 65-6, 80, 82, 91, 98, 107-9, 121, 132, 144
Longscar Pike 91, 94, 96-8, *colour plate 20*
Lord's Table *111-12*
Low Longrigg (see Burnmoor)
Low Raise 86, 115
Lowther 65, 66, 71, 91, 144, *colour plate 15*

Macehead 109
Maryport 30, 144 (see Ewanrigg)
Maughanby *48-50*, 137, *colour plate 11*
Mayburgh 7, *14-15*, 16, *56-8*, 59, 60, 61, 62, 63, 65, 83, 86, 114, 135, 138, 140, 142, 143, 144
Mazonwath 16, 21, 108-10, 143
measurement, prehistoric 32, 60, 61, 136-9, 141, 142
megalithic tomb/chamber 10, 51, 65, 72, 83, 121
megalithic yard (see measurement)
Meldon Bridge 141
Middleton Hall 12, *129*, 131, 143
Moor Divock 16, 19, 25, *71-8*, 83, 94, 133, 138, 142, 143, 144
mortuary enclosure 12

Mossthorn (see Newton Reigny)
Motherby, Stone Carr *68-9*, 138, *colour plate 17*

natural mounds 10-11, 18, 25
Newton Reigny 63, *64*, 144
numbers, preferred 137-8

Oddendale 10, 21, 37, 88-9, 92, *93-6*, 133, 136, 138-9, 142-5
Old Parks 11, *50-3*, 143-4
Origins 139-41
Ormstead Hill *62-3*
Orton Scar 98, *99-100*, 143
oval mound (see long mound)

paleo-environmental 20-23, 34, 36-37, 50, 71, 85, 86, 89, 97, 102, 120, 145
Penhurrock *100-1*, 102, 133, 138
Penrith henges 14-15, 56, 65-6, 69-70, 140, 144 (see also Mayburgh, King Arthur's Round Table, Little Round Table)
perimeter form 34, 40, 42, 59, 88, 133-4, 137-8,139, 140, 144
pit alignment 12, 67
place names 18
Plasketlands 133, 144-5
portals 14-15, 28, 40-1, 46, 57, 58, 60, 88, 129, 132, 138, 137-41
pot
    accessory vessel 52-3
    beaker 10, 24, 25, 30, 52, 54, 63-4, 66, 75, 127, 129
    collared urn 10, 13, 20, 28, 30, 37-9, 50, 53, 65, 67, 74-5, 84-5, 104, 116, 123
    food vessel 24, 30, 64, 67, 72, 95
    grooved ware 93
    other 22, 26, 31, 48-9, 52, 63, 66, 70, 72, 96, 104, 105, 117, 121, 123
    Peterborough ware 13, 64
Potter Fell 125, 136, 138
purpose/function 134-135, 140, 142, 143

Rafland Forest 84 (see White RaiseRF)
Raisbeck 14, 16
Raise Howe 94, 97, 98, 102
Rasett Hill 111, *colour plate 21*
Rawthey Bridge 130
Rawthey Cave 145
Rayseat Pike 66, 105, *107-8*, 109, 133, 134, 143, 144
Redhills 70, *colour plate 2*
regional variation 132

Index

Riddingley Top 72, 78, 143
ring bank 71, 82, 86-7, 119, 128, 133 (see also ring cairn)
ring ditch(es) 12, 13, 30, 37, 41, 51, 64, 112, 132, 139
Ringingstone (see Ringlen)
Ringlen 32
Robin Hood's Grave 101

Samson's Bratful 32
Sandford 13, 16, 20, 113-14, 138
Seal Howe 94, 95, 96, 98, 142-3
sequences 17, 34, 47, 49, 51, 53, 75, 84-5, 95, 117, 123, 129-30, 133, 142
settlement(s) 7, 12, 26, 30, 37, 38, 67, 85, 86, 119, 123, 125, 127-8, 131, 139, 144
Sewborrens (see Newton Reigny)
Shap 7, 9, 10, 19, 20, 80-3, 85, 88, 136, 140, 142, 144
Shap Moor 87
Shapbeck 13, 87, 88, 137, 138
Shiel Knowe 24, 143
Sizergh Fell 10, 100, 127, 133, 135, 140, 141, 143, 144, 145
Skelmore Heads 121-2, 135, *colour plate 24*
Skirsgill 62-3, 70, *colour plate 2*
Solden Hill 25
Southern Scotland 23, 132, 142, 144
spacing of sites 135, 144
spring 45-7, 58-9, 78-9, 80, 98, 107, 144
Stainton Ground 119-20, 142-4, *colour plate 23*
Standing stones, West Cumbria 32
Stanton Drew 132
Stockdale Moor 32, 144
Stone Carr (see Motherby)
stone
    shape 28, 49, 83, 136, 141-2
    kerb 31-2, 37, 50, 62, 73, 88, 94, 96, 101, 105, 127-9
    line 11, 52, 73-5, 92, 144 (see also avenue)
    outlier 26, 28-9, 33, 36, 54-5, 110, 137-8
    paired 36, 65, 86, 121, 133-4, 137, 144
    standing 7, 10, 22, 24, 31, 44, 53, 62-3, 71, 82, 85, 107-8, 119, 122, 124, 135, 144 (see also boulders/eratics)
Stonehenge 7, 133
Studfoldgate 8, 31, 138
Sunbiggin 110
Sunbiggin Tarn 21-2, 105, 108
Sunbrick circle 19, 122-3, 134, 140, 142-3, 138, 144 (see also Birkrigg)

survival/taphonomy 8, 9, 12-13, 2 (see also distribution)
Swarthbeck Gill 78-9
Swinside 39-42, 120, 128, 135-6, 138-40, 143-4, *colour plate 10*

tarn 21, 22, 23, 29, 34, 37, 67, 71, 114, 135, 144
The Cockpit 77, 134, 138, *colour plate 18*
The Copstone 71-2, 133
The Kirk (see Kirkby Ireleth)
The Standing Stones, MD 72-3, 97, 138, 143-4
Thorborough 48
Threaplands 90-91, 93, 136, 138
timber monuments 22, 28, 37, 40, 95, 107, 139-41
Tower Brae 7, 9, 24
Trainford Brow (see Lowther)
Troutbeck 124
types of site/monument form 7, 12, 132-7, 140, 142-3

Ullock 31
unenclosed cremation cemeteries 7, 13, 67, 143
Urswick 10, 21, *colour plate 7*

viewshed 20, 23, 25, 28, 31, 48, 55, 59, 66, 71-2, 77-9, 85, 88, 90, 94, 96-8, 100, 105, 120, 122, 131, 140

water 48, 56, 83, 144 (see spring, tarn, wetland)
Wessex 132
wetlands 20, 22, 30, 34, 37, 38-39, 42, 77, 116, 136
white 29, 47, 53-4, 76, 84, 95, 117, 120
White Hag 92, 97, 98-9, 133, 136, 138, 143, 144
White Moss (see Burnmoor)
White Raise, MD 72, 73, 75-7, 143
White Raise, RF 85-6, 142 (see Rafland Forest)
Wicker Street 96-8
Wilson Scar 87, 88, 138
Windrigg Hill 90, 91, 94
Wiseber 20
Woodhead 139
Woodhenge 17
Woundale Raise 124

Yamonside 16